100 British Documentaries

WITHDRAWN

100 BRITISH DOCUMENTARIES

BFI SCREEN GUIDES

Patrick Russell

First published in 2007 by the
British Film Institute
21 Stephen Street, London W1T 1LN

The British Film Institute's purpose is to champion moving image culture in all its
richness and diversity across the UK, for the benefit of as wide an audience as
possible, and to create and encourage debate.

Series cover design: Paul Wright
Cover image: *Gallivant* (Andrew Kötting, 1996, Tall Stories)
Series design: Ketchup/couch
Set by Fakenham Photosetting Ltd, Fakenham, Norfolk
Printed in the UK by The Cromwell Press, Trowbridge, Wiltshire

British Library Cataloguing-in-Publication Data
A catalogue record for this book is available from the British Library

ISBN 978–1–84457–195–6 (pbk)
ISBN 978–1–84457–194–9 (hbk)

Contents

Acknowledgments ix
Introduction 1

24 Hours, 2000 9
Any Man's Kingdom, Tony Thompson, 1956 11
Artists Must Live, John Read, 1953 13
At Work in Manchester and Milan (*Neighbours*), Richard Guinea,
    Manfred Voss, Enrico Platter, 1974 15
Baby's Toilet, 1905 17
The Battle of the Somme, 1916 19
Beauty, Bonny, Daisy, Violet, Grace and Geoffrey Morton,
    Frank Cvitanovich, 1974 22
The Big Meeting, 1963 24
Britain at Bay, 1940 27
Children Learning by Experience, Margaret Thomson, 1947 29
The Coal Board's Butchery (*The Miners' Campaign Video
    Tapes*), 1984 31
Coal Face, Cavalcanti, 1935 33
The Complainers, Dominic Savage, 1997 36
The Conquest of Everest, 1953 38
Conservative Party Election Broadcast 23/4/79, 1979 40
Crowd Bites Wolf, 2000 42
A Day in the Life of a Coal Miner, 1910 44
Desert Victory, Roy Boulting, 1943 47
The Devil Is Coming (*The Great War*), Tony Essex, 1964 50
A Diary for Timothy, Humphrey Jennings, 1946 52

Drifters, John Grierson, 1929 55

Drinking for England, Brian Hill, 1998 58

Education for the Future, Derrick Knight, 1967 61

Every Day Except Christmas (*Look at Britain*), Lindsay Anderson,
    1957 64

The Face of Britain, Paul Rotha, 1935 68

The Family (*Week 12*), Franc Roddam, Paul Watson, 1974 70

Five and Under, Donald Alexander, 1941 72

Gallivant, Andrew Kötting, 1996 74

The Great Recovery (*Britain under National Government*), 1934 76

Guinness for You, Anthony Short, 1971 78

Handsworth Songs, John Akomfrah, 1986 80

Health and Clothing, H. W. Bush, 1928 82

The Heart of the Angel, Molly Dineen, 1989 84

Heroes of the North Sea, A. E. Jones, 1925 86

Housing Problems, Edgar Anstey, Arthur Elton, 1935 88

I Think They Call Him John, John Krish, 1964 91

The Intimacy of Strangers, Eva Weber, 2005 94

The Irishmen: An Impression of Exile, Philip Donnellan, 1965 96

*John, Aged Seventeen Months, for Nine Days in a Residential
    Nursery*, James and Joyce Robertson, 1969 98

Johnny Cash in San Quentin, Michael Darlow, 1969 100

Johnny Go Home, John Willis, 1975 102

Jubilee, Herbert A. Green, R. Green, 1935 104

Land of Promise, Paul Rotha, 1946 106

Let It Be, Michael Lindsay-Hogg, 1970 109

Listen to Britain, Humphrey Jennings, Stewart McAllister, 1942 112

Lockerbie – A Night Remembered, Michael Grigsby, 1998 114

London, Patrick Keiller, 1994 116

London 2012: Make Britain Proud, Darryl Goodrich, 2004 119

London's Contrasts (*Wonderful London*), Frank Miller, Harry B.
    Parkinson, 1924 122

March to Aldermaston, 1958 124

Marion Knight (*Citizen 63*), John Boorman, 1963 126

Market Place (*Look at Life*), 1959 128

McLibel, Franny Armstrong, 1998/2005 .130

Mining Review 4th Year No. 12, 1951 132

Mirror (*Video Nation*), Gordon Henscher, 1994 134

Morning in the Streets, Denis Mitchell, Roy Harris, 1959 137

Moslems in Britain – Cardiff, G. Fares, 1961 140

The Negro Next Door (*This Week*), Peter Robinson, 1965 142

Neil Kinnock, Hugh Hudson, 1987 144

New Year's Eve (*Police*), Roger Graef, Charles Stewart, 1982 146

Night Mail, Harry Watt, Basil Wright, 1936 148

Nightcleaners, Berwick Street Collective, 1975 151

O'Connell Bridge, 1897 154

Out to Play, Harold Lowenstein, 1936 156

Portrait of a School, Vivian Milroy, 1957 .159

A Portrait of Ga, Margaret Tait, 1952 161

The Punk Rock Movie, Don Letts, 1978 163

A Queen Is Crowned, Castleton Knight, 1953 165

Returning the Serve (*Loyalists*), Sam Collyns, 1999 168

The Rival World, Bert Haanstra, 1955 170

Royal Family, Richard Cawston, 1969 172

The School, 1978 175

Seven Up! (*World in Action*), Paul Almond, 1964 177

The Shadow of Progress, Derek Williams, 1970 180

The Shadows in the Cave (*The Power of Nightmares*),
 Adam Curtis, 2004 182

Snow, Geoffrey Jones, 1963 184

The Song of Ceylon, Basil Wright, 1934 187

Song of the People, Max Munden, 1945 .189

South – Sir Ernest Shackleton's Glorious Epic of the Antarctic,
 1919 192

S.S. Skirmisher at Liverpool (*Mitchell and Kenyon 235*), 1901 194

Sunday by the Sea, Anthony Simmons, 1953 197

Supersocieties (*Life in the Undergrowth*), Stephen Dunleavy, 2005 . .200

The Sword of the Spirit, Henry Cass, 1942 .203

Television Comes to London, Dallas Bower, Gerald Cock, 1936 205

Time Is, Don Levy, 1964 207

Today We Live: A Film of Life in Britain, Ruby Grierson,
Ralph Bond, 1937 209

Touching the Void, Kevin Macdonald, 2003 212

Tracking down Maggie, Nick Broomfield, 1994 215

Two Victorian Girls (*Yesterday's Witness*), Stephen Peet, 1970 217

UCS I, 1971 219

The Vanishing Street, Robert Vas, 1962 221

View from an Engine Front – Ilfracombe, 1898 223

Vox Nova Scientiae, 1936 225

A Wedding on Saturday, Norman Swallow, 1964 227

Western Approaches, Pat Jackson, 1944 229

Westward Ho!, Thorold Dickinson, 1940 .231

When the Dog Bites, Penny Woolcock, 1988 233

Winter (*Secrets of Nature*), 1923 235

Wisdom of the Wild, Mary Field, 1940 237

Yarmouth Fishing Boats Leaving Harbour, 1896 239

Appendix 242

Notes 251

Further Reading 255

Index 257

Acknowledgments

Thank you to Rebecca Barden for commissioning the book and to Sarah Watt and colleagues for seeing it through to publication.

I am grateful to my senior colleagues Darren Long, Richard Paterson and Heather Stewart for their support of the project.

All writing about British screen heritage owes much to the work of my archival colleagues at the BFI National Archive, and to their predecessors and successors. Warm thanks go to my immediate curatorial colleagues, not only for their support during the writing of this book but also for introducing me to several of these films in the first place. They are Ros Cranston, Bryony Dixon, Katy McGahan, Jez Stewart, Rebecca Vick and Sue Woods.

For providing access to BFI-held films, documents and stills, many thanks go to: Anita Horne and Lynn McVeigh; Kathleen Dickson; Charles Fairall and David Briggs; Mike Caldwell and Nigel Arthur; Carolyne Bevan and Janet Moat; David Sharp and all his colleagues at the BFI National Library.

Other documents were accessed via BBC Written Archives, the British Library, Guinness Storehouse Archives, the National Archives and Nuffield Foundation. Thanks go to their archivists and librarians.

Advice and information pertinent to individual films was kindly supplied by the following (at the BFI and elsewhere): Tim Boon, Simon Brown, Steve Bryant, Bryony Dixon, Christophe Dupin, Leo Enticknap, Steve Foxon, Jon Hoare, Kathleen Luckey, Peter Todd and Stephen Toulmin.

Portions of the text were read and commented upon by Tim Boon, Ros Cranston, Margaret Deriaz, Bryony Dixon, William Fowler,

Andrea Kalas, Deirdre Russell and Phil Wickham; and by the publisher's anonymous readers. All prompted improvements: any remaining errors are mine.

I am grateful to the film-makers who made time to provide comments for the Appendix.

My greatest debt of thanks is to my wife Aileen McAllister for her constant support, encouragement and forbearance. This book is dedicated to our daughter Clementine.

Introduction

The documentary impulse has long stirred in British culture. Documentary is usually associated with realism, widely considered the most characteristically British of artistic stances. Actually, the bond between these concepts is pretty knotty. But it has underpinned claims that documentary is, for good or ill, *the* British film genre. Oddly, this assumption is contradicted by standard write-ups of UK cinema and television history, in which documentary makes brief, monolithic appearances before mysteriously vanishing for years or decades at a time.

British documentary *has* frequently been marginal. But it has a continuous history, comprising many mini-histories. This book is a selective introduction, celebrating it as varied, interesting and – against all expectations – fun.

100 British Documentaries

The films discussed in this book, though very wide-ranging, were selected because each illustrates something specific about the many forms British documentary has taken, and the numerous uses to which it has been put, as it has developed historically. The intended result is an accessible map of a national documentary heritage, using 100 films as coordinates – not an inventory of the best, or of the most historically noteworthy, or of personal favourites (though many entries do fall into at least one of these categories). The absence of (say) *The Death of Yugoslavia* (1995) doesn't mean that it's not outstanding or important. And the presence of *Market Place* (1959) (for instance) doesn't mean that *it* is. However, every film is treated as having intrinsic value: even those included only because they are examples of broader categories are unique works. Every film is also treated as having positional value: even those considered masterpieces resonate with the others on the list, reflecting its broader patterns. The choices are personal, but not designed to corroborate a grand theory of documentary or to sell any one historical variant ahead of others. Nonetheless, the following comments on concepts and history provide helpful context.

100 British *Documentaries*

Documentary has been perennially dogged by problems of definition. For instance, John Grierson's famous formulation – 'the creative treatment of actuality' – has been welcomed as insightful summary; rejected as self-contradictory; dismissed as vague obfuscation; and acknowledged as a brilliant statement of the obvious. See the Appendix for further reactions!

At the very least, it's an unusually enduring soundbite, and it does distil a common core from the diverse films included here. They all differ (to varying degrees) from fiction films, which depend less decisively than do documentaries on a claimed relationship with reality. But, just as importantly, these 100 films differ (again, to varying degrees) from non-fiction films that *aren't* documentaries and which depend less crucially on the manner by which they have been constructed, and the interpretation brought to them. Counter-intuitively, questions of style, technique, sensibility and viewpoint are as important to documentary as to any other kind of film – arguably more so. This has caused some writers to question the very integrity of the documentary form. Others have sensibly argued for the intelligence of viewers, appreciative that documentaries seek to (and can only) *represent* reality, not to duplicate it.[1]

For Grierson, 'actuality' made documentaries potentially *superior* to fiction films, while 'creative treatment' made them more advanced than 'mere records' and 'illustrated lectures'. What his definition most appreciably lacks is reference to film-makers' intentions and audiences' expectations. Documentaries are *designed* to represent reality, and watched as such by viewers. Two particular areas of film history – early film with its 'cinema of attractions',[2] and experimental film-making – clarify the distinction. Many works in both categories contain 'actuality' (the very term adopted in early years to label the large quantities of non-fiction then produced). And many 'creatively treat' it (a given of experimental artistry). But for some of these films, the creativity is its own end, the actuality merely its source material: these are not documentaries, because they lack a documentary function. Conversely, some films make use of fiction, precisely to fulfil a documentary function.

However, 'documentary' needn't be a documentary's sole function. Hybrids are the rule, not the exception. Many films in this book are experimental *and* documentary in nature, or are documentary *and* entertainment, *and* political weapon, promotional tool or educational resource. While these fused functions can be mutually compromising, they can also be mutually enriching. Some readers will object to the presence of political broadcasts or classroom teaching aids in a list of documentaries, but those included were carefully chosen precisely because they bring the language of documentary heavily into play while simultaneously fulfilling other functions. Such 'instrumental' uses of documentary are rarely discussed but merit close attention.

Cutting across functions are a range of approaches. One writer has influentially divided documentary into 'modes': poetic, expository, observational, participatory, reflexive, performative.[3] But these, too, are more often mixed than served neat. Documentary also works within several different possible narrative structures: some established in its prehistory, others gradually added to its repertoire. Films are based around events, places, journeys, processes, individuals, communities, institutions or marked passages of time. They might approach a general subject by scrutinising a case study (or by contrasting several). Or they might do so via personal report, compilation of existing materials, or indeed illustrated lecture as decried by Grierson (rather hypocritically: he and his protégés made their fair share). Most of these 100 documentaries combine such formats just as they do modes and functions.

Numerous variables, then, may be found interacting in a single documentary. Each possesses its own treasurably unique structural DNA. However, the one thing documentary isn't is abstract. Its variables interact in and with specific places and times: in this case the United Kingdom, during the twentieth century and a few years either side. Its *cultural* DNA is complex stuff.

100 *British* Documentaries

Branches of an intricate professional family tree linking documentary film-makers within and between generations are glimpsed in these pages. Enabled and constrained by evolving technologies, one generation's preoccupations and problems may find direct or distorted echo in another's. British documentary's story is one of contrasts and continuities. This book broadly traces that story, along the way suggesting certain revisions to received versions, which are sometimes too tidy. Imposing rigid divisions between sectors, phases and movements on British documentary history doesn't really work (given the UK industry's small size, it would be surprising if it did). This applies even at the level of *mise en scène*, where observational and orchestrated styles are rarely mutually exclusive. American 'Direct Cinema' may have exalted 'observation' above all else (French cinéma vérité did so to a lesser extent, while also promoting 'interaction'). But this was rarely imported wholesale into Britain. And for decades, films making heavy use of other elements such as directed re-enactment had also incorporated 'observational' material. Their makers were untroubled about mixing methods, leaving transitions between them unlabelled. (Also, they generally referred to the 'observational' bits simply as 'actuality' sequences: note how earlier terminology had persisted, while slightly changing meaning.)

Conventional histories also tend to leave gaps (this book leaves its own gaps, of course). Typically, once lip service has been paid to early actuality films, documentary disappears, resurfacing in 1929. The intervening decades' documentaries and 'proto-documentaries' deserve some attention. *Much* attention has been given to the 1930s' 'documentary movement' associated with Grierson, especially to public information documentaries made, before propaganda became a dirty word, at three state institutions: the film unit at the Empire Marketing Board, which begat its successor at the General Post Office, which in turn became World War II's Crown Film Unit. However, these were not the only settings in which the movement worked, and the range of films and film-makers it encompassed is often underestimated. Also it had a complicated, sometimes overlooked, coexistence both with more radical and with more commercial film-makers.

The period between 1939 and 1945 is rightly recorded as a major documentary moment, but shortly thereafter documentary appears to evaporate rapidly once more, this time reappearing as Free Cinema in the late 1950s. The Free Cinema group professed dislike for the documentary movement (their admiration for Humphrey Jennings being the exception that proved the rule). But a telling similarity is that both made conscious, determined efforts at thrusting themselves, via writings and screenings, into cutting-edge film culture and thence the history books. This is significant in itself. But it doesn't follow that none of the documentaries – and there were many – made in the decade preceding Free Cinema is worth watching.

Nor does the marginal post-war presence of Grierson and certain key colleagues prove that their 'movement' had entirely collapsed. It continued, in much modified form and circumstances, until about 1980. Several examples of its output are included here. This book also takes an interest in the phenomenon of 'sponsored' communications usually identified with the documentary movement but also practised elsewhere, and up to the present day. Frequently thought of as the fatal flaw in Griersonian documentary ('sponsorship meant self-censorship'),[4] as a foundation for cultural endeavour it has a longer history than unfettered free expression does. This doesn't mean any film-makers represented here are Mozarts or Michelangelos, just that sponsored craftsmanship can yield quality products, as well as interesting tensions.

If documentary film declined after 1945, it was a slower, more complicated, much more interesting decline than generally realised. A related historical problem is the complex relationship between cinema and television documentary: more accurately, projected and broadcast documentary. This book focuses on the documentary 'film'. But television having undeniably become its principal outlet, and source of funding, several television 'films' are included. This portion of the list does not aim at a full account of television documentary in its own right (that would require another book). Rather, it surveys the ways in which television refined then increasingly modified documentary as it had developed beforehand. Significant modifications (most with 'film' antecedents but never so pervasively applied) include: association of documentary with journalism; use of interviews; use of presenters; sustained use of the observational mode; documentaries forming ongoing series; and single documentaries being shown in scheduled 'slots'. All of these interact with patterns of consumption very different from those of film – an interaction now heavily mediated by the processes by which broadcasters commission programmes from producers.

This all said, the distribution histories of many films on this list indicate some continuing relationship between broadcast and non-broadcast spaces, small and large screens – not necessarily in cinemas. Grierson long ago claimed that 'non-theatrical' venues were the ideal destinations for documentaries (probably to rationalise his failure to get them into cinemas). With the emergence of digital screen networks and 'webumentary', new 'non-theatrical' spaces are emerging and their relationships with 'theatrical' and 'broadcast' ones are up for renegotiation.

Documentary is witness to a century of extraordinary change. Certain key events are regularly referenced in these pages: two world wars, for starters, and two massively reforming governments on opposite sides of the political spectrum. They provide settings, subjects or subtexts (sometimes years after the fact) for many of these films. Others register broader trends, from rising affluence to declining deference. And, these films all reflect Britishness in its contradictory complexity: brave, staid, ugly, inventive, hypocritical, refined, rebellious, haunted. And, of course, fixated with class: witness a long line of documentarists from relatively privileged backgrounds speaking to, for or about the British working class.

Like all cultural artefacts, these 100 films will accumulate different sets of meanings for different generations, outside their makers' control.

100 British Documentaries

Every film in this book has a complicated archival history, influencing the ways in which it is currently available to us: a history whose details are unique to each production. Unlike some documentaries, all of these films at least still exist: all preserved in some form, mostly by the BFI National Archive, BBC Broadcast Archives or the Imperial War Museum, sometimes by their rights-holders or in specialist, regional or overseas collections.

The scope and value of much past writing about documentaries has been severely constrained by their limited availability. However (partly with the aid of digital technologies), access to documentary heritage is widening: necessarily gradually, given the complexity of the technical and legal issues and the huge costs involved in overcoming them. As a companion to this book, most of the 100 films discussed can be viewed as part of the BFI's Mediatheque initiative: <www.bfi.org.uk/mediatheque>.

Watch them, enjoy – and make up your own mind. Then get to work on your own list of *100 British Documentaries*.

Note on the Entries

Where a film is clearly part of a series, the series is listed in brackets after the individual film title. If the film belongs to a looser cycle of films, or was screened within a non-sequential television slot, this is usually referred to in the entry itself rather than in the header.

Many films have no credited director, are entirely uncredited, or were made in production circumstances in which the role of 'director' was not recognised. For this reason, a 'possessive credit' has usually been included in headers only where a director *is* credited (e.g., *Snow* – Geoffrey Jones), or where a 'producer' has been credited and their creative role clearly corresponds to that of director as generally understood (e.g., *The Shadows in the Cave* – Adam Curtis). More thorough listings, sometimes including personnel or organisations not credited on screen, can be found at the bottom of each entry, but these are necessarily selective. Readers seeking detailed credits are directed to <www.bfi.org.uk/filmtvinfo/ftvdb/>.

24 Hours
2000 – 25 mins

By the turn of the century, Channel 4 Television was suspected of straying from its mission (it was set up in 1982 with a remit to transmit non-mainstream material). For some, the *Big Brother* (2000–) franchise typifies its recent preference for ratings-chasing infotainment over documentary and other parts of its founding mission. In an increasingly deregulated environment, though, such successful programming helped subsidise vestiges of the channel's 'alternative' remit. An example is *Alt.TV*, a slot allocated to independent film-makers, albeit reaching comparatively tiny late-night audience shares.

 24 Hours was coincidentally screened in the slot on the third night of *Big Brother*'s first series. Produced by Brian Hill's company, it consists of '24 cameras, 24 one-minute films' made by young independent film-makers across London at different hours of one day. As a kaleidoscopic portrait of London, the resulting anthology is uneven but very watchable. As a compendium of documentary strategies, it's fascinating:

 Canary Wharf Print Room documents production processes counterpointing sound and actuality images, 'observed' and 're-enacted'

 Bond Street Russian Twins depicts a person and his milieu, interspersing footage and interview

 South Bank The Eye's poetic soundtrack accompanies cityscape stills

 Blackheath Going to School shows a boy leaving for school, under his own voiceover

 Soho Courier is a montage of subjective travelling shots

 Dean Street outside Dave interviews a homeless person

 In *Wardour Street Restaurant* kitchen staff explain food preparation processes as they undertake them

 West End Passengers' protagonist recites poetry to camera (split screen is used)

Lewisham Primary School documents a school break, mainly via a
child's camera

Chelsea Beauty Parlour's 'fly-on-the-wall' observes a conversation

Camden Funeral Parlour (the best of the 24 shorts) mixes workplace
interviews, observed conversation and documentary footage

Leicester Square Joking consists of 'vox pops'

Wandsworth Tea Time is a home movie compressed into swiftly
edited highlights

Soho Birthday Party similarly evokes an office party using quick cuts

University College Hospital Waiting describes an institution, using
unhurried montage and counterpointed sound

Clapham Going out borrows stylised imagery from advertising and
music video

In *Tower Hamlets Bedtime* footage of a boy's hobby is accompanied
by his narration

West End Curtain Down records an event and contextualises it with
retrospective interview

The subject's voiceover describes *Clapham Grandma's Cafe*

Smithfield Meat Market portrays a place, using edited observational
material

Croydon Prayer Room is another observational record

Epping Podium plays interview sound over documentary material

Islington Insomniac is a character portrait, combining images of the
subject and his informative commentary

City of London Dead of Night stylises street scenes by using
superimpositions

These short films are products of documentary's multifaceted evolution
from the one-minute films made a century earlier. All the formats, styles
and techniques described above (and the overall film's 'day-in-a-life' format)
are found in unique combinations among the ninety-nine films that follow.

Prod Co: Century Films; **Prod**: Kate Baillis.

Any Man's Kingdom
1956 – 22 mins
Tony Thompson

The post-war expansion of public ownership generated new clients for documentary's services. In 1949 British Transport Films (BTF) was set up to serve the newly nationalised public transport network. It went on to produce 600 films for the Inland Waterways, London Transport and, principally, British Rail. Producer Edgar Anstey stated:

> bodies like the Transport Commission are aware that films on the public services can be made that will play an effective part in creating a new psychological pattern from the public as owner, the public as worker and the public as user.[5]

For the owner, BTF documented improvements in transport technology and services. For workers, it relayed staff information and instruction. For the user, BTF turned out handsome colour portraits of Britain as reachable by rail. These enjoyed cinema release then long shelf-lives in BTF's busy non-theatrical library. *Any Man's Kingdom*, ranging across Northumberland, exemplifies this film cycle's superior and subtle quality: vibrant colours applied to stately compositions; an imaginative score by Elisabeth Lutyens, alternately warm and sinister; and allusive, elegiac commentary – 'now between tide and tide there is only the heraldry of holidays in the horned bays where Geordie comes up from Tyneside'.

Anstey employed both old hands like J. B. Holmes and John Taylor and younger film-makers like Tony Thompson, who directed several evergreen BTF classics. His visual approach recalls much 1940s' documentary, seamlessly blending actuality (rural faces at fairs and dances) with choreographed action. BTF's half-realistic, half-escapist picture of post-war Britain yielded scores of fine films and has won it great nostalgic popular affection. It has attracted little academic notice, assumed to be of greater interest to train buffery than to documentary studies, perhaps inheriting Paul Rotha's contemporary (envious?) judgment: 'conventionally competent output which lacks real creative inspiration'.[6]

Had such films retreated from artistry and social meaning? The high quality of their craftsmanship is actually far more consistent than that attained by any previous documentary unit, though sometimes too slick. Many exude a certain complacency. In this, however, they advance rather than betray social documentary's long-stated mission of expressing, even forging a national mood. After turbulent years, Britain was meant to look to a future of modernisation and social solidarity, while reconciling itself to its heritage. Underlying *Any Man's Kingdom* is acquaintance between Northumberland's present and its distant, sometimes turbulent pasts ('dusk and dawn are banks of the one river and time is only a bridge'). Potentially trite or twee, this theme is quite creatively handled. A prosaic visual of travellers boarding a rural bus is made ageless by the ghostly music played over it.

Moreover, serving a public monopoly before mass car ownership, BTF didn't have to hard-sell. More pressing was the need to conform to internal policy. There are no trains in *Any Man's Kingdom*. The aforementioned bus sequence was hastily shot and inserted into the film to replace a shot of the equivalent train service when it was realised that the Transport Commission was about to withdraw it. During the 1950s some 2,000 miles of railway line were closed, before the next decade's better-remembered Beeching axe was taken to further chunks of the system.

Prod Co: British Transport Films; **Spons**: British Rail; **Dir**: Tony Thompson; **Prod**: Ian Ferguson; **Phot**: Robert Paynter, Reg Hughes.

Artists Must Live
1953 – 30 mins
John Read

'A BBC Television Film': given its early date, it gives some idea how television documentary looked and sounded when confined to a single BBC channel broadcasting for only a few hours a day. The relative paucity of surviving, let alone accessible early television material makes its study as much a blend of archaeology and history as is study of the early films of half a century before. On the evidence of this film, the analogy with early non-fiction film isn't entirely specious. The film-makers appear to be both reinventing documentary for a new medium and borrowing from existing models. Where early actualities might have drawn on photography and other pre-cinematic crafts, here the precedents are film documentary – and BBC radio, from which early television technicians were as likely to have come.

The programme concerns 'the artist's place in Britain today' and in particular the financing of visual art. Director John Read remained associated with BBC arts output for many years. Eyes closed, it's easy to hear his film as a radio broadcast. The pictures often merely illustrate, even during wordless sequences leisurely surveying paintings and sculptures to the strains of the BBC Orchestra. Inherited from radio is the role of the host with specialist expertise, occupied here by art historian Basil Taylor. A cinema antecedent was Jill Craigie's 1944 *Out of Chaos*, a survey of wartime painting by Kenneth Clark, who later personified the technique's refinement in the lavish BBC series *Civilisation* (1969). This film has much lower production values than either.

Taylor is sometimes on screen, wandering around galleries. Other scenes comprise actuality footage of locations or of artists at work. Several artists, both struggling and established, are used to illustrate the theme: some, like John Piper and Patrick Heron, still remembered, others forgotten. Interviews with artists and patrons already have a televisual 'look' (over-the-shoulder shots, cutaways to Taylor, shots in which both

Taylor and the interviewee appear). These mostly upper-middle-class subjects are as stilted as any interviewees of the time.

Post-dating (by four weeks) the Coronation broadcast which expanded the television audience, *Artists* would nonetheless have reached a mere fraction of homes. Unlike many early television documentaries, it continued to be available for non-theatrical hire for many years. The Arts Council, with whom the BBC made the film, became a significant sponsor both of documentaries about art and experimental films *by* artists. Its backing explains this film's sequence promoting it as the 'chief agency of state patronage' of art. Read doesn't make a thematic connection between this and another section on 'enlightened advertisers' who commission posters from artists. *Artists Must Live*, a sponsored television film, falls somewhere between the 'enlightened advertising' that had hitherto brought most documentary to the screen and mature factual television which would come to consider it an unacceptable compromise.

Prod Co: BBC, Arts Council of Great Britain; **Dir**: John Read; **Prod**: John Elliot.

At Work in Manchester and Milan (*Neighbours*)
1974 – 22 mins
Richard Guinea, Manfred Voss, Enrico Platter

Educational films haven't had armies of scholars invading them.
Nonetheless, histories seeking to encompass the full range of cinema
practice have found a place for film-makers like Mary Field. The vaster
output of television schools programming since the 1950s is
comparatively less well documented, much less systematically interpreted,
despite its far more thorough integration into curricula.

In the absence of such a critical literature, this programme is included
as an arbitrary example: a reminder not to overlook educational
television's use of documentary. It should be added that, following its
first broadcast, this film was also available for 16mm hire. With widely
available video recorders still a decade away, the presence of schools
programmes in educational libraries was essential for teachers juggling
complex timetables.

Neighbours: Four Families in Europe was a series for ten- to thirteen-
year-olds. Anglo-German co-productions, each was a short documentary
comparing everyday lives in different countries of the Common Market,
recently joined by Britain. This episode thoroughly mixes the 'day-in-the-
life' and the 'comparative study' documentary formats. 'Both these
workers are employed in large modern industries. Today we'll see some
of the differences between a white-collar and a blue-collar worker.'

The subjects are electronics-firm foreman Ted Conway and
Domenico Fasoli, a tyre-factory worker. The film's divided into several
sequences contrasting their daily schedules: clocking in, working, having
lunch, more work, heading home, enjoying an evening out. For example,
Conway walks home to a meat-and-veg lunch (cooked by his wife, who
also works full time), while Fasoli enjoys pasta, bread and red wine in his
staff canteen. Also included are sequences detailing manufacturing
processes, and interviews with the men and their wives. The most
discursive, socially interesting scene compares gender attitudes.

Mrs Conway holds respectably egalitarian views, shared by her husband
– to a point. The Fasolis embrace rigidly traditional roles.

Narration supplies context, relaying facts and figures (for instance,
comparative national pension provisions). A difference between this and
older schools films is that the producers haven't made archetypes of their
characters. They include personal details to flesh out the individuals,
though extraneous to international comparison. Still, when the final
narration concludes that 'though both men are workers, we've seen
some striking differences in their ways of life', it's clear that decades
from its black-and-white antecedents, this schools documentary still
prizes clarity above all else.

At Work in Manchester and Milan is an unremarkable film put
together with a professionalism and honesty easy to respond to. As often
with youthful ephemera encountered in adulthood, it's even rather
moving, still recent enough to evoke bittersweet nostalgia: the more so,
perhaps, given the unlikelihood of any of the thousands who saw this
film now remembering doing so. The jolly music and opening jigsaw
graphics will momentarily transport any survivor of the 1970s right back
into them. Narrator Brian Trueman (a regular children's TV presenter)
adds to the strange familiarity. Low-key idealism runs through the
project's attempt at getting Europe's children to understand each other
better. And the closing sequence, cutting between Mr Fasoli's male social
club and the Conways' suburban pub, is warmly executed. Respectful
portraiture of ordinary lives lived.

Prod Co: Granada Television, Bayerischer Rundfunk; **Dir**: Richard Guinea, Manfred Voss,
Enrico Platter.

Baby's Toilet
1905 – 3 mins

The films of producer Cecil Hepworth, a giant of early British film, encompassed many genres. Their interesting challenge to documentary history arises from their resistance to having sharp distinctions between fiction and non-fiction imposed on them, suggesting instead a spectrum along which the proportions are variably mixed from film to film. Our patchy knowledge of Hepworth's intentions compounds the difficulty of placing them, but scenic 'panoramas', 'phantom rides' and events reportage undoubtedly lie towards one end of the scale whereas, say, his film of scenes from *Alice in Wonderland* (1903) definitely lies at the opposite end.

Nearer the middle, firmly on the fictional side, is *Rescued by Rover* (1905), the story film regularly cited for influential contributions to film grammar, but played by Hepworth family members (and dog). *Baby's Toilet* is just to the other side of the divide. At first sight a home movie of a baby (Hepworth's daughter Elizabeth) handled by a nursemaid, its listing in Hepworth's 1906 catalogue indicates that it was distributed like any other commercial film. It was listed in two categories, 'Comic Films' (under the subheading of 'Babies') and 'Domestic Scenes', seemingly implying fiction and non-fiction respectively. But *Rescued by Rover* was also listed as a Domestic Scene. The fact is that original categorisations made for sales purposes are potentially as misleading as anachronistic attempts to fit films into later genres. What's clear is that this film's 'story' is constructed to quintessentially 'documentary' specifications. By this point, film-makers had added 'processes' to the stock of non-fiction formats, complementing 'events', 'places' and 'journeys'. *Baby's Toilet* transposes the emerging pattern of industrial films, including Hepworth's, from the workplace to the household. Separately photographed sections combine to depict routine procedures: baby being bathed, dried, weighed, dressed and fed. A Hepworth historian notes that there is clear evidence that Hepworth's *A Day in the Hayfields* was not shot in sequence but was edited together to create the depiction of process. That was early 1904: there is no reason to assume therefore that *Baby's Toilet* was not also constructed, therefore falling under the banner of creative treatment of actuality.[7]

It remains only to add that *Baby's Toilet* is the earliest film in this book, of many, dealing with the subject of childhood which, with its universal resonance, bestows on documentaries an appeal as wide as that usually reserved for fiction. As Hepworth liked to point out, his baby – unlike all others – was silent.

Prod Co: Hepworth Manufacturing Company.

The Battle of the Somme
1916 – 80 mins

By several calculations the most successful film in British box-office history, *The Battle of the Somme* is also the first British artefact to have been placed on Unesco's Memory of the World Register.

Cameramen J. B. McDowell and Geoffrey Malins took the footage. With Charles Urban, Malins also edited it, discarding most of McDowell's rushes. Three-quarters of *The Battle* is made of Malins's footage. That it hadn't been intended as a single film when they shot it shows in its bittiness: some fifty short discrete sequences introduced by intertitles. Individually, many could double for brief newsreel stories. Though they would barely cohere without the intertitles, together they had massive contemporary impact. Much footage is shown out of real-life sequence. The penultimate scene of soldiers cheerily heading off to replenish the

A justly famous image from *The Battle of the Somme* (Photograph courtesy of the Imperial War Museum, London, Q79501)

battlefield was filmed before the 'earlier' offensive had taken place. The shaping of messily disparate rushes into an articulate cinema statement marks this as a documentary production.

It divides itself into five parts of roughly ten sequences each. The first covers the preparations, detailed technical processes occurring amid regular hostilities across no-man's-land. There is great emphasis here and throughout the film on Howitzers and other advanced machinery of war. This was partly to motivate home-front munitions workers.

The second part charts the build-up to the offensive. It includes the first casualties – two horses. The third part is the centrepiece, the beginning of the battle, commencing with the famous scenes of men filmed from behind going over the top, chums falling at their rear. This material is now accepted as 'faked'. In this it followed an existing tradition. Numerous short Boer War films had sensationally reconstructed battles in Blighty's back yards. But it's handled with unusual gravity and the footage surrounding it depends on this dramatic highlight for meaning.

The fourth part deals with battle's aftermath, famously including quite extensive coverage of German *and* British dead, in long and in medium shot: 'The Toll of War'. The final part is more spirited, emphasising the strong start given to the soldiers marching off for more. This film helped establish rules for modern propaganda: lies are best anchored in truths. Careful calibration was necessary by 1916, when illusions about the nature of modern warfare had been shattered. If the film lacks a purposeful narrative – so did the event. In fact *The Battle* only covers the opening stages of the battle, still being fought as the film opened in thirty London cinemas. By its conclusion, over 1 million lay dead, and the Allies had advanced about five miles.

Certain images, frequently reused, have entered the subconscious. One is the heroic soldier with his ghostly look at the camera as he carries a wounded comrade on his back. But if these are some of the clearest single images we have of the Somme, our overall picture of it is sourced more from written history, fictional portrayals and family folklore. World

War I had traumatic effects on national, and individual, psychologies that took generations to work themselves out. How much is our understanding of so cataclysmic a happening influenced by its celluloid record? The answer testifies to the limitations of documentary film as well as its powers.

Prod Co: British Topical Committee for War Films; **Spons**: War Office; **Prod**: William F. Jury.

Beauty, Bonny, Daisy, Violet, Grace and Geoffrey Morton
1974 – 52 mins
Frank Cvitanovich

Geoffrey Morton is a man. Beauty, Bonny, Daisy, Grace and Violet, the eldest, are horses. Morton's farm is an agricultural anachronism, powered entirely by shire horses. Director Frank Cvitanovich had difficulty getting backing for this idea for a film, until mentioning it in a corridor to Thames executive Jeremy Isaacs, who told him to go ahead.

For the metropolitan 1970s, his subject must have sounded dull, even naff. But it had roots. British documentary had always had a bucolic side, bringing to screens a countryside in which rural reality and urban imagination were crossbred, and where continuity and modernity could mingle or clash. Cvitanovich, a television film-maker much of whose work dwelt in a grittier Britain, translated these thoughts into modern documentary language. His film, like Denis Mitchell's urban *Morning in the Streets* (1959) before it, won an Italia prize.

The pre-credits sequence adjusts the audience to the timbre, and the prioritisation of different technical components. We see the moon, then pull back to the field on which it shines. Then we hear crows, see a house, a light coming on and finally a man coming out. Then we hear his voice, off screen. The film's final shot rhymes these opening scenes, mimicking cyclical nature.

The surprisingly busy camera zooms as well as pans, often held by hand. Individual shots glisten. A ploughing sequence stands out. But the tempo remains unruffled. There is muckiness: the sex and scatology that go with animal breeding. Morton's voiceover is unpretentious, factual, sometimes philosophical as in his musings on the relationship of horse to man as a surviving remnant of a Nordic past. On-screen conversations are also heard, but their sounds are no more important than the horses' clip-clopping or intrusive modern car noises.

The film doesn't ask us either to admire or to question Morton's lifestyle, simply to look and listen (contemplation *can* prompt questions: can there really be harmony between farmer and farmed?). Nothing much happens (some will find the film tedious) but a climax does come: a foal's birth. The noisy nativity is followed by a delicate sequence of the newborn's first barnyard moments with its mother, then later ones of it running and playing in the fields. Sweetly orchestrated strings and piano play over these slowly dissolving shots. Coming after the real-time, synch-sound messiness of the birth, at the end of a film into which music has but sparingly intruded – it's rather exquisite. Amazing, now, that such serene film-making was once screened on ITV at 9pm.

Prod Co: Thames Television; **Dir/Prod**: Frank Cvitanovich; **Phot**: Mike Fash.

The Big Meeting
1963 – 26 mins

An astonishing *1,000*-odd films were produced for the National Coal
Board (NCB) over four decades. Buried treasure, they constitute an
undervalued collection in post-war British film – perhaps the medium's
definitive expression of the era's 'Butskellite' social consensus. Labour
Leader Hugh Gaitskell actually makes several appearances in the NCB
documentary *The Big Meeting*. By the time it was released, he had died,
aged 56.

The film opens on eight painterly shots of Durham. 'The Big Meeting'
is the Durham Miners' Gala, one of the world's largest annual gatherings
of miners and their families. The film is a visual record, attended by
narration delving into everything from the event's history to the
symbolism and physical materials of union banners. An intriguing facet of
the NCB's film output is its tributes to the workforce and its union,
incorporated into what are authorised statements by the body running
the industry. This potentially precarious balancing act can be sensed in
the mixing of industry news items and community stories in the long-
running *Mining Review* series. In *The Big Meeting* the union's history and
community presence are foregrounded. The principal narrator is a
veteran regional union officer, supplemented by many other community
voices. For instance, a genial sequence showing brass bandsmen
practising before the big day, while their wives dutifully bake for them,
has overlaid comments from several men and women.

The well-worn technique of multiple commentaries is here updated
by their unrehearsed naturalism: the film might be described as
traditionalist social documentary with concessions to contemporary
styling. Its documentary pedigree is impeccable. Founded some years
after the NCB began sponsoring films, its Film Unit was headed by
Donald Alexander, part of the documentary movement since 1936.
As with British Transport Films, a close parallel, the unit brought together
documentary veterans and younger colleagues. According to one,

Working-class tradition at *The Big Meeting*

The Big Meeting was 'very much a pet project of Donald Alexander' though it isn't clear whether he or others directed it. There are no credits 'because Donald decided that no one person should take the credit; he was modest in giving himself credits'.[8] This, too, reflects a tradition drawn towards film as a tool to shape civic values rather than towards documentary subject matter as fodder for artistic statements.

A better-known film entitled *Gala Day* provides an instructive, rarely made comparison. This independent short was funded by the British Film Institute, responsible for subsidising much broadly experimental post-war production. Released the same year, it covers the same subject, and even has an identical running time. Many scenes are direct analogues: parading, a Durham Cathedral service, speeches, dancing and fairground entertainment. *Gala Day* includes some drunkenness and mess, coyly absent from the NCB film, but itself omits the latter's attention to build-up and context. Overall, it substitutes for documentary classicism a more contemporary Free Cinema-influenced style, befitting a slightly more oblique view of the subject matter. Both films have their own sincere allegiance to the documentary 'truth' of the situation, and their relative merits are matters of taste. What's fascinating is that it's the 'official' production that possesses the more uncomplicated generosity towards working-class culture. And that it pays unequivocal tribute to the Labour Movement, though made during a Conservative administration. Such were the times.

Prod Co: NCB Film Unit.

Britain at Bay
1940 – 8 mins

The title-card says that *Britain at Bay* is 'by J. B. Priestley'. Why the attribution of personal authorship to a writer-narrator?

First, this is a 'compilation film', meaning it's assembled (supervised here by Harry Watt) out of footage from various sources: material shaped by editing but made meaningful by the viewpoint imposed upon it by commentary. A well-established form before 1939, the compilation documentary became tremendously useful in wartime.

Second, Priestley was an esteemed and popular writer and broadcaster: a middlebrow cultural celebrity. He's heard here but not seen, unlike the stars of the personality-fronted documentaries that television would make its own thirty years later. The film resembles an illustrated version of his radio 'postscripts', a weekly fixture of the BBC's Home Service. Priestley's was a trusted voice – and effective propaganda needs these.

Third, the themes resonate with Priestley's work in other media. This is where his authorship melds indivisibly with the GPO Film Unit's. In 1934, Priestley's *Zeitgeist* travel book *An English Journey* told of 'Three Englands', pastoral, industrial, suburban: all recurring characters in the same decade's documentary. Now, France fallen and Britain alone in war, they had to stand together in common defence. *Britain at Bay* compiles instantly resounding landscape images: green and pleasant, dark and smoky. Big Ben, defiant even when filmed behind barbed wire: whoever took this shot may not have intended symbolism, but the compiler certainly did. And Dover's white cliffs, not yet clichéd. Shots of sea and sky complement Priestley's invocation of a national history so olden it brushes eternity. Compiled in juxtaposition are the present's unnatural intrusions: the bombs, the refugees. And compiled in retort: Britain's forces, its voluntary services. Recruitment is specifically encouraged but the overriding purpose is simple – to boost morale.

Churchill's legendary 'fight on the beaches' is quoted, and a shot found to illustrate every subclause. Some propaganda documentaries were seen only at home, some abroad. *Britain at Bay* was released to UK cinemas *and* distributed overseas (as *Britain on Guard*). In both guises it speaks of unity. Priestley had socialist sympathies, but all ideologies were now subsumed. References to poor social conditions at home are soft-pedalled. The flattering characterisation of the British as a tolerant people who ask 'only to be left to do what we like with our own', who 'ask for nothing belonging to others' doesn't square with the biggest empire in history. But in 1940 something worse was being withstood. To express the heroism, and to feed it, was a cultural duty.

Prod Co: GPO Film Unit; **Spons**: Min of Information; **Music**: Richard Adinsell.

Children Learning by Experience
1947 – 32 mins
Margaret Thomson

In 1946, the Central Office of Information (COI) replaced the Ministry of Information (MOI) as the government's centralised communications facility. Initially, like the MOI, it commissioned films from both the Crown Film Unit and from independent producers. *Children Learning by Experience* and companion piece *Children Growing up with Other People* (1947) were made by the Realist Film Unit, for the Ministry of Education, via the COI. This example of the COI's varied early work was described by director Margaret Thomson:

> It was presumed that when the war ended there would be lots of people coming out of the forces who wanted to be teachers but they wouldn't know children at all . . . an HM Inspector had thought up the idea of making two films purely about children at their own ploys . . . we'd go all over London looking for children, playing by the river . . . in youth clubs, on bomb sites. Then we did more structured things by going into schools and watching the classes and playgrounds and crafts.[9]

A cameraman commented:

> I could never quite understand her way of working . . . she had the idea we'll just turn the camera on and we'll see what happens. I thought this is a little odd, but still it was the right thing to do.[10]

These remarks betray the subordinate status of 'observation' among documentary's mixed practices *c.* 1947. Basing an entire film around it was unusual. But it was not a Direct Cinema end in itself, merely the style chosen to serve the film's function. Also, it applies only to the cinematography, itself integrated into more conventional structures. The narrator states: 'There is commentary to point the way but the actions of the children are shown for you to interpret and discuss . . .. They're so absorbed that the camera is forgotten and this behaviour is natural and spontaneous.' These images are organised into logical sequences introduced by instructive intertitles. The commentary is subtler, often asking questions rather than making statements, gently underlining the footage's inherent, unforced charm. A scene filmed in a cinema is lovely. Whereas scenes with matches and lighters are alarming!

There is a disarming epilogue revisiting the opening scene with synchronised sound. The children were hitherto 'seen but not heard', though not due to Victorian attitudes. The film is relatively liberal: 'adults should respect children as young people with interests of their own'. The absence of live sound was at the time a virtually universal technical limitation on documentary shorts, transcended by creatively combining music, commentary and other sounds. Here the film-makers are happy to leave action genuinely silent for longish stretches when the narrator isn't speaking, ensuring attentive viewers will observe the children's behaviour closely.

An intriguing facet of Britain's documentary film tradition was its relatively large number of female directors. Women like Evelyn Spice, Budge Cooper, Jill Craigie and Kay Mander directed many films before and during World War II: far fewer afterwards. This is one respect in which post-war documentary *does* seem to have regressed (a few, very neglected younger film-makers can be found, such as Sarah Erulkar). Margaret Thomson was an exception. Having begun with Gaumont–British in the 1930s, she was still directing in 1970. *Children Learning by Experience*, probably her best-known film, remains engaging – partly because of its subject, partly because of its handling.

Prod Co: Realist Film Unit; **Spons**: Central Office of Information, Min of Education; **Dir**: Margaret Thomson; **Prod**: John Taylor.

The Coal Board's Butchery (*The Miners' Campaign Video Tapes*)
1984 – 15 mins

The Grierson Award for Best Documentary in 1985 surprisingly went to a group of short, hastily produced, technically substandard films. Never televised, they were circulated among working-class communities in the form of some 4,000 VHS tapes. The award wasn't a tribute to their quality so much as to a passionate intervention into a polarising national event.

The three *Miners' Campaign Video Tapes*, each containing two short polemical documentaries, were a collective contribution by politicised film-makers to 1984's nationwide miners' strike against threatened pit closures. An impressive roll-call of groups across the independent production world contributed to the project. The principal producers were London-based Platform Films (a video offshoot of Cinema Action) and Newcastle-based Trade Films.

The films weren't analysis or poetry. They were part of the strike, now widely seen as post-war collectivism's failed last stand against the Thatcherite onslaught. The second film on the first Campaign tape, *The Coal Board's Butchery*, is defiant, ending with an exhortation to fight, to organise. Yet with hindsight it's impossible to miss strong undercurrents of defeatism. The principal message proved accurate: 'no pit is safe' from closure.

The film summarises the strikers' case using a rudimentary blend of several documentary ingredients. Central to it are the *vox pops* of miners recorded at demonstrations. The mix of accents reflects filming around the UK coalfields. But they form *a* collective voice rather than several individual ones: *the* voice of the film. It has a monolithic viewpoint, unlike the strike's 'balanced' television coverage. It is bolstered by extracts from speeches by union leaders Arthur Scargill, Peter Heathfield and Kim Howells (now a New Labour minister) and political supporters like Tony Benn; loaded imagery presenting a brutal police force as

'Thatcher's political army'; and statistics charting the industry's decline. These are often captioned over monochrome coal-industry footage literally drawn from the stock imagery of classic British documentary, and newsreel footage of the 1926 General Strike. The video's own shots of bleak pit villages echo a documentary past. This gives it a paradox, shared with the strike itself. Margaret Thatcher's government, Conservative in name, reactionary in certain respects, had radical aims and methods. And 'while Scargill may have had a radical political philosophy, the strike itself was called for the most conservative of reasons – to preserve a traditional lifestyle'.[11]

The project's financial backers are listed in the credits. They fittingly include Ralph Bond and Ivor Montagu, elderly survivors of 1930s' socialist film-making. Like their films, the tapes found and shaped a distribution network to the left of the mainstream, showing, according to one commentator, 'just how much can be achieved without the conventional broadcast media. If television consistently ignores or misrepresents those in conflict with the State they in turn will increasingly start looking to the alternatives offered by the new technology.'[12] These remarks now read both presciently and anachronistically, referring as they do to productions mastered on the clunky Lo-Band Umatic video format. The inferior quality, the keyboard-generated captions, even the Heaven 17 soundtrack: all contribute to *The Coal Board's Butchery*'s period fascination. Few films in this book are more poignantly trapped inside their own historical moment.

Prod Co: Miners' Campaign Tape Project.

Coal Face
1935 – 12 mins
Alberto Cavalcanti

> 40 million tons of coal are sold every year for household use, 10 million
> tons for the production of electricity, 12 million tons for locomotives . . . .

The narrator's phrases are baldly, urgently factual. Yet also formal, decorative, intricately patterned into a low-budget polyphanous soundtrack of drummed rhythms, discordant piano notes, individual and massed voices, Welsh choirs: 'an oratorio of coal mining'.[13] This makes *Coal Face*, like a mistranslated textbook, prosaic and poetic, straightforward and weird.

Coal Face's first movement is like an overture introducing us to its self-contained world, bounded and guarded by vast pitheads seen in longer then in closer shot. The phrase that begins and ends the film – 'coal-mining is the basic industry of Britain' – seems to open and close the door on that world, created as much of sound as of image. This is rather paradoxical given that the socioeconomics of the off-screen world supply the film's subject.

Its second movement consists of maps of the main coalfields and statistics on the number of men employed, the tons of coal extracted, by each. Then the key sequence begins, a shift down the mine: more an artistic representation of miners' shifts in general than a record of an actual, individual one, despite references to the location of some of the footage and unconvincing dialogue dubbed over a scene of miners eating their sandwiches underground. But it's striking film-making. Even more impressive than the musical roll-call of miners' names on the track as they descend into the mine is their re-emergence into the open air as a female choir bursts into song and the next sequence begins, outlining coal communities' dependence on the industry dominating their localities. A swift camera movement across to swaying trees is worth the admission price.

Pitheads – a recurring image in British documentary – in *Coal Face*

The final sequences show how excavated coal is processed and the uses to which it's put throughout Britain's economy. Then several dissolves pull us away from the film's world clustered around Britain's coal faces. *Coal Face* exhibits strong social conscience, drawing attention to harsh realities by references to long shifts, cramped positions and the scale of death and injury in British mines – but stops short of explicit protest. And the aesheticisation arguably reconciles the audience to these realities.

Coal Face was credited to a non-existent organisation, Empo: apparently Grierson's *nom de guerre* for the GPO Unit when making films too far from the beaten artistic track to be released under its own name. In its own day it received limited release to mixed reviews, only in later decades becoming a documentary movement classic. Its initial impact was mainly on the 'movement' itself. Though most of the shots were stock material directed by GPO employees like Basil Wright and recent recruit Humphrey Jennings, the imaginative soundtrack was principally the work of Alberto Cavalcanti (uncredited on many prints). This émigré film-maker's relatively brief appearance in the British documentary world (as a Grierson employee then as his successor as head of the GPO Unit) was to have a decisive effect on it. His soundtrack collaborators on *Coal Face* included Benjamin Britten and W. H. Auden, then as young and hungry as the GPO's staffers. All three would make crucial, and credited, contributions to 1936's much more widely seen *Night Mail*.

Prod Co: Empo; **Dir**: Alberto Cavalcanti; **Prod**: John Grierson.

The Complainers
1997 – 51 mins
Dominic Savage

It's a tried-and-tested documentary recipe: explore a subject by looking
at how it plays out in the lives of two or three human case studies.
Documentarists used this approach in the 1930s and 1940s, if at a
distance. On television, helped by synchronised sound, their successors
have employed it repeatedly. The 1990s' love of docusoap 'characters'
has added another dimension. In the case of *The Complainers*, David
from Maidstone, Barry from Brighton and Alan from Greater Manchester
illustrate the topic of compulsive complaining by consumers. This is
explored mostly by interviews with them and with others commenting on
them (principally Alan's long-suffering ex-wife and daughter). And also
by actuality scenes in which they are filmed showering testosterone-
fuelled fury on those unfortunate enough to have supplied them with
shoddy products or substandard service. Some are minor incidents like
Alan's complaint at the number of fries in his takeaway. Others are
setpieces, like David's confrontation with a manager at the local Tesco,
a regular site for his rage. The manager proves patient beyond the call of
duty.

These techniques are conventional, applied to a trivial-seeming
theme and to initially unlikeable characters. But stylistically there is more:
the film opens on frighteningly extreme frontal close-ups of the three,
testifying as if in judgment rather than confession. And in the opening
titles they're grouped together on a windswept hill as the camera frames
and glides over them (they're never seen together in the film itself). The
effect of this stylish beginning, half-dramatic, half-comic, is to signal the
lifting of 1990s' factual entertainment to the level of mock-cinematic
morality play. The viewer immediately pays attention, sensing that the
film will offer more than meets the eye.

Despite the consistently light tone, there is a strand of acute
psychological portraiture. All three men have experienced misfortunes

mentioned in passing which we surmise have contributed to excessive displacement activities bringing evidently little pleasure. But this is also engagingly ambivalent social comment. We may be horrified that these people can become engulfed with rage at mere consumer disappointment. But we're hardly immune from consumerism. And isn't the British willingness to moan, but never to act, hypocritical?

The film climaxes on Barry, the most disproportionate character (a partial source for Ricky Gervais's David Brent?) upturning his desk and brutally frogmarching a hapless employee out of his office. Director Dominic Savage's later *Rogue Males* (1998), also aired in Channel 4's *Cutting Edge* slot, attracted controversy when scenes were revealed to have been staged, but in this case we sense that the crew's presence has contributed to Barry's *own* impulsive decision to drive himself to new extremes. Strangely, this enhances rather than diminishes the tragic-comic effect. His rage subsiding, the stylised hillside grouping of he and his fellow complainers reappears over the closing credits, walking away as if from a high noon gunfight's bloody aftermath.

Prod Co: Cicada Productions; **Dir**: Dominic Savage; **Prod**: Frances Berrigan.

The Conquest of Everest
1953 – 80 mins

John Taylor, Leon Clore and Grahame Tharp formed Countryman Films to make short natural-history films in the *Secrets of Nature* tradition. Taylor and Clore's credits elsewhere in this volume suggest their diverse careers; Tharp had worked principally for Shell and the NCB. On the suggestion that they film the upcoming Everest expedition, they embarked on a labyrinthine fundraising process descending to farce when one studio guaranteed financing if they could guarantee the expedition would reach the top! Eventually, public funds were provided on condition Countryman share credit with the Grierson-led subsidised company Group 3. *The Conquest of Everest* proved one of its few moneymakers. The producers were relieved when Grierson fell ill before editing, sparing them inevitable interference.

This film has no director. The biggest credit is to Thomas Stobart for 'filming', though he shot only sequences nearer ground before falling ill. Most of the material was photographed by George Lowe, occasionally on screen as part of the expedition party. His 16mm footage was later blown up to 35mm. The producers shaped the material in London, padding it to feature length by adding footage of J. B. Noel's 1924 expedition, and Coronation scenes. The taking of Everest was announced the day the Queen was crowned.

Once the story begins the strongest echoes are from World War II. Taylor and Tharp had made many films for the war effort. As in classic 'mission' movies, the team are shown researching and preparing, then doing it for real. The narrator singles out individuals, often when engaged in practical tasks, but there's little hint of inner lives. It's a group effort, against a respected foe. Everest's forbidding image dominates the screen, to stirring, swelling music.

Stobart's and Lowe's expedition footage is mixed with other elements to prevent monotony. Expedition members' retrospective comments are inserted into the soundtrack, coming across today like

over-rehearsed DVD commentaries (John Hunt, outlining the plan of
ascent over diagrams, is stereotypically, stiffly English, Edmund Hillary
more natural). Exposition otherwise depends on narration, always in the
present tense, often pointing out what's happening on screen as if
making the viewer vicariously present. Poet Louis MacNeice's script isn't
above turgid excess:

> Everest remained a challenge, aloof, inviolate, murderous . . . a land
> rushed upwards by subterranean violence . . . the ice is always on the
> move, cracking, rumbling, roaring . . . what bliss it would be to get down
> again, down from this blighted and wind-ravaged chunk of the moon
> where everything stops but the wind.

Phew! The music, though effective, is too insistent. It's a relief when
wintry ambient sound takes over. But the biggest disappointment is the
anticlimax of Hillary and Tensing's arrival on the summit. Lowe wasn't
with them: the necessary insertion of a still feels cheap.

Those anticipating unthinking racism may be surprised by the film's
humanism. Nepalese culture is presented positively if exotically and
Nepalese team members treated as respectfully as their comrades,
though they're reduced to a collective credit, while each white climber
is listed. The commentary's final reference to only two men reaching
Everest's summit, 'one of them born in New Zealand, the other born
under Everest' keeps Little England nicely at bay.

The Conquest of Everest exemplifies cinematic good taste c. 1953.
Not for the first time, an expedition overseas supplied cinemas with a
popular documentary feature proclaiming Britishness in an attractively
self-effacing form.

Prod Co: Countryman Films, Group 3; **Phot**: Thomas Stobart, George Lowe; **Ed**: Adrian de
Potier.

Conservative Party Election Broadcast 23/4/79
1979 – 10 mins

Britain was decisively, divisively altered by the 1979 General Election
result: and its party politics were altered by the preceding campaign.
This process kicked off the previous year when Margaret Thatcher's
Conservative Party appointed advertising agency Saatchi and Saatchi to
manage its image. Notwithstanding Thatcher's reputation for 'conviction
politics', policy positioning became closely bound with public relations
underpinned by market research, the result a deeply thought through
advertising crusade in which documentary film was a significant tool.
Saatchi's midterm 'Labour Isn't Working' poster lives in the collective
memory, having often been reproduced, unlike the agency's cinema and
television work. But in 1979 its election broadcasts were recognised as
groundbreaking, and generally considered electorally influential. Four of
the five pieces were shot on 35mm film before the election was even
announced, and the second in particular was clever, crude, classic
polemical documentary. Its very first shot distils Britain's 'winter of
discontent' into a single stark picture: snow-covered heaps of uncollected
rubbish. A pointed documentary of contrasts follows, reminiscent of past
left-wing assaults on the establishment. The phrase 'Crisis – What Crisis?'
(inaccurately attributed by tabloids to Labour Prime Minister James
Callaghan) is repeated five times, each time followed by news footage of
dysfunction: cancelled flights, empty shelves, picket lines.

 The remaining seven minutes intersperse a patrician fireside chat by
Conservative politician Humphrey Atkins with more imaginative sections:
effectively, several mini-documentaries combining to fashion a lively
lesson in monetarist economics. This is directly aimed at the target voters
identified by Saatchi's research, most blatantly in scenes of brightly
conceived and staged political symbolism. Several innocent citizens stand
in a courtroom dock, receiving 'punishment' for their initiative and
ambition in the form of heavy taxation. They represent key sections of
the electorate: women, aspirant families, owners of small businesses,

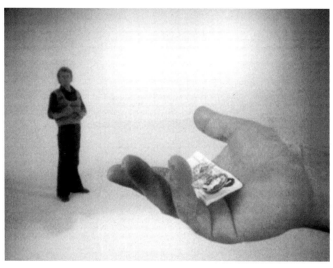

Conservative Party Broadcast: Little Man versus the state

pensioners. And in particular, skilled workers: a scene comparing their take-home pay with Continental equivalents (cue gallery of stereotypes) further stirs their resentment. Another shows a literally frozen wage packet. Another uses deep focus to portray Everyman forced to chuck his hard-earned cash into the state's literally giant hands.

Many of these people had voted Labour since 1945. Many did indeed switch to the Conservatives. Some flourished in the 'property-owning democracy' established by eighteen years of Conservative government and never looked back. Others saw their industries collapse, joined dole queues longer than those depicted by the famous Saatchi poster, and forever regretted it.

Spons: Conservative Party.

Crowd Bites Wolf
2000 – 23 mins

Ever-widening access to affordable, easy-to-use digital video equipment
has coincided with the advance of consumerism. And with that of its
discontents: locally and internationally politically active but rejecting
conventional national politics. The result of these phenomena coinciding
is 'video activism', eschewing mainstream media. This loose umbrella
term masks diversity as great as that found in earlier generations'
oppositional film cultures. Many campaign videos and video newsreels by
groups like Undercurrents and Conscious Cinema are effective
contributions to campaigns and community awareness-raising, whereas a
film like *Crowd Bites Wolf* combines extreme politics with forcefully
stylish aesthetics. The work of an obscure (now defunct?) anonymous
collective named Guerrillavision, it's a documentary of sorts about the
huge anti-globalisation protests staged in Prague in 2000 during an
IMF–World Bank summit. Its coverage of demonstrators stoning police
lines includes a police helmet being framed and followed as if the target
in a videogame: an inventive, witty, but morally problematic use of digital
editing software. The film was decried by respectable radical George
Monbiot as a 'fetishisation of violence, a sadistic pornography of pain'.[14]

While demonstration footage makes up much of the content, the
narrative focus is on one Flaco Blag. Part of the film-making team off
screen, within the film his persona is both fictional and non-fictional.
He is its journalistic presenter, interviewing demonstrators with a
handheld mike, and proferring political analysis in front of the camera
and in voiceover (for example, his scathing attack on World Bank
President James Wolfensohn). But he is simultaneously a character in a
flimsy fictional narrative constructed around the real events, a British
visitor intent on a boozy weekend in the Czech capital but swiftly drawn
into the insurrectionist maelstrom erupting on the barricades. Creatively
speaking, *Crowd Bites Wolf* is something of a zero-budget *tour de force*,
in equally confident command of dynamics and of graphics, gleefully

mixing angles, colours, speeds (and film and sound material borrowed from other sources, doubtless without copyright clearance).

The film was distributed in a compilation with two similar Guerrillavision pieces: 'stylistic hard hitting films which pull no punches. But be careful, watching all three together will have you reaching for a rock and heading for the nearest symbol of capitalist oppression.'[15]

The proliferation and increasing sophistication of nonetheless ephemeral born-digital moving image content presents as many practical problems for archivists as it does analytical ones for historians and critics. *Crowd Bites Wolf* stands out from the crowd for its disturbingly invigorating take on political documentary.

Prod Co: Guerrillavision.

A Day in the Life of a Coal Miner
1910 – 10 mins

Many silent actuality films contain prototypical documentary elements, but the 'interest' films made by Charles Urban's Kineto company come as close as any to being fully fledged documentary before the fact. *A Day in the Life of a Coal Miner* shares a textbook place in British documentary's evolution with an earlier film by another company, the 1906 *A Visit to Peek Frean & Co's Biscuit Works*. The differences are as striking as the similarities. Both closely document workplace processes, but in *Peek Frean* the workers have no stronger a presence than the machines. By combining the 'process' documentary with another, not yet codified format, the 'day in the life', the Kineto film adds the human to the mechanistic.

The intertitles anticipate the various tones adopted by the narrations of later sound documentaries. Most are explanatory: 'Locking the Lamps'. Some are playful: 'Belles of the (Black) Diamond Field'. Others veer into understated symbolism: 'Light after Darkness'. Scene for scene, much of *Coal Miner* is old hat. Female surface workers waving at the camera could have come out of a factory-gate scene filmed ten years earlier. But the film is more than the sum of its parts. That it's book-ended by staged scenes arguably strengthens rather than weakens its claim to be a documentary, 'creatively treating' rather than simply recording actuality. The sight of the eponymous miner leaving and returning to his family transforms our interpretation of the colliery footage in between (some of it also staged, underground cinematography not yet technically feasible). Still more obviously dramatised is the final scene, depicting a wealthy family enjoying an evening by their coal fire. This too anticipates a standard documentary device, the contrasting case study. Here it locates the preceding action inside a class structure literally fuelled by the mineworkers' toil. It's crudely effective, and surprising. Given the film's sanctioning by the Wigan Coal and Iron Co., ascribing subversive political intentions to it would probably be an interpretation too far. Could the contrast have shaken middle-class viewers from their complacency? Or were class expectations so ingrained that the final scene merely balanced grit with glamour?

The coal industry would go on to supply British documentary with resonant, ideologically charged images for many decades: *Coal Miner's* academic status, as a link in the chain ending in documentary proper, seems apt given its subject. It's primitive in various ways. By later

Faces staring from the past in *A Day in the Life of a Coal Miner*

standards, editing of shots within sequences is particularly sloppy, and photographic exposures inconsistent. Yet it's moving as well as informative. Placed halfway through is a shot of a haggard female worker (doubtless much younger than she looks) and a very young male one staring out at the viewer – abjectly, it seems. In narrative terms this shot is extraneous, but it adds a layer of meaning. The inclusion of footage unnecessary to the 'plot' but crucial to its impact on the viewer is another unintended anticipation of the creative documentary of the future.

Prod Co: Kineto; **Spons**: London & North Western Railway.

Desert Victory
1943 – 60 mins
Roy Boulting

The Western Desert is a place fit only for war.

Desert Victory recounts the second Battle of El Alamein, in which Montgomery's Eighth Army forced the retreat of Rommel's German and Italian forces. In *The Battle of the Somme* vein, it turns what might have been several discrete newsreel reports into a lengthier composite statement, but this time the joins don't show. Like World War II itself, it's clearer, better organised, more advanced, morally more convincing – less alienating – than its predecessor. But modern viewers should remember that, prior to this desert victory, Britain was losing the war. This helps explain the film's persuasive tone of qualified jubilation. But that it rings true is also down to its having emerged from within the forces, a co-production of the service film units set up in 1941. Further feature-length campaign documentaries were to follow, all as vividly authentic but adding extra doses of sentiment and reflection.

Miles of actuality material shot by frontline cameraman (and some captured German footage) were honed into documentary shape under the supervision of Roy Boulting. Boulting had directed some non-fiction but is famous with brother John for later lightly satirical farces. Alongside these the presence of the deadly serious *Desert Victory* might seem peculiar. It shouldn't. In war Captain Boulting had a different job than in peace, like the men in his film.

The background and progress of battle are explained by lucid narration, helped by maps. With its constant musings on subtle shifts in Rommel's strategic thinking, it betrays the same grudging admiration that Montgomery had for his nemesis. As for Rommel's army: the bodies of the German dead (and the exoskeletons of their dead tanks) are treated with a certain matter-of-fact dignity, but no more than that.

No energy is expended on pity or regret. For every Commonwealth casualty, it's proudly reported, there were five on the Axis side: 'bombed, blasted and machine-gunned, they tasted what they had administered in France and Poland'.

There are brief, important references to the home front, appearances by Churchill as well as Montgomery, and even a stiffly plummy officer's lecture to camera on being 'fighting fit and fit to fight'. But attention is

Military camaraderie in *Desert Victory*

focused on the common soldier. The unquestionable highlight, the sequence covering the initial offensive, is difficult to forget. The sights of the troops' last evening before the attack will breed butterflies in your stomach. Then, to show night descending, the frame is plunged into ominous darkness, the soundtrack hushed. After a full two minutes have passed, the building tension is exploded. Shells and gunfire are mingled with roaring voices; flares illuminate swiftly moving men. This sequence was constructed from a mixture of material recorded on the spot, and shots filmed in Pinewood. It's a frequent reference point for debates about the validity of staging in documentary reportage: further echoes from the Somme. The reconstruction parts are necessary to the impact of the whole, necessary to *suggest* the experiential reality of battle to those of us who can't know it. The offensive takes three minutes of screen time. In life it lasted five hours. According to legend, the noise was so loud that the gunners' ears bled.

Prod Co: Army Film Unit, RAF Film Production Unit; **Spons**: Min of Information; **Dir**: Roy Boulting; **Prod**: David MacDonald.

The Devil Is Coming (*The Great War*)
1964 – 26 mins
Tony Essex

Three stills combine into horrible triptych under rostrum camera. It moves down from a silhouetted soldier aside a memorial cross to a mangled skeleton beneath, then left to a soldier staring ahead as if indicating he knows he is a ghost. The photograph, taken shortly before the Battle of the Somme, subject of *The Devil Is Coming*, was shown at the start of every episode of the ambitious, influential BBC series *The Great War*. As the thirteenth of the twenty-six episodes, *The Devil* is chronologically as well as emotionally at the series' heart.

It had long been predicted that 'the retrospective historical film may become increasingly important as the back-log of factual historical material becomes longer'.[16] *The Great War* is usually seen as setting a template for television history, further refined by *The World at War* a decade later. This is all true. But it was itself refining a template bequeathed by cinema. In *The Devil* the words of Michael Redgrave as narrator and of several other thespians reading from contemporary letters, accounts and poems (Ralph Richardson voices General Haig) are edited to achieve machinegun-like rapidity. They are interwoven into a dense mosaic of footage, photographs and maps that feels as much like older multi-voice compilation films, as the history programmes to come.

The Great War's vital inflections of compilation documentary included its extended length and multipart format. This in turn necessitated more thorough scholarship – it was scripted by historians. It also prompted the professionalisation of footage reuse. No fewer than nine film researchers are listed on *The Devil*'s credit list. A vast amount of source material was drawn upon, including, of course, footage from *The Battle of the Somme*. The Imperial War Museum, holding much of the material, co-produced with the BBC. Film was 'stretch-printed' so that its action would not be speeded up when replayed at 24 fps. More debatably, synch sound-effects were added to the silent images.

Finally, television could now add interviews with eyewitnesses: soldiers who were there, and the sister of one who never made it back. Their old-world reticence is moving, given that they are recounting experiences more extraordinary than those of any later generation. It contrasts with the loudness of almost everything else in the film.

Like some other episodes, *The Devil Is Coming* sparked production disagreements. Scriptwriter John Terraine intended a sober explanation of the battle in its strategic context, advancing a revisionist view that it was not merely the futile waste of popular memory, and pointing out the scale of German as well as British death and suffering. This in particular comes across: the film ends quoting from a German soldier's letter: 'Hans is dead, Fritz is dead. There are many others. I am quite alone in the company . . . if only peace would come'. However, subtle analysis, though present, is easily lost under the visceral onslaught insisted upon by producer Tony Essex (whose background was in BBC current affairs). This contributed to the series' instant status as landmark television: this episode was especially singled out. But it contributes, now, to its also feeling 'cinematic'.

Prod Co: BBC, Imperial War Museum, Canadian Broadcasting Corp., Australian Broadcasting Commission; **Prod**: Tony Essex.

A Diary for Timothy
1946 – 38 mins
Humphrey Jennings

'Made in the years 1944–45', *A Diary for Timothy* is addressed to
Timothy Jenkins, born five years after war's declaration. Off-screen
narrator Michael Redgrave talks him through events of his early life
and the later stages of the war raging around him. Four adult lives are
also glimpsed, outside Timothy's own middle-class milieu: miner
Geronwy; farmer Alan; railway engineer Bill; and convalescent fighter
pilot Peter. The hallmark combination of many great films,
documentary or fiction, is here: simplicity, fineness and a gently
unyielding inscrutability. The premise is simple and effective, the
narrative touching, their execution delicately accomplished. Yet after
the twelfth viewing as after the first, it's still difficult to pinpoint,
firmly, why *A Diary for Timothy* so stirs the heart.

But the following are factors. The unforgettable small moments in
this film: Christmas 1944 brings two of them, the concurrent toasts,
nationwide, to 'absent friends'; and the close shot of Timothy,
dribbling in his cot as the choir sings, of the infant Jesus, 'Come let us
adore him'.

Few films so effectively touch the mixed feelings stirred in us by the
arrival of young lives alongside our own. The coal fire crackles by
Timothy's cot as Geronwy labours for such coal, and as a war is painfully
won. Innocent, mysterious infancy lays amid the familiar, wounded
grown-up world to which it will become accommodated. 'There's bad
luck in the world, Tim, as well as good. It's a chancy world. People get
hurt in peacetime as well as in war – though that shouldn't be.' If
Redgrave is the film's 'Voice of God', then this is a benevolent but not an
omnipotent God, omniscient over the present but as ignorant of, as
powerless over, the future as the baby. It will be made by Timothy's
generation when grown. The only thing we can predict with certainty is
that his innocence will fade.

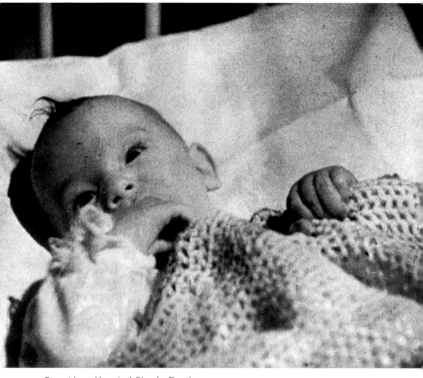

Our cot-bound hero in *A Diary for Timothy*

These emotions are intensified by Timothy's birth having been into an unusual historical moment, beautifully evoked by the film. His country is on the threshold between war and peace. And between one kind of society and another, one less deferential but perhaps less self-assured. Many viewers sense a tension between the stated hope that war and poverty be banished and an unstated fear of some unnamed loss. The film's several very evident flaws (structural imbalances, Redgrave's over-patricianism and sometimes false aspirations, Peter's stiffness) fit this theme, legacies of the pre-war world about to be put to pasture. However, the claim, frequently made, that the film's power rests partly on dramatic irony, our knowledge that its higher ideals will be betrayed, simply doesn't stand up. Timothy's generation has been among the most privileged in history. But older generations, battered by two wars and a depression, couldn't have known this.

The 1940s' documentary is a uniquely moving vehicle for this subject. The diary concept, the juxtaposition with the other characters: these could have been rendered entirely as fiction, with the themes intact but less memorable. Equally, today's documentary television could and has used the diary format, probing the details of everyday lives, yielding a more useful bequest to future anthropologists, maybe, but a less moving summing up of an age than *Timothy*'s furtive but respectful glances at its subjects.

Though Humphrey Jennings's direction is very fine, it is at the nexus of a collaborative project. A collaboration including Basil Wright (producer in his capacity as head of the Crown Film Unit): the film's tenderness is his as well as Jennings's. Including E. M. Forster, the scriptwriter selected by Wright, a generation older than his collaborators. And including composer Richard Addinsell. The minor-key violin chords over the final image of the film help send a chill down the spine, bring a tear to the eye.

Prod Co: Crown Film Unit; **Spons**: Min of Information; **Dir**: Humphrey Jennings; **Prod**: Basil Wright; **Phot**: Fred Gamage.

Drifters
1929 – 50 mins
John Grierson

Sir Stephen Tallents, head of the Empire Marketing Board (EMB), was an imaginative civil servant dedicated, in his phrase, to 'the projection of England'. The first lasting product of this project is *Drifters*, a very particular projection of Britain. Its unpromising premise, a herring drifter followed down the east coast from departure in Scotland to market in East Anglia, yielded a potent intervention into national culture.

The EMB sought to promote Empire trade and 'bring the Empire alive'. The choice of the modern herring fishing industry as its second film's theme was pragmatic politics. Director John Grierson felt an affinity for the subject, but also undertook extensive research prior to shooting.

A vision of thriving industry: *Drifters*

Not to be forgotten is the contribution of cinematographer Basil Emmott, with the experience his director entirely lacked. But *Drifters'* impact was largely due to Grierson's opportunism. He seized the chance to put theories into action then promoted the result to the right people. The month before *Drifters'* West End premiere, its first audience was the cineaste community attending the London Film Society meeting at which *The Battleship Potemkin* (1926) also had its first British screening.

Critical applause was widespread, spanning the journalistic spectrum. The left-liberal *Manchester Guardian* and conservative *Daily Mail* were both positive. For the *Sunday Worker*, *Drifters* was 'a work of art . . . that has some social purpose'. For the *Daily Telegraph* it was 'emphatically a very worthy British film'.[17] *Drifters'* equivocation set a pattern for mainstream documentary. It projected national identity, but not through flag and crown. It celebrated the worker but as a symbol. It balanced its enthusiasm for progress with a hint of nostalgia for fading pasts. It was open to fortuitously recorded events: the appearance of a whale in the film was a matter of luck. But it incorporated them into a construction assembled to represent the intended reality. Below-deck scenes were necessarily recreated on shore. More to the point is Grierson's recollection of waiting for weeks to get 'a real storm, an intimate storm, and if possible a rather noble storm'.[18]

Crashing waves had been in the cinematic toolbox since 1895. Commercial fishing as source material was almost as ancient. Industrial processes had been documented on film since Edward VII was on the throne. Journeys between places had been supplying a narrative framework for decades. But Grierson fused these into something more complex and exciting. The waves took on metaphorical as well as visual force, the processes a national as well as technical significance. Montage (overly gentle, admittedly) made connections.

It's creaky now. The lack of interest in the fishermen's psychology is beside Grierson's point but leaves the film with a gaping absence, which would matter less in a short than in a feature. And the underwater fish sequences are interminable! *Drifters* was a public-relations tool which ultimately did its best PR on its own behalf. Grierson later commented, tongue slightly in cheek, that it was 'more important to make a myth than a film. And *Drifters* was one such. It even got to the point that people wrote about it without ever having seen it, and that always tickled my propagandist fancy.'[19] It would be easy to advance revisionism by claiming that today's audiences inevitably emerge from screenings scratching their heads wondering what the fuss is about. But that would be another oversimplification. Viewers still spot the film's vigour and ambition as quickly as its defects. *Drifters* the film doesn't stand up too badly for its age. *Drifters* the myth is still working magic on many who haven't seen it, and even on those who have.

Prod: EMB Film Unit, New Era Films; **Dir**: John Grierson.

Drinking for England
1998 – 58 mins
Brian Hill

Drinking for England was produced for the BBC's *Modern Times* slot. Its broadcast was a revelation for many viewers, refreshing parts other television documentaries couldn't reach by imaginatively dispensing with convention. It could equally be argued that Brian Hill's film is so striking because it dares to *mix* idioms, some long dormant (rather than completely new).

The subject is the close bond many people have with alcohol. Conventionally enough, it's pursued by following parallel case studies, in most cases interviewing their protagonists and observing their drinking in bars or at home. But constantly interspersed are jolting sequences in which they address the audience, speaking rhyming verse. Two well-spoken twentysomething ladettes jointly recite the mantra:

> We open with lager then move on to wine
> And spirits and cocktails, one at a time
> 'Til we're holding as much as we're physically able
> By which time we're shitfaced and under the table.

Audio interviews had been sent to poet and regular Hill collaborator Simon Armitage who wrote verses reflecting the feelings and speech patterns, to be performed by their inspirations under Hill's direction. Two of the poems are set to music – the film is twice transformed into full-blown documentary musical. Hill/Armitage's subsequent *Feltham Sings* (2002) took this process even further.

Surprisingly, it isn't gimmicky. The standard and unorthodox techniques have complementary documentary uses. A retired gent of the shires is revealing when speaking spontaneously: 'my drinking isn't a problem . . .. It just slightly governs the way I lead my life.' But his reading better expresses the rhythm of his consumption: 'steady flow and a constant stream'. Sometimes, as if under the influence, the film collides the spontaneous and the choreographed. At one point, the twentysomethings slur their recitation as they literally spill onto the street at closing time.

It was once not uncommon for documentary-makers to put words into people's mouths. The difference here is that the words serve to explore individual psychologies. Another character, the only self-described alcoholic, is shown with her young son and mother, before heading off to a rehabilitation clinic. While there, she is filmed performing a Lloyd-Webberish production number ('Sherry and me, we're a fact of life/I'm a widow to sherry as well as a wife'). The former scenes are conventional, moving indications of the effect of her disease on others. The latter suggest alcohol's transformative if ultimately destructive power over her inner life, and her latent power to fight back.

Though interested in the individuals, the film suggests national cirrhosis via its title and its social cross-section of drinkers. A ten-pints-a-

'A Thinking Man' sings in *Drinking for England*

day man ('Sean that's me/Who likes the craic of knocking back the lager with the lads') is wedded to unpleasantly unreconstructed masculinity. His wife, for whom 'long-suffering' could have been coined, picks up him from the pub every night. Another is a likeable pub philosopher ('Thinking's a beautiful thing for a man/Thinks from a bottle and thinks from a can'). His love of drinking is joyous, if, in his song, laced with melancholy. The film celebrates the pleasures of consumption, rather than presenting it as simply a problem. But a young woman who appears only once, reciting her verse and not contributing interview, supplies its saddest section: 'Know it's true/Tell you why/Mother drinks/So do I'.

Documentaries can be playful *and* thought-provoking. Realism isn't identical to naturalism. And serious documentary doesn't always mean deep sobriety.

Prod Co: Century Films; **Dir/Prod**: Brian Hill; **Phot**: Gerry Law.

Education for the Future
1967 – 10 mins
Derrick Knight

Party political broadcasts (PPBs) became an occasional fixture of television schedules in the 1950s. Most were studio-bound addresses to camera by senior politicians, or forelock-tugging interviews broadcast (or recorded as if) live. More advanced early 1960s' PPBs mimicked contemporary discussion programmes with film inserts interpolated into studio chat. Genuine 'films' remained rare and the potential of documentary conspicuously untapped. The Labour Party in particular had long proved surprisingly apathetic about creative, campaigning use of film despite the documentary community's generally leftward leanings.

Then in 1967, Labour, urgently needing to fill some midterm slots, approached producer-director Derrick Knight's company. His firm, a fascinating transitional hybrid of old-fashioned documentary unit and youthful independent production house, willingly took on industrially sponsored projects, while investing the proceeds to produce socially committed or artistically inventive shorts: here was an opportunity to bring these strands together. It proved partially successful due to the film-makers' determination to produce a politically useful, artistically valid piece. And a partial failure because of the sponsor's half-hearted commitment and inadequate financial support. Documentary units expected this of routine industrial sponsorship, but perhaps not when working for Britain's governing political party!

Educational reform was one of the more dynamic projects of Harold Wilson's government. The first of the two resulting films was about comprehensive secondary education, which began supplanting the two-tier selective system in 1965. Rather than handmaiden a dull current-affairs lecture, the producers proposed a location documentary shot at a school, selecting one in Hull (a staunchly Labour-supporting town, presumably smoothing the school's agreement to being used for partisanship). Mobile, handheld shots taken in available light in the middle of classroom activity reflect the production company's stylistic history. It had earlier pioneered incorporation into British documentary film of lightweight 16mm cameras and synchronised sound, so suitable for recording unstaged action (this contribution has gone largely unsung, probably because the films' subjects and audiences were more specialised than their American and French equivalents). But for their political meaning these scenes depend heavily on what was now a standard *small*-screen documentary practice, statement to camera. The school's charismatic, articulate headmaster, speaking passionately about the role of comprehensive education in forging the good society, is supplemented by the less confident but telling contribution of a pupil's mother.

Given its severe production constraints, the film is inevitably serviceable rather than stylish, but its efficient techniques did bring out the idealistic underpinnings and human effects of government policies. It was unexpectedly popular, by its much maligned genre's standards. PPBs had always been one-night-only affairs, permanently shelved after their initial transmission. But this one, divorced from its original purpose, went on to enjoy an active afterlife as a non-theatrical film when the British Council picked it up. For decades this body had been commissioning and distributing British documentaries to promote UK culture abroad: since the main body of Knight's film contains no direct references to political parties, its succinct record of Britain's changing schools system was easily repurposed. For several years it remained available for international booking under the title *Education for the Future*.

Meanwhile, the potentially promising rapprochement of party politics with professional film-making had proved abortive – at least for the time being. Sadly, political communication, since then, thoroughly professionalised, has become tainted, associated either with negativity or with slick superficiality. Though *Education for the Future* attained, for

1967, a decent level of professionalism transcending semi-professional circumstances, what impresses now is its unaffected optimism, seriousness and direct engagement with an issue that divided the parties and the nation.

Prod Co: Derrick Knight & Partners; **Spons**: Labour Party; **Dir**: Derrick Knight.

Every Day Except Christmas (*Look at Britain*)
1957 – 40 mins
Lindsay Anderson

As a devotee of John Ford as well as Humphrey Jennings, Free Cinema's head boy Lindsay Anderson doubtless enjoyed its infiltration of cinema's memory banks. He and his cohorts began 'printing the legend' even as their films hit the screen. Repeated often enough, it became a fact. In practical terms, the Free Cinema 'movement' amounted to six screenings at the National Film Theatre, only three of them devoted to British films. But those films were distinctive enough – and well enough publicised in the right places – to become a noted cultural phenomenon.

The most ambitious, subsequently most anthologised, of these films was Anderson's prize-winning *Every Day except Christmas*, about Covent Garden market. It was included in the third Free Cinema programme. The programme's other highlight was Claude Goretta and Alain Tanner's *Nice Time* (1957), an interesting contrast. *Nice Time* was made entirely independently, with financial support from the BFI. *Every Day Except Christmas* was the first of three films in a shortlived series funded by Ford Motors (the next was Karel Reisz's *We Are the Lambeth Boys*, screened in a later Free Cinema programme). This was commercial sponsorship of the kind the documentary movement had once sought – enlightened patronage rather than base self-promotion.

Anderson's film projects a divided artistic personality: sometimes animated by the people and processes forming its raw material, at others forcing an affected response to them (perhaps, in view of Anderson's other work, even masking misanthropic dislike). Moreover, if a Free Cinema 'aesthetic' can be deduced from the films screened under its banner, in *Nice Time* (and in Anderson's 1953 *O Dreamland*) it is undiluted, while *Christmas* mixes it with others. Its arresting poetic visuals, experimentation with sound, sporadic use of improvisation and dependence on its director's vision were all signatures of Free Cinema though not unique to it. But they sit inside a classical structure, chronologically outlining twelve hours in the life of the market though filmed during four weeks, and following its products' journey from farm to market stall. Alun Owen's softly Welsh-accented narration has classic public information rhythms ('through cities and country towns and down the long, arterial roads the lorries are coming to London with apples from Kent and Evesham, potatoes from Norfolk, oranges and lemons from the western ports'). The punchline – 'we all depend on each other's work as well as our own' – has the same interest in conveying workers' dignity that earlier films had, and similarly risks patronising them.

Certainly the people are sometimes the dignified 'types' beloved of older documentary-makers: witness the final, lively montage of their faces. But sometimes individuals whose mysterious uniqueness briefly flowers: the fastidious lady, the camp young man and the furrow-browed gentleman caught on camera in the bustle of an all-night café. They sometimes prompt thoughtful reflection: the lady who has been selling flowers since 'Victoria was Queen and every gentleman wore a buttonhole, a long time ago'. And they are sometimes simply part of the film's vivid atmosphere, alongside the poetry conjured from the simplest material. At the gently beating heart of the film is an exquisite lyrical sequence in which tender music plays as the camera surveys the cups, caps and hats of a café's sleepy customers then pans across rows of flowers – dissolves – and tilts up to darkness.

Prod Co: Graphic Films; **Spons**: Ford Motor Company; **Dir**: Lindsay Anderson; **Prod**: Leon Clore, Karel Reisz; **Phot**: Walter Lassally.

(*Next page*) An atmospheric moment from *Every Day Except Christmas*

The Face of Britain
1935 – 18 mins
Paul Rotha

Paul Rotha, already a groundbreaking film critic, found his way into the industry under Grierson at the EMB but, unlike contemporaries, was too headstrong and individualistic to work under Grierson's patronage. He was soon out on his own, tirelessly extolling his own version of the documentary gospel while chasing after film commissions in an attempt to eke out an insecure living. 'The most left-wing member of the Documentary Movement', certainly the most iconoclastic, worked much more often in the private sector, often under capitalist sponsorship, than many of his colleagues. In 1934 he fetched up in the not entirely congenial surroundings of Gaumont–British Instructional where he made one of its least, one of his most, characteristic films. *The Face of Britain* actually had some public sponsorship, from the Central Electricity Board, then working towards a fully national electricity grid. Its sponsorship supplies the film's ostensible subject, the power of electricity to transform the country, but the deeper theme came from the director: a fervent love–hate relationship with Britain itself. Rotha later judged that it was 'an over-ambitious film trying to say too much in too short a screentime and with not enough resources',[20] an accurate assessment of most of his films but unreasonably harsh on this one.

Rotha's documentaries are both cerebral and passionate – sometimes an unstable combination. But his films better than anyone's support the argument that documentary's lineage is less in the literary tradition of journalism than in the oratorical tradition of rhetoric. *The Face of Britain* is principally concerned to advance a hypothesis, appealing to fact and reason but simultaneously depending on the exercise of style – see particularly the dazzling montage of the film's second part, which really must be viewed on the big screen for full impact. (Another Russian trapping, common in documentary movement films, is Rotha's frequent use of low-angle shots of people against landscapes.)

Like so much 1930s' documentary, the film references Britain's different topographical personae, but goes further, by explicitly organising itself around their historical relationship in dialectical fashion. The first section, 'The Heritage of the Land', tables the thesis: the idyllic Britain of farms, village churches and market towns. The second chapter, 'The Smoke Age', presents its antithesis, a nightmarish industrial Britain clambering out of its coalfields, bringing in its wake progress and wealth, and poverty, degradation and ugliness. The final sections, 'The New Power' and 'The New Age', foretell a synthesis in which the power of electricity is harnessed to create a new Utopia out of the wreckage of Britain's imperfect pasts.

By explaining historical processes as if from a cosmic vantage point outside them, the commentary (by liberal journalist A. J. Cummings) deserves the 'Voice of God' epithet more than most, though it's hardly disinterested. Politically, the film is hard to place if viewed through the prism of our own ideological spectrum. In the mix: strong social conscience, bucolic nostalgia and an explicit revulsion for manufacturing industry. It is here that the film's rhetorical components are in tension: the second chapter of industrial antithesis is much the most exciting.

The final section argues for a planned economy, the building blocks of which were tentatively put in place before World War II, and vigorously built on afterwards. For the 'face' of Britain, then, read its landscape . . . and from its landscape, the film-maker argues, we can read its psyche . . . its heritage . . . its future.

Prod Co: Gaumont–British Instructional; **Dir**: Paul Rotha.

The Family (*Week 12*)
1974 – 29 mins
Franc Roddam, Paul Watson

In his powerful 2006 film *Rain in my Heart*, Paul Watson stresses to viewers and potential participants that he is making documentary, *not* reality television – aware that many regard him as having sown the seeds for docusoap in his series *The Family*. This series involved three months of a crew filming for eighteen hours a day inside the home of an 'ordinary working-class family', the Wilkins of Reading. It was partly modelled on a similar US experiment, *The American Family* (1973). An important difference was that the American version was in the can before any of the films were screened. Watson and team were shooting and editing well after Episode 1 had been televised. Accordingly, the final film takes into account the massive controversy generated by earlier instalments, becoming in large part a reflection on its own making and meaning. Early in *The Family*'s final episode the surreal intensity of its production is summarised by clips of cameras whirring around family members, and of them being interviewed by programme staff, whose voices sound uniformly posh compared with the Wilkins'.

The films raised two debates. One, hard to credit now, was that of television's responsibilities for national moral rectitude. Here, Mrs Wilkins accurately summarises the four things that made her family 'different' and therefore controversial as a representation of British domestic life. An extended family was living under one roof. It included her daughter and fiancé, clearly having premarital sex. Another daughter had a 'coloured' boyfriend. Her own son had been born out of wedlock.

The other debate, very resonant today, was over the status of the films as documentary, and their implications for the future of television. Was this sociology or gimmickry? Was reality being observed or altered? Were people driven to watch by curiosity or prurience?

Both debates are aired in the film, partly by including interview material in which the subjects reflect on the experience of being filmed, on how they came across and on public and press reaction. As throughout the series, the boundaries between formal 'interview' and relaxed 'conversation' are blurred: this later became increasingly common in factual television. Intercut is footage of a radio debate about the series, compered by popular DJ Jimmy Savile, and featuring Mr Wilkins, Watson and opponents of his programmes.

Ultimately *The Family* doesn't feel like reality television, more like 1974 film-making prefiguring some of its aspects. Made on 16mm, its shooting ratio, generous for the time, pales in significance to later video output. It has a filmic artfulness, announced at the beginning and end of every film by its beautifully crafted credits sequence. In the films themselves it's evident in the stills formally introducing family members, and especially in the editing. Short, expressive snatches of scenes, punctuated by black, are assembled into an arc more thematically than chronologically determined. A telling moment arises from Savile's question of Watson: has he lumbered or helped the family? He doesn't believe he has lumbered them, but thinks they might have experienced self-discoveries on the strength of the juxtaposition of shots that he, the producer, has consciously chosen in order to make *his* statement of how *he* sees *them*. He claims that this exercise has validity as national social enquiry, because the family's life is entwined with the social conditions of its time, but not because the Wilkins are a 'typical' family – there is no such thing. Many aspects of his practice and that of programme-makers who have followed are questionable. But they do underline a sound maxim: the only normal people are the ones you don't know very well.

Prod Co: BBC; Co-dir: Franc Roddam; Co-dir/Prod: Paul Watson.

Five and Under
1941 – 16 mins
Donald Alexander

The war that brought Britons together into vital collaboration prompted many to reflect on how collective effort might be continued afterwards. These feelings began finding expression in documentaries groping towards the post-war world even as war raged, films often betraying their makers' political leanings. *Five and Under* is a good representative of these Janus-faced wartime documentaries and the varied, imaginative techniques they employed. It opens with a title-card stating that 'Women are in the war as much as their men', then poses the question as to what has happened to the children they would otherwise be looking after. Footage documenting various childcare arrangements is interspersed with scenes in which the female narrator (voice supplied by character actress Beatrice Lehmann) interacts with on-screen working mothers and nursery nurses, speaking direct to camera about their experiences.

Breaking the fourth wall like this is now virtually never done in 'serious' documentary (unlike in advertising and educational films). Comfortably mixing non-fiction genres, this film's makers have taken their subject matter and much of their footage from real processes, people and relationships, then combined these with constructed and reconstructed imagery in part to convey these realities and a particular view of them, but also to affect behaviour. And stylistically, though they never really try to be lyrical, they switch between several other approaches – informative, analytical, emotive – depending on which other genre their documentary is interacting with at any given moment. As a public-information film, *Five and Under* summarises the main childcare options: baby-minders, nursery schools and day nurseries. As a work of reportage, it touches fairly honestly on challenges such as understaffing and child behavioural problems (in a striking staged sequence, a group of unattended children begin to run amok before a matron arrives and intervenes), and the inherent tragedy of the war itself (the safe interiors contrast with frequent images of rubble-strewn streets). Finally, as propaganda, it at first indicts society ('We allowed two things to happen – slums and war') then looks forward to better future social provision. Though Paul Rotha Productions, like other independent documentary producers, was willingly co-opted into working for Britain's wartime coalition government, films like this are easily seen today as foreshadowing the rhetoric and policies of the Labour government elected four years later.

Twenty-first-century viewers will feel the film-makers' progressive sentiments are undermined by their unconscious sexism. They clearly imply that the need for widespread institutional support will diminish once mothers return to their rightful place at home. And portrayals of working-class women are less than convincing (incidentally this is the point at which the film begins using clearly directed performances). But even as a social document, *Five and Under* is of topical as well as historical interest. Today, as in 1941, many mothers work outside the home, whether from choice or necessity, and finding affordable, appropriate childcare is as big a problem as ever.

Prod Co: Paul Rotha Productions; **Spons**: Ministry of Information; **Dir**: Donald Alexander.

Gallivant
1996 – 99 mins
Andrew Kötting

Andrew Kötting's *Gallivant*, like Patrick Keiller's *London*, was among the later films funded by the BFI. Co-funded by Channel 4, they both saw cinema release before being televised. Both were memorably unconventional reinventions of travelogue; and both feature film debuts in the documentary form by artists previously responsible for experimental shorts. But *London* (and its sequel *Robinson in Space* [1996]) is a purposely immobile, deceptively dispassionate, certainly pessimistic meditation on location. *Gallivant* is constantly on the move, a picaresque journey among people as well as places, as far from metropolitan Britain as it's physically possible to get on its mainland.

The small crew spent three months travelling round the coastline, from Sussex to Cornwall, round Wales, via Lancs and Cumbria to Scotland, back down the east coast from John O'Groats, ending where they began in the faded-genteel resort of Bexhill-on-Sea. With them much of the way were the director's talkative octogenarian grandmother Gladys and seven-year-old daughter Eden, who has Jouberts Syndrome, communicates through yelps and limited sign language and isn't expected to live to adulthood. Their growing attachment is subtly charted, as they converse on deckchairs and boats, in tents, on cliffs, down pathways and astride the Anglo–Scottish border. Chronicled meanwhile is the party's journey through contrasting landscapes, encountering *en route* stubbornly quirky local customs and assorted folk. The adventure arises, as with many documentaries and most family holidays, from the collision of serendipity with logistical planning (of which there is rather more than the film itself lets on). Kötting, with his maddish, slightly laddish persona, comes over as an offbeat investigative reporter, brilliantly able to put his chance interviewees at their ease.

There's poignancy in the premise, but no sentimentality in its handling. The mythical undertones of this odd odyssey aren't overstressed. And although there is much formal experimentation, it's never pretentious. Kötting's most frequent experimental trope, the speeding up of footage, brings out the weirdness in the everyday, in which permanence and transience jostle. His frequent use of Super-8 stock evokes vintage holiday home-movie traditions (underscored by a scene in which he and Eden post a completed roll of film to the developer). Most refreshingly, the film is free of cynicism and condescension. Most of the people met are courteous, interesting and humorous. The many themes emerge in the viewer's responses rather than from any direct, consistent statement. Yet the national and the personal, the cultural and existential, seem to interconnect. So, though the scene in which Eden walks unaided before her father and great grandmother, is extremely emotional, another in which Kötting humorously banters with an elderly Cumbrian lady and her middle-aged son is in its own way as touching.

The film loses focus when Gladys and Eden are (for good reasons in the real world) absent from the expedition. Its pace later flags. A late scene in which Kötting battles a large fish is distractingly brutal amid the film's gentleness. Another in which celebrated English folk musician Martin Carthy gives a seaside accordion rendition seems contrived where an earlier encounter with two anonymous characters singing 'Do You Ken John Peel' felt marvellously fresh.

But the final moments are among the most simply affecting in 1990s' cinema. If everyone has a novel in them, but perhaps just one, maybe everyone has one feature-length documentary in them. It seems significant that Kötting has since largely returned to smaller-scale experimental film-making. Almost every viewer emerges from *Gallivant* informed, entertained and almost literally revitalised: ready to embrace our own curiosities and affections while we still can.

Prod Co: Tall Stories; **Dir/Sc**: Andrew Kötting; **Prod**: Ben Woolford; **Phot**: N. G. Smith.

The Great Recovery (*Britain under National Government*)
1934 – 10 mins

The Great Recovery in question is from the Great Depression. The film was made in support of the Conservative-dominated coalition government struggling with the Depression's effects, and was merely the latest in a line of films produced by the Conservative Party. Ironically, it was the most progressive of British political parties in adopting new technology for mass political education. Via its Conservative and Unionist Film Association, Central Office had been commissioning films since 1926, for back-projection in a fleet of 'mobile cinemas' driven to meetings across the country: satirical cartoons, films of speeches and a simple series of compilation documentaries, *Britain under National Government*.

Farms, steel plants and coal mines represent the economy, industries failing at the beginning of the film (fallow fields, stopped mines), thriving by its end (belching smoke, fiery sparks, laden coal trains). And a compilation of shots of individuals represents the socially diverse nation depending on them: from the bearskin-hatted guardsman to the policeman, postman, the typist, 'the man in the street, the woman in the home'. Much of this socially inclusive imagery could have been borrowed from the more artistic documentaries of the time. A shot of a cup-final crowd to make a key point adds a populist touch. But all of this sits alongside the more traditionalist symbolism of Big Ben, Britannia and the union flag, and illustrates an analysis of the government's tasks and achievements. Diagrams explain the balancing scales of income and expenditure. Footage of an Empire trade conference evidences enthusiastic British promotion of imperial trading. Much is made of the balance of imports and exports. The film's appeal to commonsense realism is characteristic of right-wing rhetoric, in this case directed against rather than for free trade: the Conservative Party of 1934 was strongly protectionist.

The Great Recovery is an illustrated lecture. Virtually every shot is directly related to the commentary: 'look at this abandoned coal mine . . . here is a shot of the treasury . . . let me now summarise . . . '. The bathos approaches absurdity when the narrator's reference to gathering storm clouds is duly accompanied by a shot of a cloudy sky. And there are technical defects. At one point, the narrator, presumably recorded in one take, can be heard clearing his throat. At another, a figure mistakenly enters the frame briefly. There is a puzzling resort to captions halfway through making a point. At one juncture no fewer than twelve factual statements hurtle at the viewer in silence, taking up a full minute of the running time. The library footage used to contrast recovering Britain with other countries ('Who wouldn't rather live in Britain under a National Government?') is more dramatic and better photographed than anything else in the film. But many of these oddities are explained by how such films will have been seen: in large meeting spaces, introduced by speakers, watched by potentially noisy crowds. The film is no cruder than those produced on the left, but was seen by far more of the unconverted. Whether it changed votes is hard to say, but, like its socialist counterparts, it's a valuable inheritance from a decade still well within living memory, yet politically, culturally – and financially – lifetimes away.

Prod Co: Conservative and Unionist Film Association; **Spons**: Conservative Party.

Guinness for You
1971 – 15 mins
Anthony Short

Documentary and advertising are sometimes placed at opposite ends of the filmic spectrum: soberly elevated vs crassly exploitative. Neither characterisation is always accurate. Moreover, the two forms have many connections, conceptual and historical. Both seek to convince viewers of their own veracity; sponsorship caused them to mingle; and many documentarists have filmed commercials, if only to pay the bills. Analysis of commercial breaks would show documentary practices jostling among several others. A more easily established connection is via longer 'promotional documentaries'. Sydney Box illuminated it back in 1937 while listing categories for his Handbook on the Production and Distribution of Propaganda Films:

> *Industrial:* This was the first type of publicity film to be made and it still enjoys considerable favour. Its object is to tell the audience how the sponsor's product is made . . . people are notoriously interested in 'how the wheels go round', and nearly every manufacturer knows that if he could show prospective customers the care and ingenuity lavished on manufacture, he would be well on the way to increased sales. As the technique of the cinema developed, this reporting became more expert, and a film of a factory improved on the factory itself. Out of this change grew up a new method of screen journalism known as: *Documentary.*[21]

Thirty-fours years younger than Box's statement, *Guinness for You* is a lively, experimental take on the venerable 'process' documentary. Promoting Guinness Stout (emblematically Irish but popular in Britain where it has a full manufacturing and marketing operation), Guinness described it as:

> An impressionistic film which without uttering a word delights the eye and ear to evoke the magic of taste in every bottle of Guinness. Interweaving images of all the elements that go to its make up . . .

accompanied by cleverly composed sound effects and some impressive modern photography.[22]

Although jump-cuts, reverse action and sudden changes of focus date the film, it still works very well, benefiting from a strong colour scheme of burnished oranges, yellows, browns – and black, of course. The director gets round Arthur Elton's 'first law of industrial sponsorship' ('the impact of a sponsored film upon its audience will be in inverse ratio to the number of times the sponsor insists on having his name mentioned') by repeatedly foregrounding the famous harp logo on bottles, caps and glasses. But otherwise it's not unsubtle. Tristram Cary's eerie soundtrack bestows an almost sci-fi ambience. Rather than replicating the exact sequence of production, the film switches locations and times, reinforcing connections between the product and several abstract concepts: nature (barley and hop fields), history (engravings of Arthur Guinness and historic Dublin), science ('laboratory' scenes) and consumer pleasure (regular cuts to a bar in which Guinness is being served and drunk).

Such associative montage is a mainstay of creative documentary. *Guinness*'s production origins also mark it out as a documentary product. Unit 7 was one of several companies in the Film Producers Guild, which channelled and distributed documentary sponsorship between participating units. Writer-producer Eric Marquis is an interesting, overlooked film-maker responsible, as director, for films on topics as serious as mental illness and terrorism. He remembers *Guinness for You*, without affection, as 'advertising' (see p. 248). The company described it, approvingly, as 'documentary'. It's both. Guinness's publicity work, from John Gilroy's 1930s' posters to Jonathan Glazer's *Swimmer*, is renowned. Its 1971 foray into documentary is stylish enough for teetotallers to enjoy the technique. But, by the time a bubbling vat of fermenting liquid cuts to an enticing glass of creamy, black stout, even they might find themselves thirstily rushing to the bar. *Slainte*!

Prod Co: Unit 7 Film Productions; **Spons**: Guinness; **Dir**: Anthony Short; **Prod/Sc**: Eric Marquis.

Handsworth Songs
1986 – 61 mins
John Akomfrah

An interesting 1980s' crossover between film and television documentary resulted from the 'Workshop Agreement' guaranteeing BFI and Channel 4 subsidy to the independent production sector. Surviving collectives from the previous decade's activist film-making (notably Cinema Action) were among the beneficiaries. Others were newer film and video workshops, several emerging from minority communities once largely disenfranchised from media production. The resulting films were both distributed non-theatrically, or even in cinemas, and broadcast, often in Channel 4's 'alternative' slot *The Eleventh Hour*.

In 1985 rioting had erupted in multiracial urban areas such as Birmingham's Handsworth district. *Handsworth Songs* is a multi-layered 'documentary essay' exploring the meaning of these events. By including footage of TV crews filming, and a television discussion programme being set up, the film clearly falls within a tradition of documentaries explicitly positioned to the left of mainstream reportage, purporting to expose ideological processes behind newsworthy events. Admittedly, *Handsworth Songs*' methods are more sophisticated than, say, *Jubilee* (1935). It interweaves extracts from the riots' extensive coverage with older archive material, interviews, stills, newspaper headlines and specially shot footage of inanimate objects symbolic of British colonialism: the union flag, a pith helmet, chains. At one point there is a cut from the chains to archive extracts showing metalwork factories, an edit typical of the film's juxtaposition of disparate images to imply a relationship (here indicating Britain's white workforce was simultaneously victim and agent of exploitation). Sound and picture are often deliberately distorted, imagery of past and present frequently correlated, images combined with unexpected sound to prompt reinterpretation. Above all, two soundtrack voices recur in constantly shifting guises, suggesting a plurality of possible interpretations, as does the film's title:

Handsworth Songs rather than, say, *The Song of Ceylon* (1934). However, as with many 'multiply voiced' documentaries, the material is weighted so as to favour some general conclusions.

Handsworth Songs, often cited as a major work both of British documentary and of 1980s' British cinema, divides viewers. Following its broadcast, two leading non-white intellectuals clashed in print over its merits. Stuart Hall praised it for challenging common representations by breaking with conventional documentary methodology. Salman Rushdie attacked it for empty pretentiousness. Their debate echoed those caused by earlier films documenting social issues while experimenting with form. *Handsworth Songs'* avoidance of the obviousness of much 1980s' politicised film-making is commendable and its resurrection of the multi-voice film interesting, but it has otherwise dated badly, mainly due to flaws of execution rather than conception. Lacking a strong enough interior logic to make it more than the sum of its parts, its source materials are more fascinating than the means putting them together. Publicity handouts claimed it attempted 'to excavate hidden ruptures/agonies of "Race" in both its historical and contemporary movements. *Handsworth Songs* looks at the riots as a political field coloured by the trajectories of industrial decline and structural crisis.'[23] It's never a good sign when film-makers resort to academic jargon to promote their work. It's difficult to avoid suspecting that inverse racism, fuelled by proper concern at continuing ethnic media under-representation, has played a part in the overpraising of *Handsworth Songs*.

Prod Co: Black Audio Film Collective; **Dir**: John Akomfrah; **Phot**: Sebastian Shah.

Health and Clothing
1928 – 15 mins
H. W. Bush

'Sponsored' documentaries are those funded by bodies outside the film industry, often conveying messages relevant to their work. A sponsorship *infrastructure* was a 1930s' development. But sponsored films, though scattered, were far from uncommon beforehand. Of the several surviving 1920s' examples, this one is a product of one of the more thoroughgoing attempts at using film to fulfil organisational remits. To suggest it's great film-making is less to overrate than to misrepresent it. It has no artistic intentions: its charm lies elsewhere.

In 1923 a Labour majority was elected to Bermondsey Borough Council, local authority for an impoverished working-class part of London. Its public-health department embarked on ambitious health campaigning, at its most intensive through the 1920s though continuing for three decades. Some thirty films were produced. Like many communications documentaries, they were part of a multimedia effort (incorporating pamphlets, posters and newspaper advertisements). They were often screened within lectures also including lantern-slides in public buildings, and at local associations and open-air meetings. The council even had its own projector van.

The films were made by a small team of council officers showing no interest in film other than as a means of advancing policy objectives. If later mainstream documentary is obliquely tied to an ideology of state social democracy, these films are the product of an earlier political tradition of social reform pursued by local government. Bermondsey's films were part of an innovative political project nonetheless due to be superseded. Perhaps this is why *Health and Clothing* feels vivid *and* archaic.

Municipal socialism was geographically constrained but activist, paternalistic but close to its people. It follows that its adherents might take interest in progressive communication tools (as film still was) to present the populace not with symbolic representations but with facts to influence behaviour. One of the film-makers, Bermondsey's Medical Officer of Health, stated that films' advantage over slides was that they 'could demonstrate a process, and thus relate cause and effect', via 'simple continuity of ideas throughout' and intertitles which 'must be simple and accurate . . . concise and pointed'.[24] This suggests a homemade anticipation of later schools' films, though *Health and Clothing*'s target audience is clearly adult women. After an opening comparison of animal and human worlds reminiscent of *Secrets of Nature* (1922–33), it goes on to use a classic classroom instructional technique: building an argument in stages prior to a summarising conclusion. It's divided into chapters listing different characteristics of healthy clothing. Interestingly, chapter by chapter different documentary options are energetically taken. These include records of process (wool being sheared), staged scenes (a woman putting up the laundry indoors while her man reads his paper) and actuality footage (shots taken of public places). There are fun 'demonstration' scenes shot in the producers' makeshift studio. Check out the bemused reaction of the cute child being divested of numerous layers of heavy outer clothing. Also included are rudimentary animation and graphics, even crude historical reconstruction. The year '1560' is amusingly fluffed and overacted; '1890' is more realistic but equally obsolete when viewed from modern, resourceful Bermondsey. The year 1890 preceded projected film. But in 1928 it was well within living memory.

Spons: Bermondsey Borough Council; **Dir**: H. W. Bush.

The Heart of the Angel
1989 – 40 mins
Molly Dineen

The Heart of the Angel was an edition of *Forty Minutes*, a social
documentary slot running to some 320 films screened between 1981
and 1994 on BBC2. Like several later ones, this episode was produced by
an independent company. It augmented director Molly Dineen's budding
reputation as a distinctive television documentary auteur. But its listings'
blurb nonetheless accurately hints at a film stationed somewhere
between the crafted 'day-in-the-life' single-film documentary of yore,
and the disreputable docusoap series of television's then near future:
'Every day the Angel tube station struggles to cope with its load of
15,000 commuters. Weary travellers lose their tempers with a frustrated
staff, who try to smile through all the traumas.'[25]

Dineen covers two days and the night in between, rather than the
standard working day, or twenty-four-hour time-slice. This gives her film
a tidy overall construction of three distinct sections, though the material
sitting inside is authentically untidy. One effect is to represent the
station's cyclical existence. Largely the same collection of daytime ticket-
sellers, guards and supervisors appear in the first and third days, even if
reacting to slightly different events (a lift breakdown and an injured man
supply respectively the main dramas of the two days). Sandwiched
between these, the nighttime sequence is arresting, with its darkness and
an entirely different cast: gangs of female cleaners and male
maintenance workers, at the physical heart of the station, in the middle
of the documentary's running time. The station's life depends on their
pounding activity just as bodies depend for life on hearts beating out of
sight and earshot. When these cavernous nightworkers emerge into
daylight, from a documentary history perspective it's *Coal Face* (1935)
that comes to mind, though Dineen is not interested in visual stylisation.
Instead, she mixes the Direct Cinema, vérité and journalistic approaches.
Much is purely observational: operating her own camera, Dineen comes

closer to the viewer's visual perspective than most directors. The sequence with the male nightworkers contains highly impromptu interviews. Other scenes are even less formal: employees' casual utterances as they go about the business Dineen is filming, or conversations sparked off between them. A critic has commented: 'Dineen's documentaries, more clearly than many, are negotiations between the reality before she intruded, and the artificial environment generated by her presence. Within this, Dineen is perpetually oscillating between relinquishing and asserting control.'[26]

The film's final conversation is with a ticket-seller who has been sparring with customers and with Dineen throughout. He shares his worldview, quintessentially British: gloomy, pragmatic and humorous.

Dineen's questioning voice became a marked feature of more ambitious later projects. Here, it's intermittent. The dialogue scenes are shot through with a jokily self-aware *faux naïveté*, mutual between film-maker and subjects, with their class and gender differences a constant undercurrent. But she is an opportunistic rather than theoretical documentarist. When opportunities for arty camerawork present themselves, she quickly takes them: a *Vertigo*-like shot of the lift-deprived passengers descending the spiral staircase. When she encounters lively customers (off-their-face teens or feisty octogenarians), she duly turns her camera towards them. All of this is edited so as to produce a lively, open piece without a telegraphed meaning. Notably, it doesn't stress for political ends the chronic state of investment in the London Underground, though the events caught on film make this obvious.

Prod Co: Allegra Productions; **Dir/Phot**: Molly Dineen.

Heroes of the North Sea
1925 – 23 mins
A. E. Jones

Like several films discussed here, *Heroes of the North Sea* has physically survived largely by chance and, so far as most cinema histories are concerned, might just as well not have. Apparently the solitary item on the filmographies of its production company and director (the cameraman has credits on a handful of forgotten, mostly fictional works of the 1910s and 1920s), it's as unsung as most of silent cinema's supporting programme two-reelers. But its subject happens to be remarkably close to that of *Drifters*, made four years later, demonstrating that Grierson's film didn't burst on the screen as if from nowhere (at least not with respect to its narrative framework). It was actually in a fairly long line of documentaries accompanying fishing trips (an even earlier example is *A Trip to the White Sea Fisheries* [1909]). Which is not to accuse *Drifters* of plagiarism, rather to assert that appreciation of it should be informed by acquaintance with its forebears.

This forebear shares certain of *Drifters*' key features, principally its concern to bring the fishing industry's workers to the screen: *Heroes* accompanies a boat belonging to the National Mission to Deep Sea Fishermen, a charity formed in 1881 to improve fishermen's circumstances. Several intertitles relay statistics on the industry's headcount and methods, adding that fishermen undertook minesweeping during the Great War. The intertitles, like *Drifters*', contain snatches of poetry: 'Man takes toll of the sea but the sea takes toll of man.' Both films situate industrial processes in a wider socioeconomic pattern – like *Drifters*, *Heroes* ends and, unlike it, also begins, at market. Surprisingly it comes closer to social criticism by contrasting workforce sweat with consumer ease ('fish is cheap today madam'). Meandering nature footage (seagulls, on this occasion) slows both films. But both emphasise the sheer force of the sea. Here, the camera bobs up and down from sky to sea and back, prompting humorous references to seasickness.

The 1925 film lacks the 1929 one's dynamic sense of space, despite varied camera angles for what is clearly a smaller boat. Notwithstanding the constant movement, its makers are far less in tune with their camera's kinetic capacities, following a precedent in expeditionary narratives by mimicking still photography, as in the introduction of the crew coming out on deck. Some shots are fetching, others poorly exposed. And the editing eschews montage, cuts being at best determined by changes of subject, at worst arbitrary. But the film-makers, with their playful moments and corny humour, lack Grierson's solemn self-importance. The film also refers to its own making and permits the men to look at the camera. Occasional attention to individual characters contrasts sharply with *Drifters'* abstract evocations.

It's certainly a work of lesser artistry but *Heroes of the North Sea* nonetheless bolsters the case for *Drifters'* vaunted invention of British documentary resting partly on prior foundations. An interesting footnote: this forgotten short supported the British premiere of F. W. Murnau's German Expressionist classic *The Last Laugh* (1924), at London's Capitol Cinema. The souvenir programme stated:

> A. E. Jones, who was responsible for the making of the film, and his operator, Frank Grainger, deserve the greatest credit for this enterprise; and we congratulate ourselves upon being able to show you a British picture which we think is eminently suitable to Capitol needs. But please write and tell us if we are making you feel too sick, and we will reconsider the matter![27]

Prod Co: R & J Films; **Dir/Prod**: A. E. Jones; **Phot**: Frank Grainger.

Housing Problems
1935 – 13 mins
Edgar Anstey, Arthur Elton

Housing Problems, funded by the gas industry, is a sombre exposition of slum housing conditions (in London's Stepney district) and its favoured solutions to them, with stark visuals of grimy interiors and observational shots of surrounding streets, unadorned by music. Instead, the film's sound is a mixture of Voice-of-God narration, authoritative commentary by Stepney's housing chairman and statements made, *on screen and in synch*, by slum residents. It's with these memorably jolting scenes that *Housing Problems* entered documentary history. Its innovative cinema technique, achieved despite technical difficulty, was later an easily accomplished commonplace of investigative television reportage.

These 'interviews' have been celebrated as 'spontaneous' and debunked as 'staged', but were neither. The answer given to the question by cinematographer John Taylor should surely settle things:

> Q: Who in effect did the interviewing? Or were they staged pieces rehearsed?
> A: Ruby coached them through it.[28]

Taylor refers to production member Ruby Grierson (*Housing Problems* is best credited not simply to directors Anstey and Elton but, as with many documentary movement films, to its entire production team). 'Coaching' would then have been necessary for anyone unaccustomed to being recorded. The stilted deliveries reinforce the authenticity of what, it's been pointed out, are *testimonies* not interviews.

Housing Problems has been attacked for middle-class timidity, and for techniques that 'endistance' the slum-dwellers. For sure, the film-makers' backgrounds were advantaged ones (Elton's positively aristocratic) and of course this institutionally funded film isn't exactly insurrectionary. But its anonymous narrator is used functionally more

A new estate's caretaker interviewed for *Housing Problems*

than ideologically, and the 'expert specialist' narration by the housing chairman is exactly that. The camera's distance from its subjects is a matter of decorum (and technical factors), and the film's reluctance to dwell on the most disgusting consequences of living in slums likewise as courteous to its subjects, surely, as to audiences (intelligent enough to understand that the surface of a grim subject has merely been skimmed). The film's 'solutions' may be over-optimistic, but it ends on a sound montage of residents' comments on their slum circumstances played over final backstreet shots. It's a powerful, deceptively artless close, reminding viewers that fellow citizens' housing problems are not all solved.

Anstey and Elton were two of their movement's less brilliant directors but, of all its leading figures, they enjoyed the most stable post-war careers: on different sides of the mixed economy, as senior figures at British Transport and Shell respectively. Lindsay Anderson later explained his rejection of their tradition with reference to

> the weakness of the traditional documentary movement . . . their work was essentially social-democratic propaganda of a kind that in the thirties seemed to be progressive . . . after the war the work had no kind of progressive quality . . . [they] ended up as pillars of the establishment, in British Transport Films or the Shell Film Unit or the Coal Board. That was as far as their revolutionary zeal took them.'[29]

It's possible to accept Anderson's factual analysis while finding his judgments too harsh. In the 1930s, social democracy *was* progressive, and partnerships between public bodies and commercially owned utilities such as the gas industry a pragmatic way to advance it. From 1945 social democracy, now national policy, *did* transform society. To this extent, documentary's shift from eager reformism to state corporatism reflected not disheartening conformity but commendable constancy. Britain had resolved never to return to the world of *Housing Problems*.

Prod Co/Spons: British Commercial Gas Association; **Dir**: Edgar Anstey, Arthur Elton; **Phot**: John Taylor.

I Think They Call Him John
1964 – 28 mins
John Krish

John Krish, a committed, undervalued film-maker, was a Crown Film Unit alumnus whose career proves that the 'message' documentary enjoyed a long life beyond VE Day. From 1948 he directed films on various subjects in differing styles for numerous sponsors – with whom he was prone to clashes. Though sacked by Edgar Anstey in 1953 from British Transport Films for his much-loved but unauthorised 'last tram' film, *The Elephant Will Never Forget*, he was no rebel against the restrictions of sponsorship *per se*. The conflicts were generally over *treatment*, used not to subvert the messages but to bring them to audiences as freshly as possible.
It's unsurprising that textbook film history has marginalised films like *I Think They Call Him John*. They had outgrown their roots in wartime documentary, though informed by its public-service ethos. But they were

A powerfully claustrophobic composition from *I Think They Call Him John*

equally at odds with competing developments in Free Cinema and television journalism.

One longstanding function of documentary, often commissioned by charities, was to raise funds or consciousness on behalf of good causes. This film's purpose was to awaken concern for the elderly but it was initiated by the director himself, his producer then securing funding from the charitable Craignish Trust to enable its making. It's thus analogous to earlier documentaries' use of sponsorship to fund 'personal' projects as a break from the norm of sponsors supplying the brief. Produced on 35mm, it was also available to the 16mm non-theatrical circuit (and was unexpectedly booked for screenings to those studying geriatric care).

John Ronson. Retired. Old miner. Old soldier. Old gardener. Old-age pensioner. Widower, no children.

The film depicts the daily routine of an old man in his flat: shaving, breakfasting, cleaning, reading, watching television, ironing. It's conveyed through minimalism and claustrophobia: no music, sparing commentary. The only words from this solitary man are whispers to his caged canary. Taut narration spoken by Victor Spinetti deftly blends the factual and the tersely poetic, often drawing on Ronson's life story. The film pauses for tellingly placed shots that deepen rather than advance the narrative: family photos; World War I medals; a treasured Home Guard certificate. As Ronson dozes in his chair, distant gunfire is heard as the camera slowly pans across heirlooms atop an upright piano, ending on a photo of young Ronson that dissolves to his present aged face as he wakes. By the time Spinetti eventually delivers the film's message, the audience is committed to it.

This outstanding film was made the same year as *The Great War*, in which other elderly men gave lengthy interviews. If filmed by a television crew, Ronson would certainly be heard speaking. Free Cinema or vérité directors would equally have rejected Krish's methods, whereby voiceover is crucial, improvisation rejected, set-ups composed, scenes rigorously directed. It's a style best described as sensitive but controlled. The film seems realistic though it's neither an observation of events nor a fiction, rather an encapsulation of a real subject's meaning, possible only by constructing events for the camera.

Speaking recently, Krish (now older than his subject) reflected:

Beware documentary directors who espouse good causes – it's almost certainly a severe case of guilt transference. They can make themselves believe that instead of taking the time to do something for somebody, making a film is enough – whereas it would do more good having a cup of tea with him once in a while. We filmed John Ronson on two weekends. When we said goodbye he was upset. We'd been company and he was going to be alone again. My family and I went to see him every Christmas Eve, but I knew I should have seen him more often. Then the year came when there was no reply. He had died a month earlier. John Ronson had done plenty in his life. I don't know how many people I've filmed but this gallant, haunted man is one I never want to forget.[30]

Once you've seen the film, neither will you.

Prod Co: Samaritan Films; **Spons**: Craignish Trust; **Dir/Sc**: John Krish; **Prod**: Anne Balfour-Fraser; **Phot**: David Muir; **Ed**: Kevin Brownlow.

The Intimacy of Strangers
2005 – 22 mins
Eva Weber

A now established (though not guaranteed) route into the moving image industry is through accredited tuition at establishments like the London International Film School and the National Film and Television School, whose documentary alumni include Molly Dineen, Nick Broomfield, Dominic Savage and Kim Longinotto. Where television might once have been the obvious sector for documentary graduates to aspire to enter, the tentative renaissance of non-broadcast documentary culture is now presenting young film-makers with different career options. Eva Weber, the director of *The Intimacy of Strangers* says that it 'could never be made for television or a broadcaster because it is shaped through the material you get, and that is something very difficult to sell to a broadcaster. So the film had to be made independently.'[31] A graveyard-slot transmission is anyway unlikely to have brought it the awards and profile it has won on the strength of festival screenings, competition entry and a dedicated promotional website.

Aptly, *Intimacy* brings a classic model for short-form documentary *film* technologically and socially up to date. Its closing titles state: 'This film consists entirely of overheard mobile phone conversations of real people, filmed in public places in London.' These ephemeral moments 'found' by the film-makers form in the editing suite a denser, deeper pattern of life as it's lived now – listening to Britain in an era of techno-solipsism.

Despite hinting at big themes, the film is extremely accessible. Its other notable achievement (physically for the crew as well as creatively for the director) is to have balanced spontaneity of content with formality of style, bringing a hovering tension to the viewing experience. It's studded with snatches of random conversation: 'Yvonne's divorce is through'; 'I'm in Euston'; 'I can't see you – you're married. I'm sorry'; 'I look like shit'; 'You're *not* a burden'. Mostly these soundbites are synchronised to the picture, but sometimes used in counterpoint. The shots are sturdily composed. There are cutaways to even more carefully framed, almost static images of buildings, bus stops – and transmitter stations. Sombre chamber music regularly intrudes then recedes. And the conversations, mostly about relationships, are edited into a loose but definite narrative curve. This has a verbal climax: one of the film's most regularly quoted subjects says: 'it feels like there's a gap somewhere, I'm not quite sure what the gap is: it's only talking to you that that's come to the surface'. Then a visual one: another breezily ends her call, dabs her eyes and stares . . . before rekeying her phone pad.

Many viewers find it difficult to believe the phone scenes were genuinely unstaged, perhaps because the film is so tightly coiled. Or perhaps because certain conversations seem 'false', as real conversations and people sometimes do. Considerable ingenuity was required to enable audio to be captured (in some scenes sound equipment is barely hidden, for instance behind a skateboard). But it seems that there was no staging (though there was limited re-recording for continuity purposes). At the time of writing, though, Weber is developing a fictional feature based on the documentary premise of *The Intimacy of Strangers*.

Prod Co: National Film and Television School; **Dir/Prod**: Eva Weber.

The Irishmen: An Impression of Exile
1965 – 50 mins
Philip Donnellan

Philip Donnellan, like Denis Mitchell, had a radio background prompting a 'contrapuntal' use of sound against image in television documentary. Unlike Mitchell, Donnellan had political motivations:

> the key to radical documentary was the juxtaposition of the visible with the lyrical complexity offered by our DIY technology. Grierson had said it already . . . the difference between us and the old documentary was that we lived with it: 'industrial Britain' was all around us.[32]

Donnellan, upper-middle class, was an establishment rebel, based at BBC Birmingham, safer from higher-ups than in London, closer to provincial realities. He saw some fifty impassioned documentaries through to transmission. *The Irishmen*, a quintessential work, didn't make it over that final hurdle.

Intrigued by his own suppressed heritage, Donnellan proposed to document the contemporary phenomenon of 'McAlpine's Fusileers', the Irish male casual workers on Britain's post-war construction sites and motorways. Borrowing the 'musical documentary' approach of the BBC's acclaimed *Radio Ballads*, he hired as collaborators the radio series' producer Charles Parker, and its balladeers Ewan MacColl and Peggy Seeger to provide heartfelt Irish folk-song renditions for the soundtrack. No presenter or narrator: sequences of men labouring by day, carousing by night, are bathed in the music, or accompanied by off-screen voices. Recurrent shots of rugged Irish landscapes show us the world they've left behind. Threaded through all this is a narrative element: a young man's journey from Connemara. The film ends on his arrival in a London which, viewers can assume, will offer little welcome. *The Irishmen* doesn't exactly flatter its intended audience! There are plaintive moments, some (in their view of Ireland) romantic to a fault. But they can't disguise an intense bitterness.

Donnellan's superiors had agreed to commission the film but, after seeing it, BBC1 controller Richard Peacock advised him: 'Both Dick Cawston and I found it shapeless, pretentious and, to be frank, boring.'[33] It's difficult to imagine two more incompatible sets of aesthetics than those of Donnellan and Richard Cawston, then Head of BBC Documentaries, later unfairly characterised by his adversary as 'an extremely unimaginative programme maker and a very conventional mind'. Donnellan was predictably incensed; the film was refused transmission. Instead it lived a non-theatrical half-life at Irish clubs and societies.

Cawston's scepticism was probably sincere: the film *is* defective, too relentless to grab the uncommitted. But the BBC response was philistine: not partisan but surely an instinctively conservative reaction to a project daring to veer off the middle of the road. And a misunderstanding of the stated method: to give an *impression* of a subject, not a carefully balanced report.

One man, filmed in his digs, says his father had loyally fought as a pre-Independence British subject in World War I. He denounces the prejudiced English, and the Irish government for forcing him to find work in the UK. This rough-faced, bitter man is an embarrassing reminder to 'Celtic Tiger' Ireland as well as Britain of recent pasts they've both conveniently lost. The man's young children are seen in the frame as he speaks. Where are they, *who* are they, now? Most likely they're fully integrated UK citizens with a Celtic heritage to be proud of. But for generations, being Irish in Britain wasn't cool, as this angry keepsake reminds us.

Prod Co: BBC; **Dir/Prod**: Philip Donnellan; **Phot**: Michael Williams.

John, Aged Seventeen Months, for Nine Days in a Residential Nursery
1969 – 43 mins
James and Joyce Robertson

This film wasn't made for theatres or for television. It and its makers are invisible from histories of documentary as a film genre. Yet if documentary were to be evaluated solely by measurable effects on the off-screen world then perhaps this would be the best documentary in this book.

One of documentary's most powerful, least celebrated uses is as a specialised tool in professional settings. James and Joyce Robertson were developmental psychologists associated with pioneer psychoanalysts like Anna Freud and John Bowlby. Working at Bowlby's clinic in the 1950s, James made films documenting the psychological effects of hospitalisation on children: initially contentious, eventually influential on paediatric practices. Later, he and Joyce initiated the project *Young Children in Brief Separation*, monitoring infants who had been separated from their parents for several days.

John was the most famous film of several to emerge from the project. With both clinical objectivity and compassion, it maps a well-adjusted boy's experiences in a residential nursery while his mother is giving birth to a sibling. Competing with more boisterous children, he struggles to form attachments with besieged nurses. His changing reactions to his father's visits mark his building distress. He turns increasingly to a giant teddy for comfort. By the eighth day he is being force-fed. His withering look at his returning mother is unforgettable. Reviewed in psychiatric journals rather than film periodicals, this was a controversial *cause célèbre*. Ultimately it was used in Britain and abroad for social services training, government ministers received private screenings, and prevalent systems of group care were reformed, partly due to its influence.

James Robertson's camera captures a permanent chronological record of John's psychological trajectory, using his medium to isolate it from the distracting, clamorous circumstances in which it unfolds. The four minutes of footage taken each day supplemented Joyce's extensive written observation, enabling her narration to interpret visible events authoritatively (incidentally, she is occasionally seen, when John goes to her in search of comfort he can't find elsewhere). She is careful not to condemn the nurses (not unkind, merely overwhelmed), nor to oversimplify maternal separation's significance. Refining Bowlby's theories, younger psychologists like the Robertsons didn't focus on mothers to the exclusion of other potential attachment figures.

They use film to get at the truth, but also to communicate it impactfully:

> *John* is a simple story of a type found in journals, short case notes which make little impact before the page is turned over. A story that could be told in twenty lines of textbook without causing comment, in its visual form struck deep and provoked emotional turmoil in most viewers.[34]

Even silent black-and-white 16mm stock was expensive. That *John* could be made at all was thanks to a Kodak award, but its technical limitations intensify its force. In monochrome silence, viewers focus intently, mentally supplying distressing absent sounds. Because the psychologists' professional practice was grounded on observation, its extension into film-making strikingly resembles (even with voiceover) Direct Cinema and vérité documentaries, styles that at their least fatuous were *deceptively* anti-dramatic. Paradoxically, this clinical study is also riveting existential drama. Amid a cast of antagonists with whom he has shifting relationships, the protagonist's personality inexorably breaks down before us. Initially overwhelming – then shattering.

Spons: Tavistock Child Development Research Unit; **Makers**: James and Joyce Robertson.

Johnny Cash in San Quentin
1969 – 50 mins
Michael Darlow

When Johnny Cash performed for the incarcerated of San Quentin state prison, he was not only famously recorded by CBS records, but also filmed by Granada Television. Only in 2006 were their products brought together, when a deluxe CD of the classic album *At San Quentin* was released with an accompanying DVD of Granada's film. Since his death, Cash has gone from iconic to legendary status, and the film had become a valuable commercial asset for both industries. Originally, however, the two projects had different motives, the two companies very different cultural perspectives. Part of the fascination of *Johnny Cash in San Quentin*, not even seen in the US until after Cash's death, is its extremely British documentary take on a very American subject.

In the film's peculiar preface, sepia photos and clips from Westerns are shown as a strident commentary sketches American mythology in the broad, telling strokes characteristic of Granada documentary. The ambivalence towards American culture, critical yet in thrall to the romance, is classically European, and a crucial set-up for what follows, as the narrator disappears and the film properly starts when 'the past and the present come together when Johnny Cash enters this jail'. He's seen doing so, then once on stage kicks into 'I Walk the Line'.

There is no information provided on Cash (described as a 'folk-singer' rather than as a country star), no interviews with him or his entourage, no coverage of the background to the concert. Instead, the Man in Black is the Greek Chorus providing troubadorial framework for a gritty social documentary. During the twelve concert performances, excitingly recorded by multiple cameras, there are cutaways to ominous, telling actuality images captured by the crew in the days leading up to the concert: cells, yards, lines of prisoners, their few possessions, wardens' keys and guns. Between songs, the film includes numerous snatches of inmates' comments to the crew, sometimes related to the subject of the song (as in the references to family accompanying 'Daddy Sang Bass'). The comments are articulate, intelligent and often angry: one prisoner states that he and his fellows are mostly merely 'guilty of being poor'. Only one guard is interviewed, and he too is reflective, though largely conservative in his opinions. The film offers no direct judgment, though some of these men are murderers. Just as the 'concert documentary' reaches the gospel-music section with which Cash concluded all his concerts, the 'prison documentary' climaxes with stark shots of the gas chamber, and words from the guard and a condemned man on California's death penalty. Capital punishment had been abolished in Britain in 1965.

The high point comes earlier, as the musical and social documentaries again coalesce in Cash's 'San Quentin', written for the occasion. Splendid reaction shots capture thrilled responses to Cash's bitterly written and delivered lines ('San Quentin I hate every inch of you . . . San Quentin may you rot and burn in hell'). But the film-makers, too, succumb to Cash's immense, disquieting American charisma. With each cut back to him, the camera is closer, its angle lower. Cash later commented that at this moment he could have started a riot if he'd wanted. You'll believe him.

Prod Co: Granada Television; **Dir/Prod**: Michael Darlow; **Phot**: Ray Goode, David Wood.

Johnny Go Home
1975 – 120 mins
John Willis

In his commentary John Willis says 'For us,' referring to the crew, 'the story began here in the cold doorway of Euston Station. Before it was over we were to find ourselves caught up in violence, exploitation and finally the most brutal murder.'

The title of the film that now begins echoes an earlier *cause célèbre* on the same subject, homelessness. Ken Loach's *Cathy Come Home* was fiction with a famed documentary style. *Johnny Go Home* is crusading investigative journalism in the form of a prestigious primetime documentary film. Because of the events that unexpectedly occurred during shooting, *two* related investigations are reported, one of general issues, the other of specific incidents. The intended social-problem documentary became *Johnny Come Home Part 1: The End of the Line*, shown across the ITV network at 9pm. It finds its way into its big subject by following two case histories, of Annie, a seventeen-year-old hardened to the homeless life; and of twelve-year-old Tony, seen arriving at Euston as the film begins. With his fresh face, about to age prematurely, Tony immediately reaches viewers who might not otherwise pay heed to the Dickensian sights or the grim statistics in Willis's pithily forceful voiceover. Tony clambers out of a cardboard box, suited and booted, as morning breaks. Annie clambers across derelict land which looks as if it has just been bombed. Such arresting images are neither stressed nor contemplated: pace and tone stay steady. Finally, as Tony enters a hostel, Willis's narration sets up *Part 2: The Murder of Billy Two-Tone*, which was screened after the 10pm news bulletin.

Willis recalled:

The story of the killing which had taken place while we were filming in the hostel unfolded to us through our hostel contacts. It was so bloodcurdling it almost defied belief . . . we had, in effect, filmed a murder before it happened, with motives, personalities, even participants. The only thing missing was the police side of the story. We approached them and they agreed to co-operate with us in presenting the story.[35]

The unit hadn't filmed the victim himself: William McPhee, Billy Two Tone. Interviewees recall him; photographs record his face. Graphic police footage shows his fly-blown corpse. His coffin is lowered at his funeral. In a series of clearly marked sections, the film-makers forensically uncover the facts behind this funeral, centring on the hostel's owner. His housing empire turns out to be based on sexual exploitation, religious cultishness, financial corruption – and bureaucratic ineptitude unable to recognise these facts behind his persuasively respectable front.

The film's two parts have similar styles, but the second has greater urgency, a tighter 'storyline'. Sometimes it feels an arbitrary, maybe misleading way to further dramatise the theme of homelessness. But *The End of the Line* is cleverly recalled by *The Murder of Billy Two-Tone*. Footage of Tony being taken into the hostel's care is replayed: scenes which *had* seemed innocent, even encouraging. The interview with Billy's mother echoes that with Tony's. Both are respectable, concerned middle-aged Scottish ladies. But one is in a black veil.

The film isn't crass enough to suggest that Tony is headed for the same fate as his older compatriot. But both entered the same dangerous world, inhabited by thousands, at Euston's cold doorway.

Prod Co: Yorkshire Television; **Dir**: John Willis.

Jubilee
1935 – 10 mins
Herbert A. Green, R. Green

While in some respects the documentary movement lay to the left of
mainstream commercial cinema, its politics are better characterised as
loosely, and inconsistently, progressive rather than radical. To its own
left, the 1930s also witnessed a lively movement of socialist film-makers
committed to using film as an ideological tool: the ancestors of today's
video activists. While some individual industry professionals were
involved, notably Ivor Montagu and Ralph Bond, these were very much
collective activities. Bond wrote:

> The documentary type of films is the one most suited to our aims. We
> can take our cameras out into the streets and at the expense of little
> more than film, patience and an infinite capacity for taking trouble,
> photograph our material as it actually exists. Through the camera we can
> speak to the workers in terms they can understand and appreciate. And if
> we do this we are at the same time exposing the stupidity and false
> values of the commercial film.[36]

Jubilee, critiquing the Silver Jubilee of King George V, illustrates
these ideas perfectly, not least by its shot of newsreel men busily turning
their cameras on the events: an acerbic exposé of dominant media
production. By means of a documentary technique, the contrast of one
reality with another, *Jubilee* advances the view that such media
dishonestly serve an establishment agenda. It begins with street parties,
bunting, flags, cheering crowds, and the Royals on ceremonial show in
East London, before switching to a darker section documenting the East
End's slums and lines of unemployed. An historian of left film-making
argues that such 'deadly parallels' were its quintessential modus
operandi.[37] The intertitles here relate them to specific political
arguments: that the Conservative-dominated national government was

using the Jubilee to deflect attention from reactionary policies, not only ignoring the Depression but simultaneously rearming. The most emotive image is of legless World War I veterans. The film then returns to the Jubilee imagery, military parading, now of course deconstructed. The film's final words and images state that Britain is preparing for future warfare.

Several prints credit the Workers' Film and Photo League (WFPL), one of the socialist film community's major production organisations. In fact, the film was shot (on 35mm, surprisingly) by two brothers (both teachers) as an amateur effort. They subsequently brought it to the WFPL who helped improve it with additional footage and recutting. Kino, the major distributor for the workers' film movement, then distributed the film on 16mm. Ignored by commercial cinema programmers, such films set a long pattern for left-wing documentary, that of preaching to already converted non-theatrical audiences, mixing left-wing intelligentsia with politicised members of the working class.

The montages ending both sections, presumably the result of the WFPL's interventions, provide the film's most impressive moments. But it's vivid throughout, notwithstanding amateurish faults: poorly focused or badly composed shots and visible film splices. Aside from its politics, *Jubilee* exemplifies two further important points about non-mainstream 1930s' documentary. Documentaries made by serious amateur film-makers became much more common than in previous decades. And film had not broken with silence in 1930. Many non-theatrical documentaries (including almost all amateur, and most political, ones) continued to be made without sound for several years thereafter.

Prod Co: North London Film Society, Workers' Film and Photo League; **Dir/Phot**: Herbert A. Green, R. Green.

Land of Promise
1946 – 67 mins
Paul Rotha

July 1945: Britain votes for its own transformation, ejecting beloved wartime leader Churchill, electing Attlee's Labour Party on its manifesto, 'Let Us Face the Future'.

'Made by Films of Fact Ltd 1944–5', *Land of Promise* doesn't name political parties but is the most detailed articulation anywhere on celluloid of the national thought processes late in World War II before this seismic event. Unfortunately, it wasn't released until 1946: its protracted production has left internal inconsistencies as to which precise historical instant it occupies. Predictably it proved of greater interest to cineastes and policy wonks than anyone else, but it amply repays viewing as an odd, almost absurdly grandiloquent allegory with statistics, an ambitious interpretation of an idiom long since rendered obsolete by telejournalism. Paul Rotha, director of this film of promise, would soon, barely forty, be bankrupted, eventually becoming a disappointed, sidelined witness to documentary's progressive marginalisation from cinema culture.

This 'argument about our houses and homes' has a past-present-future structure typical of Rotha's films: *Homes as They Were*, *Homes as They Are*, *Homes as They Might Be*. This it combines with archive footage evoking each epoch (the amount of appositely compiled material is impressive for the time, though aficionados will spot sizeable chunks of Rotha's own past productions), and with multiple-voice narration. Soundtrack components interact, conversing and competing as if in Socratic dialogue over the meaning of recent history's raw materials. Some are abstractions: voices of History (dominating the first section), of Hansard (quoting from parliamentary debates and reports) and of the robotic Isotype ('I use symbols to make diagrams. I am here to help. I am Isotype'). Isotype was a sociological pictogram system invented by philosopher-educator Otto Neurath, with whom Rotha had collaborated on the similar *World of Plenty* (1943). Imagine PowerPoint becoming a

Land of Promise: allegorical characters face the future

named character in a twenty-first-century documentary and you get the idea.

Other participants personify distinct British sensibilities. The central voice, that of John Mills, represents ordinary, progressive Britons increasingly confident in drawing conclusions from the multi-voice 'argument'. Straw counterweight comes from character actor Miles Malleson, embodying self-congratulatory, complacent, conservative Middle England ('good old Britisher – sense of humour, proper respect for tradition'). There are two crucial female characters. A slum-dwelling housewife appears on screen arguing against the narrators. A compassionate velvety voice dominates the *Homes as They Are* section: 'Could men not learn without a war?' Finally, two real people feature, speaking authoritatively to camera: Sir Ernest Simon and housing campaigner Father John Groser.

The first section, covering 1919–39, indicts national failures to coordinate housing policy. The second covers 1939–45, arguing that evacuation and conscription had revealed the poor health of many infant and adult citizens, but that the collectivised planning necessitated by war also proves what can be achieved in peace. The ground is laid for the film's future agenda, a planned economy driven by compassionate technocracy. In the final, surreal section several of the characters appear in a bar pondering the post-war world over a drink. Mills, in uniform, eventually joins them, supposedly from the audience, to whom he turns – delivering an impassioned, increasingly off-kilter five-minute speech that finally derails the movie.

How many other films offer the self-contradictory spectacle of social democrat rationalism gone baroque, and increasingly going berserk, before its viewers? Enthralling, fascinating and eventually exhausting.

Prod Co: Films of Fact; **Dir/Prod**: Paul Rotha; **Phot**: Harold Young.

Let It Be
1970 – 81 mins
Michael Lindsay-Hogg

Popular music has long been much the most regular, lucrative source for cinema documentary, but this famous early example originated as an intended television documentary sketch of The Beatles at work. Partly to help the band meet contractual commitments for cinema projects, the idea was expanded to the shooting of a full-length documentary on the making of what became its final album release. Michael Lindsay-Hogg was brought in to direct on the strength of previous work on promos. His small crew shot on 16mm, later blown up for distribution.

Every Beatles film yielded an iconic snapshot of their evolution and that of their decade. Their sole sustained engagement with documentary was no exception, despite its rather derivative use of Direct Cinema stylings. An historian of their films observes that *Let It Be* is 'one of the most minimalist films to have achieved a full theatrical release in Britain'.[38] Its muted colours, downbeat mood and candid observations of acrimony and boredom symbolised the group's break-up and therefore Britain's descent from the 'swinging sixties' into the dreary 1970s. Of all this book's documentaries the operative comparison is surely with the previous year's *Royal Family*. Both films turned self-consciously modern, deliberately understated technique on larger-than-life subjects in an attempt to demythologise them. The monarchy's demythologisation eventually worked too well. *Let It Be*'s very graininess and pedestrianism became *part* of the mythology of its increasingly deified 'family'. This has secured it a cultural presence that few documentaries have, that it doesn't deserve on the strength of its film-making alone, and despite its longstanding unavailability. (The ultimate proof of its resonance: a parody of its final sequence in an episode of *The Simpsons*.)

The film has a simple tripartite structure. The first third captures rehearsals at Twickenham studios, the second sessions at Abbey Road. Too often their filming is aimless. It's unclear whether musical or

interpersonal issues are their main focus, leaving both unsatisfactorily covered. But, because the music and relationships are those of the world's most legendary band, the film can't help but be studded with fascinating moments. Musically, Paul McCartney's piano ballads generally come off best, and McCartney's relationship with his bandmates dominates the group dynamics. While he's more animated than the others, some music critics have used this film to justify their antipathy to him, particularly the discomforting scene in which he patronisingly instructs George Harrison on guitar technique. Yet many viewers will be surprised, given the film's reputation, that the rancour is mostly understated, and much of the interplay good-humoured.

Only in the film's final third, the famous rooftop concert, does it overcome its weaknesses. It's the one part of the film staged entirely for its own benefit, and thus the point at which *Let It Be* shifts documentary methods. The years suddenly fall away. Bystanders, young and old, gawp from the streets. There's a splendid shot of a bowler-hatted gentleman nonchalantly clambering the rooftops to get a closer view. Lennon, McCartney, Harrison and Starr, merging late and early styles, exchange smiles. And who, with any feeling for popular culture, can *suppress* a smile? An era is fading bittersweetly before our eyes.

Prod Co: Apple Films; **Dir**: Michael Lindsay-Hogg; **Prod**: Neill Aspinall.

(Opposite page) The Beatles (with Yoko Ono) in *Let It Be*

Listen to Britain
1942 – 19 mins
Humphrey Jennings, Stewart McAllister

The title-card picture is of a gun and a violin. An early treatment was entitled 'The Music of War':

> Do you think that modern war has no music? That mechanisation has banished harmony and that, because her life is for the moment so grim, that Britain no longer thinks of singing? What an error. Listen . . ..[39]

During production, the film changed its name, and deviated from the treatment in several respects, not least by dropping this proposed opening commentary. There is no narration at all on *Listen to Britain* (excluding the introductory sequence added to some foreign prints, to the horror of the directors and most later fans). The film is, at its simplest, a collection of disparate images and sounds of midwar Britain, arranged together to suggest a typical day in the life of the nation. The epic of war broken down into unrelated moments, the fleeting, forgettable fragments lives are made up out of: together, they remain fleeting but reveal their shared nobility. And whether the music is highbrow (Mozart at the National Gallery, with the Queen and her Surveyor of Pictures Sir Kenneth Clark in attendance) or lowbrow (Flanagan and Allen at a lunchtime canteen concert), a complex, hesitant harmony emerges from the contrasting rhythms and melodies.

This description of the film, like many others, fails to convey what it is actually like. Readers are better recommended to experience it for themselves – a complex technical and artistic achievement pulled off with such self-effacement that it seems simple, almost natural. Long since rubber-stamped 'Masterpiece', it must be the shortest British film in this category. Less often commented upon: it is the only one that was seen as often in mess halls, church halls and factories as in cinemas. Yet Humphrey Jennings is admired and loved by cinephiles who otherwise shun documentary: the only British non-fiction film-maker to have ascended from its specialist categories into the certified canon of their national cinema, where a cult of personality has grown around him. Devoted to the singularity of genius, it has risked cutting it off from the artistic tradition in which it flourished (and not only by widely overlooked editor Stewart McAllister, though he's here credited with co-direction). *Listen to Britain* has the nighttime trains, the smoky chimneys, the swaying cornfields, the stalwart shoreline, Big Ben at night, the crop harvesting and the coal-mining, the dutiful soldiers on guard, the plucky girls in the factory, the children in the playground: realities and symbols with which 1930s' and 1940s' documentary is replete. Part of its fineness is that it refreshes them, and deepens the relationship of each to each, all to all. It's often said that *Listen to Britain* transcends propaganda, but it would be more accurate, and still as complimentary, to say that it perfects it.

Prod Co: Crown Film Unit; **Spons**: Ministry of Information; **Dir**: Humphrey Jennings, Stewart McAllister; **Prod**: Ian Dalrymple; **Phot**: H. E. Fowle.

Lockerbie – A Night Remembered
1998 – 51 mins
Michael Grigsby

One after another, the shots are held long, each a simple, still view of a small town at night, accompanied by reassuring sounds: bingo-calling in a local hall; TV sets blaring. A ticking clock supplies the only close views, the only movement. The hour strikes. This is Lockerbie in 1998, ten years after the infamous bombing of Pan-Am Flight 103 brought carnage to its streets and fields. But this could also be sleepy Lockerbie in 1988, moments before the plane began its fiery descent. Then the point of view shifts . . . we are moving . . . the camera is staring through the windscreen of a car driving through dark rural roads. We begin to hear soft lowland voices recollecting the events of a decade earlier, as we are driven deeper, deeper into the twilight.

When agreeing to the producer's suggestion that Michael Grigsby be hired to direct, Channel 4 knew it would get something unlike the masses of media coverage spawned by the Lockerbie disaster. Grigsby was a veteran of the 1960s' Granada Television generation, and of Free Cinema; he had even been offered his first Granada post by none other than Harry Watt, co-director of *Night Mail*, the film that inspired him to a documentary career when he had seen it at school. He brought these accumulated influences to Channel 4's anniversary study of the disaster's long-term effects on Lockerbie's local population. It harnesses television's power to capture testimony, while avoiding its usual dangers: in interview people are allowed truly to speak their minds, single takes remain on screen uncut for minutes at a time, only stopping when the magazine is emptied (*Lockerbie* was defiantly shot on Super 16mm, not on digital video). But it also harnesses other elements, those of *cinema*. When fast-forwarding it becomes striking how lengthy and static so many shots are: in real time, all seem to have exactly the right duration. Dissolves are used as often as straight cuts. The car journey continues through the film. And then there are the motionless, contemplative views, of townscape and landscape, layered with ambient sound and gently

Haunting, beautifully framed landscape imagery from *Lockerbie – A Night Remembered*

augmented by minor-key piano, each conjunction of sight and sound, shot with shot, adding to the meaning. In the final minutes, the elements come together. An interviewee makes her final, heartfelt but measured statements. The car has parked: only the wiper is moving. Then there are five shots of individual interviewees, virtually stills, respectful final views as their voices are heard for the last time. A single piano note is played as one dissolves to the next; then a shot of the town closes the film.

Several of Grigsby's earlier documentaries received a BFI release prior to broadcast; others enjoyed non-theatrical distribution after transmission. It's a pity that *Lockerbie* postdated the decline of the 16mm circuit and predated the growth of new non-broadcast environments. It received a single broadcast, then wasn't seen for some years before finally being picked up for repertory screenings. One of the best British films of its time, it translates superbly to the big screen.

Prod Co: Castle Haven Digital; **Dir**: Michael Grigsby; **Prod**: Rex Pyke; **Phot**: Adam Suschitzky.

London
1994 – 85 mins
Patrick Keiller

In his production funding application, Patrick Keiller envisaged a part fiction, part documentary, a film about London as a *place* which will attempt to create a new imagination of the city (adding, in response to the application form's request that he indicate why the project was more suited to film than to television, that 'its scale and its imaginative ambitions are more characteristic of film and more likely to be realised by it'). Later, during *London*'s release, producer Keith Griffiths complained to the BFI on their joint behalf that, by classifying it as a documentary, it was mis-marketing it: 'whilst the film clearly has a documentary base in terms of the images, we have both always insisted that the fictional aspect is *equally* – if not *more* – important'.[39] Most viewers will find their interplay is what causes the film to stand out.

Hardly unique in wedding fact to fiction, *London*'s factual apparatus is unusual, effective and, for an otherwise complex film, extremely simple. It is visually non-fictional: eighty minutes of London location shots, from central landmarks to nondescript or ugly suburban corners, all recorded without sound or camera movement, suggesting (in a documentary history context) the most primitive of travelogues, postcard views on the screen. Intertitles underscore a rapport with silent cinema: some of Keiller's subsequent work has focused on film archives, as repositories for shifting visions of urban space. The effect, bestowing disturbing strangeness on a modern, familiar place, is especially strong at this short distance from the film's making.

The soundtrack supplies the fictional element. 'The Narrator' describes his relationship with 'Robinson' (never heard or seen) and Robinson's obscurely idiosyncratic research into 'the problem of London'. His account covers most of 1992, the period in which the film was shot, referring to real events and the photographed locations: the fiction increases, but also slants, the documentary value of the actuality images.

Many shots are annotated by erudite topographical and cultural observations while, across the film, an embittered alienation emerges: from modern London, from Britain's anti-intellectual culture, from its short-sighted politics. (For further adventures, see *Robinson in Space*, Keiller's 1996 follow-up on the wider canvas of the whole UK.)

Does the Narrator share Robinson's disenchantment? Does the film endorse the Narrator's statements? There is no clear answer, but the balance seems to be between satire at the two characters' expense and sympathy for their perspectives. Doubtless, many of *London*'s enthusiastic reviewers shared politics and demographics with Robinson. Viewers outside the demographic might be less indulgent. Robinson's first thought on the Conservatives' 1992 re-election is to deride the 'miserable hearts' of the middle-class voters responsible, then to ponder the likely consequences for him personally: 'his job would be at risk and

A disenchanted view of modern *London*

subjected to interference'. True, it's quickly added that 'for the old, or anyone with children it would be much worse'. But younger viewers might despair at such displays of cosseted baby-boomer arrogance.

Those who start out suspicious of *London*'s donnish self-consciousness may be surprised at finding themselves sucked in by exquisite visuals, pokerfaced humour and Paul Scofield's soothing voice. Before Scofield was contracted, Dirk Bogarde had been one of those approached: with a different voice, *London* would be a significantly different film, as both fiction and documentary.

Prod Co: Koninck, BFI, Channel 4; **Dir/Sc/Phot**: Patrick Keiller; **Prod**: Keith Griffiths; **Ed**: Larry Sider.

London 2012: Make Britain Proud
2004 – 4 mins
Darryl Goodrich

A short film. No on-screen credits other than to the campaign that commissioned it. Filmed in real locations. Set to music of the time. Containing personalities of the day and ordinary citizens, or actors representing them, on the streets of London, their actions less caught by the camera than choreographed for it. Made for the purposes both of delivering specific information to target viewers and of projecting an image of nationhood at home and abroad. Documentary? By, say, 1944 standards, the question wouldn't even need to be asked.

Sixty years on, the film described above, 2004's *Make Britain Proud*, is *very* unlikely, in its own era, to be generally classified as documentary. *Make Britain Proud* lacks the *sine qua non* of documentary as it's come

Archetypes inflected by *London 2012*

to be defined by decades of television practice: inspection by the camera of a reality which would have physically existed precisely as recorded even without the camera's presence. Only a few travelogue location shots (the Thames, Big Ben, Tower Bridge) are 'documentary' in this sense. But, also unlike most television documentary, this film has, as one part of a multimedia operation, had the effect once intended for British documentary: not simply to record 'the real world' but to help construct a new one. Over the coming five years, Britain's infrastructure will be significantly altered (at high cost, as we now know) as a result of the campaign of which this film was a part, London's successful crusade to host the 2012 Olympics.

To the strains of 'Proud' by Heather Small (who briefly appears) runners jog through a London in which British sportspeople like David Beckham, Kelly Holmes and Amir Khan and internationally known UK celebrities such as Ralph Fiennes, Roger Moore and Helen Mirren rub shoulders with flight attendants, cyclists and policemen. A carefully directed, knowing smile appears on London Mayor Ken Livingstone's face. Almost every scene both reinforces and inflects a cliché about Britain and its capital: umbrella'd, bowler-hatted city gents – a deliberate mix of white and black men – burst into dance.

The film was distributed in different versions. For members of the Olympic committee judging London's bid, it was screened with captions informing them of the facilities London could offer competitors and visitors. Within the UK the film served as a tool to raise national support for the bid, shown in short TV 'spots' as well as in its full version. It won the Grand Prix at the 2005 awards of the International Visual Communications Association, an organisation with roots in the British Industrial and Scientific Films Assocation, of which Edgar Anstey was once president. Yes, parts of the mantle of Griersonian documentary have been inherited by the makers of 'corporate video', one of the least generally regarded of moving image forms but an industry of considerable sophistication with a £3 billion annual turnover.

Many viewers will dislike this film's slickness, and its similarities to pop video and to television advertising. Others will find its optimism refreshing. But it's undeniably a representation – *a* representation – of the reality of contemporary, prosperous, culturally diverse Britain. It will be interesting to revisit in 2012. Will it be an era-defining classic, dismally dated curiosity, or something in between? It's likely, anyway, that it will be taken exactly as originally intended, as a creative treatment of actuality, a documentary statement more than a fictional creation.

Prod Co: New Moon Television; **Spons**: London 2012, Central Office of Information; **Dir**: Darryl Goodrich; **Prod**: Caroline Rowland.

London's Contrasts (*Wonderful London*)
1924 – 10 mins
Frank Miller, Harry B. Parkinson

London's Contrasts exemplifies much 1920s' factual film-making. Most professionally produced non-fiction films were shorts padding the full cinema bill, some produced by small production organisations specialising in such work, others by small divisions of larger film companies. This film's production company, Graham-Wilcox Productions (jointly owned by Graham Cutts and by Herbert Wilcox, a producer-director who would become a prestigious mainstay of the British film industry) turned out minor features and regular non-fiction shorts for the supporting programme.

While newsreels had long since evolved from early films of particular events into compilations of several topical stories, 'interest' films lightly covered single, non-newsworthy topics. Travelogues were a common subtype, documenting exotic locations their audiences were certain never to visit, or places in the UK as in Graham-Wilcox's two 1924 series of *Wonderful London* films (and a later offshoot, *Wonderful Britain* [1926]).

The fun in viewing most travelogues is spotting what has since changed and what remained, but *London's Contrasts* briefly rewards curiosity as a piece of screencraft. Though criticised for pointless triviality, interest films could occasionally hint at serious themes: this one evidences the general frivolity *and* the occasional seriousness. And, while anticipating today's holiday programmes (also schedule-fillers), it speaks the evolving language of what would come to be called documentary. Its very theme derives from its use of a classic documentary rhetorical device: the drawing of contrasts. It begins by comparing London's West and East Ends, highways and crannies. Thereafter, sights are pointed out by a cockney horse-drawn-cab driver to his passengers, accompanied by the viewer (another documentary technique: the expert 'layman-presenter'). It's hard to be certain whether he's here an actor or a genuine cabbie but his 'type' is good-naturedly patronised something rotten. Sample dialogue: 'Look at all them oughter-go-miles! I tell you, the Nobs lie down this way.' Or: 'Lumme! A plate of cockles and you'd fancy you was at Southend.'

Travelogues of the 1920s were typically made up of several images earlier constituting entire films, even entire genres: point-of-view travelling shots, static postcard views, busy street scenes with extensive movement in the frame captured by a stationary camera. Together these comprise a documentary portrait of a place: separately they're but sketches towards one. The final intertitle betrays such films' modesty, bordering on inferiority complex: 'the Busman could go on for ever in this strain, and we *know* you must be waiting impatiently for the Big Picture'. Little more than pleasant diversion has been provided while refreshments were sold and the organist vamped. But audience members bothering to watch will have learned something about their multifaceted capital city, divided, like the provinces, by class. True poverty is barely hinted at, but London, the film says, is a city of 'light and shade, sunshine and gloom, happiness . . . and the reverse'.

Prod Co: Graham–Wilcox Productions; **Dir**: Frank Miller, Harry B. Parkinson.

March to Aldermaston
1958 – 33 mins

The 1958 March to Aldermaston enjoys landmark status in the annals of peaceful protest. Its filmed record is similarly recalled as a milestone for campaigning documentary.

CND emerged from Aldermaston as a movement uniting disparate wings of the political left with otherwise apolitical concerned citizens. The film echoes this. The committee of volunteers responsible for it impressively united different sectors of their industry from lab technicians processing footage for free, to Contemporary Films, which handled distribution. The fascinating credits list ties several of the threads making up the fabric of documentary's most diverse decade yet. Best known are those contributors who had begun making their mark with Free Cinema. Equally important were exponents of documentary cinema working outside that faction. Others came from the older information documentary tradition. Some were working in television. This mixed group was set to the work of documenting the march with a jumble of different types of equipment, and invariably logged footage ranging from straight actuality record to ennobling imagery, and plenty of *vox pop* interviews (some on camera, some only on audio). Though heavily criticised, the addition of Christopher Logue's commentary, sensitively read by Richard Burton, is surely crucial to the film that eventually emerged. It gives it surprising coherence even if it never fully resolves the creative tensions in the source material or helps the film decide if it's ultimately an impressionistic or an analytical piece.

Credited only to the Committee, *March to Aldermaston* demands appreciation as the product of selfless collaboration. By most accounts, however, Lindsay Anderson came to dominate the film at the editing stage. The crisp documentary shaped from the miles of raw footage is succinct and moving, rather than hysterical or sentimental. It doesn't flinch from criticising the Eastern Bloc as harshly as Western politicians. And in documenting the march's generally middle-class demographics, it's now a great period piece, awash with cut-glass accents, trad jazz and sensible hats and coats. (To be fair, it tries to show a broader base, as with an interview with a veteran of 1926's Jarrow March.)

Precisely because it deserves admiration for advancing its cause through documentary distribution, the film deserves the respect of being asked tough questions. It echoes the weaknesses, as much as the strengths, of the disarmament movement. CND's principal demand was for unilateral nuclear disarmament by the UK, a position that never won over more than a sizeable minority of the population. Politically, it influenced only the Labour Party, mainly to Labour's electoral detriment. It soon caused damaging divisions and, as late as 1983, Aldermaston veteran Michael Foot's landslide defeat was widely blamed on Labour's unilateralist platform. The film, too, fails to mount a convincing case for unilateral disarmament. This is the commentary's main weakness. Its best shot is the claim that Britain can set a powerful moral example, arguably reflecting a dated faith in its postcolonial international influence. *March to Aldermaston* was successful in many ways, being widely distributed abroad and in the UK. It must have had an electrifying effect at campaign meetings. But it was less likely to win over the undecided: like too many other campaigning films, it's ultimately a feelgood film for activists.

Prod Co: Film and Television Committee for Nuclear Disarmament; **Contributors included**: Derrick Knight, Lindsay Anderson, Karel Reisz, Kurt Lewenhak, Chris Menges, Wolfgang Suschitzky, Stephen Peet, Peter Jessop.

Marion Knight (*Citizen 63*)
1963 – 30 mins
John Boorman

One interesting sidelight on the documentary–fiction relationship is
provided by the career histories of film-makers who have worked in both
disciplines. Mostly these indicate that documentary is the easier field in
which to establish a career, but much the less sexy in which to spend it:
it doesn't follow that either type of film is easier to make, or that
triumph in one augurs success in another. Some accomplished film
documentarists made a disproportionately modest impact on fiction
features given their talent (examples include Paul Rotha, Pat Jackson and
John Krish). Some 'name' directors have made side-project forays into
film or television documentary (recent examples are Julien Temple and
Michael Winterbottom). A few directors have transferred their successful
small-screen documentary careers' sensibilities across into fiction (Paul
Greengrass, Penny Woolcock). Others have begun making documentaries
chiefly to enter the industry and begin flexing creative talents. The well-
known non-fiction work of Lindsay Anderson and Karel Reisz is usually
appreciated as their juvenilia. Conversely, many consider Ken Russell and
John Schlesinger as having made better youthful documentaries than
mature features.

Other acclaimed auteurs' documentary beginnings have been
scarcely considered. Little attention has been given to the factual films of
John Boorman, though in the early 1960s, as head of the BBC's Bristol
Documentary Unit, he held an unusually responsible industry position,
making films with considerable impact. This may be because they haven't
been widely available since, or maybe because they don't obviously
presage his feature-film work. It isn't easy to find seeds for *Deliverance*
or *Excalibur* in Boorman's *Citizen 63*, a very successful series at the time.
Stylistically, it slightly better resembles his flashier 1960s' features: this
episode's opening, with its jazzy music over footage of its subject and a
boyfriend on a motorcycle is swaggeringly contemporary. An arty use of

freeze-frames and of stills to open the programme proper confirms this impression. The narrator announces that 'this film is about one person . . . part of our society'. The purpose of the five-part series was to encapsulate the modern UK. The opening episode, *Barry Langford*, about a flamboyant businessman, earned the greatest notoriety. Others were devoted to a police inspector, a shop steward, a scientist and teenager Marion Knight. Almost the same age as Jennings's Timothy, Marion is similarly representative of their generation, grown up into a society whose films now documented it not just by evoking archetypes but by observing individuals (Marion is seen at school, work and having fun with her friends) and by recording their comments (Marion is interviewed in a darkened studio, some of her comments played over footage). This type of film-making was possible due to improving documentary technology, but proved suitable for reflecting social change. Many of the details of Marion's life covered in the film are specific to her, others (for instance, her education at a secondary modern school) are indicative of broader social patterns. With reference to Marion's elderly adoptive parents, represented only by stills, the film alludes to the opening of generational chasms: 1963 is often cited as the year in which the 1960s properly began. No doubt some older people found Marion's free-spiritedness disturbing, but Boorman makes sure to include interview material demonstrating that she is articulate and socially responsible. Marion and her fellow teenage rebels now seem almost comically innocent. But the film, which doesn't pass explicit comment, remains fresh and lively.

Prod: BBC West; **Dir**: John Boorman; **Phot**: Arthur Smith.

Market Place (*Look at Life*)
1959 – 9 mins

As feature films' supporting programmes increasingly shrank, the available room for documentary shrank with them. This cemented the longstanding position whereby regular production of non-fiction cinema emanated almost entirely from lowlier corners of the commercial film industry. Shorts by committed documentary-makers were largely destined for screens in other venues. It was a source of consternation to independent film-makers that virtually the only short films guaranteed exhibition with features were those in commercial cinemagazine series, produced by firms with production, distribution or exhibition interests. For ten years from 1959 some 500 issues were released of *Look at Life*, produced by the giant Rank Organisation (a similar number of issues of its much longer-established rival *Pathe Pictorial* went out during the same period). They were damned by faint praise (inoffensive, competent, colourful . . .). Yet they are an essential part of any full account of British documentary 'cinema', having become its sole instantiation. And for all their shortcomings, they are still fondly remembered, above all for vivid colours distinguishing them from black-and-white factual television of their day. Their very blandness and conformism make them great gauges of prevailing contemporary attitudes, particularly when compared with other documentaries. They often shared topics though not treatments with these. To give just one example, the *Look at Life* issue *I Protest* (1960) refers to Aldermaston marches. The issue considered here makes revealing passing references (neither PC nor extremely offensive) to Britain's growing 'coloured' population.

   Market Place is a typical early *Look at Life* in every respect except that it contains chirpy guest narration by Sid James, rather than the usual cheerily anonymous voice. Cinemagazines tend to have more of a documentary character than newsreels, less topical, concerned more with painting a picture of a subject than with logging events. A standard documentary narrative design is used here, that of compare-and-contrast. As Sid puts it: 'the supermarket and the street market – that's two sides of life in Britain today'. There are actuality scenes of London markets like Petticoat Lane ('nice friendly place where you can meet up with your mates') and Berwick St ('mostly for women'). Compare the new supermarkets: 'a street market with a top hat on . . . a bit more posh and a bit more modern'. A few loud street-traders and other characters are thrown in for good measure. Cinematography is good if anonymous, and the sound recording streets ahead of what most documentary producers were then capable of. Like every issue, this ends with an invitation: 'Take another *Look at Life* again soon.'

Prod Co: Rank Film Productions.

McLibel
1998/2005 – 53/84 mins
Franny Armstrong

In 1990 fast-food chain McDonald's sued activists David Morris and
Helen Steel for libel, for distributing a leaflet oppposing its practices. The
longest-running trial in English legal history followed. Morris and Steel
defended themselves, losing their case technically, but (arguably) winning
it morally, the judgment in their favour on several of the leaflet's claims.
McDonald's was battered by negative publicity.

As the trial lengthened, news media increasingly reported it. Several
television companies contacted the defendants about possible
documentary treatment, each dropping out after failing to be
commissioned. Instead a first-time director with a borrowed camera
began filming them, some distance in. With no broadcast commission,
they trusted her to commit to the film for its own sake, if with perilously
little investment. Funding came from contributions and by licensing
footage. Technicians were volunteers. Impressively, Ken Loach directed,
unpaid, reconstruction scenes in which Steel and Morris play themselves
questioning witnesses played by actors.

The resulting film, *McLibel*, combines an account of the process
with the personal story of the individuals at its centre, advancing two
arguments: multinational corporations are corrupt; libel law is stacked
in favour of powerful players at the expense of free speech of
defendants denied legal aid. Steel and Morris successfully pursued this
latter point to the European Court. Consequently, an alternate version
of the film exists, adding a European coda, plus additional interview
material.

Otherwise, the two films supply similar content beneath differing
surfaces. In the 1998 film, Veronika Hyks's voiceover style will spook
viewers of a certain age with reminders of yesteryear's schools
programmes. This is reinforced by the structure, divided into chapters
covering the trial's main issues: carefully announced at their opening,

adjudications summarised at their close, then recapitulated in a 'balance-sheet' conclusion.

The 2005 version replicates the structure but sexes up the delivery. Hyks is jettisoned; captions are replaced with graphics; editing is sharpened. The animals sequence, for instance, is more incisive: distressing imagery of slaughter and subsequent 'processing' cut to music. Both films are riveting because the story and issues are intriguing. Reflecting their protagonists, they're sincere, committed and unflashy. The film-making isn't distinctive, never impeding nor enhancing the story. Though the daughter of a documentary-maker, Armstrong had no directing experience, and sometimes it shows (as she refreshingly admits in interviews).

McLibel's value to this list is mainly for its production and distribution history. Like earlier films, it not only documents but forms part of a long campaign: film and campaign both symbiotic works in progress. The first version was released on VHS. The second enjoyed brief cinema release, but principally exists as an extra-packed DVD. Trailers and versions of the full film have been downloadable from Spanner Films' website. And it *was* eventually broadcast, when the BBC acquired screening rights for its classy documentary slot *Storyville*. Among the positive user comments on *Storyville*'s website is one praising the film for 'true BBC quality'. But creatively the film had nothing to do with the BBC.

McLibel – 'programme', 'video', 'film' – stands for the independent contemporary documentaries not dependent for their production on a distribution mechanism fixed in advance. And its ability to leap from non-broadcast to broadcast spaces and back is the direct result of the film-maker retaining full control over her own rights: rights she would never have had if she'd signed a television contract at the outset.

Prod Co: Spanner Films; **Dir/Prod**: Franny Armstrong.

Mining Review 4th Year No. 12
1951 – 10 mins

This is a typical issue from the National Coal Board's *Mining Review* series released monthly between 1947 when the industry was nationalised and 1982, shortly before its decimation commenced. Three months after this film's release, the Conservatives returned to government, committed to efficient management rather than privatisation of industries Labour had taken into public ownership.

Issues mixed newsreel-style reports on events with technical and social-interest stories constructed as mini-documentaries. Small units filmed items over a couple of days, but often after extensive preparation had first taken place. Subjects were selected on the advice of NCB officials or by the production company, sometimes having been contacted by local mining communities with suggestions. The series put the breezy jollity of commercial newsreels to a social mission in direct descent from those of pre-war and wartime documentary. It sought to inform miners of developments, but also to engender their sense of the state corporation as a harmonious national family (each issue included items from several coalfields). Equally, it sought to embed positive representations of the miner and mining in national consciousness. The films, distributed free to cinemas, were widely seen in non-mining areas as well as in coalfields. This makes *Mining Review* much the most successful offshoot of the documentary movement in terms of theatrical distribution. It was initially outsourced by the NCB to DATA – Documentary and Technicians Alliance – a cooperative formed by film-makers formerly employed by Paul Rotha, many of them staunch socialists.

4th Year No. 12's four items were filmed in June 1951 for the August issue. *Digging Deep* feels closest to newsreel in both tone and subject: the sinking of new shafts at a West Lothian colliery, ceremonially launched by Lady Balfour, wife of the NCB's Scottish Division chairman, watched by local VIPs and mining families (a hint of barbed social comment in the cut from dignitaries to workers?). But this is correlated with the nationwide drive to increase production, illustrated by underground footage from Lancashire.

In *Miners' Festival* the emphasis is on community rather than industry: Festival of Britain celebrations in Shotts, Lanarkshire. Cracking final line: 'it was a good do. When a mining town sets out to go gay, it doesn't do things by halves.' The issue's 'technical' item, *Personal Call*, documents processes associated with the Continuous Miner machine that helped a Leicestershire colliery beat output records. These are shown mostly in close shots, because of the cramped filming conditions. A preproduction report recommended this as 'a plain, straightforward coal getting story of more than usual interest. The human angle is about nil. The machine is a slave driver – typically American . . . the whole business struck me as being pretty inhuman.'[40] The film avoids being too mechanistic by turning the report into a personal visit down the mine by *Mining Review* narrator John Slater – anticipating presented television documentary (though he is shot silent and post-synched).

The final story, *Foxhunt*, concerns bloodsports in Wales: 'Joe Collins, sixty-two-year-old ex-miner, and his nine miner sons find good sport in doing a good turn for their neighbours' by tracking and shooting local foxes. Today this would be a controversial topic, and some of the footage is gruesome, but it's presented as an uncontentious, microcosmic glimpse into miners' leisure time.

Prod Co: DATA; Spons: National Coal Board; Dir (stories, uncredited): Peter Pickering, John Shaw Jones.

Mirror (*Video Nation*)
1994
Gordon Henscher

Video Nation is positioned at a significant midway point in documentary's gradual, latterly rapid democratisation. Two distinct historical strands have become increasingly interwoven. Non-professionals had long made their own documentaries, either by importing professional techniques into family home movies, or by shooting homemade documentaries on general subjects. Meanwhile, professional film-makers had sometimes put their resources to the service of members of the public: in 1935 *Jubilee* and *Housing Problems* represented different means of widening access, respectively by providing professional assistance and distribution to amateur production, and by enabling 'ordinary people' to place their testimonies on celluloid. Later film-makers as different as Grigsby and Graef, depicting communities or institutions otherwise inadequately represented by television, would often screen their films' first cuts to their subjects, inviting their comment. But the most systematic attempts at 'access' documentary were those of the BBC's Community Programmes Unit (CPU). For its *Open Door* (1973–83) and *Open Space* (1985–94) slots, the CPU collaborated with groups as varied as the Bogside Community Association, the Transexual Liberation Group and the British Campaign to Stop Immigration on the making of programmes then screened on BBC2.

The CPU's camcorder-era *Video Diaries* and *Video Nation* took the process further by providing Hi-8 or DV cameras to individuals who then made their own films, usually reflecting their own lives, broadcast in many different packages, often as 'filler' shorts between longer programmes, to considerable cumulative impact. The very first *Video Nation* short to be screened was *Mirror*, retired Colonel Gordon Hensher's study of old age in the form of a two-minute self-portrait.

Consciously influenced by the 1930s' Mass Observation movement, *Video Nation* echoed its complex interplay between anthropological

survey shaped from above, and spontaneous cultural expression
emerging from below. Applicants were selected partly to ensure a
suitable demographic mix:

> The idea of Video Nation was partly a response to the increasingly diverse
> nature of British society. The notion of a consensus among the 'general
> public' had clearly become an anachronism. The BBC needed to find new
> ways of reflecting the wide range of views, attitudes and lifestyles that
> were out there and the Video Nation project was one way of doing
> this.[41]

The applicants were trained to operate the camera, and their
programmes edited by the producers (but with contributor right of veto).
They were excitingly wide-ranging in subject and in style, but *Mirror* is
based on *Video Nation*'s most recognisable stylistic legacy. Opening with
three shots of mirrors, and gracefully accompanied by piano scales, the
film consists mainly of Hensher delivering a monologue to camera – 'It's
a ghastly thing to look at one's face, what it is now and what one feels it
should be inside . . . inside you don't get any older but every time you
look in that confounded mirror . . .' – concluding with him reaching for
its off button. Future *Video Nation* contributors made more varied,
ambitious films, but such confessional self-recording was frequently the
core element. Having thus entered the public consciousness as a
distinctively 'amateur' aesthetic, it has since seeped heavily into
professional documentary, and factual television generally.

Meanwhile, the rising quality and decreasing cost of digital cameras
and editing software has resulted in 'amateur' documentary content
achieving an increasingly 'professional' look. Moreover, the web has
provided a distribution mechanism removing the necessity of 'user-
generated content' being mediated as by *Video Nation*. British
contributors to <youtube.com> have occasionally attracted national
media attention, for instance, films by 'geriatric1927', a grumpier latter-
day Gordon Henscher sharing his reflections on aging with a worldwide

audience. Other websites still provide a structured framework for distribution of 'webumentary', as in Channel 4's fourdocs, which includes it in a wider engagement with documentary. Video Nation itself now lives in cyberspace, at <bbc.co.uk/videonation> where Gordon Henscher's *Mirror* can be seen alongside hundreds of old and new shorts.

Webdocs are becoming as varied as any form of documentary but it's interesting to note that, just as Victorian films often have a single technique later to be combined with others in more sophisticated productions, so these films often rely on basic building blocks. And the most common is the to-camera monologue thoughtfully used by Gordon Henscher as a member of the *Video Nation*.

Prod Co: BBC Community Programme Unit; **Dir**: Gordon Hensher; **Prod**: Chris Mohr, Mandy Rose.

Morning in the Streets
1959 – 35 mins
Denis Mitchell, Roy Harris

The BBC Northern Film Unit's *Morning in the Streets* was publicised as an 'impression of life and opinion in the back streets of a Northern City in the morning'. That city is never identified. Co-director Denis Mitchell stated, 'I wanted to show the warmth and vitality and good humour to be found there. I had no particular city in mind and scenes for the film were in fact shot in Liverpool, Stockport, Salford and Manchester.'[42] These were then combined as if capturing a single morning in one location. Because they are impressionistic rather than journalistic (there is no presenter, or narrator), this artistically licensed deceit is easily accepted. While a minority disliked the film, it was hailed as marking

Poetic detail in *Morning in the Streets*

television documentary's artistic maturity, worthy of film antecedents, and cemented Mitchell's emerging reputation as one of its first great practitioners. After its broadcast, *Morning in the Streets* became part of the non-theatrical documentary film repertory, available for years for 16mm bookings, but never again broadcast until 1991, following Mitchell's death.

Resonances with documentary's past include the almost, but not quite, seamless mix of observational scenes with staged ones (such as a family waking up in their one-room apartment early in the day). A sequence referencing slum-dwelling echoes *Housing Problems* in technique as well as in subject, with its use of an old woman's statements to camera. The Free Cinema film-makers admired the film, sensing Jennings's shade in its frequent pauses to take in telling details, of scant narrative importance but great poetic effect: streetlamps, pavement puddles, birds, cats, broken bottles, toy soldiers, tea being stirred. Common to all Mitchell's films is their transformation of everyday imagery and sounds into what feel like eternal statements by means of strong photographic compositions and telling editing.

But Mitchell was unfamiliar with Jennings, and influenced less by cinema than by radio, where his roots lay. The co-direction credit to Roy Harris reflected Mitchell's technical inexperience with the visual medium, but the film most impressed with its use of sound, which had few cinematic precursors. Sound is sometimes synchronised, recording conversations by matching the silent footage to separately recorded audiotapes. Lively shots of children playing street games are accompanied by their joyous cries. More often, passages of speech recorded only in audio form are played over unrelated visuals. These snatches of conversation are sometimes anecdotal, sometimes philosophical: 'My wife would have me back tomorrow'; 'His brain and my talent would go a long way if you know what I mean'; 'the class I belong to is the higher working class' . . ..

The music is sometimes irritating. Some thin stretches of storyline featuring an Irish tramp-cum-street-philosopher feel strained and silly.

And Mitchell's attraction to the grotesque and the bleak isn't to everyone's taste. The optimism of the final scenes of children enjoying their school lunch break is weirdly undercut by a voice having immediately beforehand referred to the contemporary threat of atomic destruction (elsewhere, an old woman remembers her husband being called up to fight in World War I). But *Morning in the Streets* is still a classic whose many imperfections almost work in its favour.

Prod Co: BBC; **Dir**: Denis Mitchell, Roy Harris.

Moslems in Britain – Cardiff
1961 – 18 mins
G. Fares

This average-quality film has one feature immediately distinguishing it
from the other ninety-nine discussed here: it isn't in English. In the post-
war films of the Central Office of Information, of which this is one
example among thousands, this fact isn't especially surprising.

The COI disappears from most histories of film in about 1952. Yet it
celebrated its 60th anniversary in 2006, having outlived by decades many
of the government departments it was set up to serve, and having
commissioned more documentaries over a longer period than any UK
organisation bar the BBC. Before vanishing entirely from critical view,
it was disparaged for having dissipated the legacy of state documentary
that had peaked in World War II (sample critique: 'It is extremely difficult
to discuss the filming activities of the COI in a detached manner . . .
it has collected over the years an image of purposelessness, petty-minded
administration and exploitation of the small and frightened film-
maker.')[43]

These criticisms are reasonable to the extent that the COI absolutely
failed to foster a vibrant culture of public film-making, but many
individual examples of fine film-making can be found among its vast
output. More importantly: even when mediocre, it's a fascinating, if
partial, continually shifting index for national concerns. This is particularly
so given that one wartime documentary project continued methodically
by the COI was the sponsoring of films about Britain for overseas
audiences. Thus, for example, two 1961 films funded by the Foreign
Office, entitled *Moslems in Britain*, documenting the life and work of
British Muslims for co-religionists, one filmed in Manchester, the other in
Cardiff – in Arabic.

Many of these films for overseas distribution were intended for
television, while some were interchangeable between large and small
screens. This film comes over as a cross between cinema travelogue and

television location report. It benefits from some good compositions and lighting, and an Arabic music soundtrack. But it is structured around an on-screen presenter, shown at the beginning driving into Cardiff and getting back into his car to drive away at the end. The main body of the film is divided between his seven different interviews of Cardiff residents, and more discursive and visual sequences bridging them, exploring Cardiff's history and character, and showing its castles, shopping streets and docks. The interviews take place in several of these locations, including a mosque, and are mostly with Muslims who have migrated to Cardiff from countries like Yemen. But they also include the city's Lord Mayor. Hers is the only interview conducted in English (her answers translated by the reporter).

The film naturally presents a mostly sunny view of Britain as a destination for Muslim migrants, at a point when its Muslim minority was small. Nearly fifty years on, it's surprising that Cardiff (unlike Manchester) should have been considered one of the two cities suitable for exploring the Muslim presence in Britain. But up to that point, the Welsh capital city had been one of Britain's more racially mixed places.

Prod Co: United Motion Pictures; **Spons**: Central Office of Information, Foreign Office; **Dir**: G. Fares.

The Negro Next Door (*This Week*)
1965 – 27 mins
Peter Robinson

Television current-affairs programming has its own history, distinct from that mapped by this book, but it interacts with documentary as with other forms. Three of the longest-running flagship series were *Panorama* (made by the BBC since 1953), *This Week* (started in 1956 by Associated-Rediffusion, later inherited by Thames Television) and *World in Action* (begun by Granada Television in 1963). Their many differences included their contrasting relationships with documentary. *World in Action* effected a thorough fusion of documentary with journalism. *Panorama* and *This Week* began as studio-based magazine programmes in which individual items shot on film approximated 'mini-documentaries', as newsreel and cinemagazine stories had. During the 1960s items lengthened, to the point of filling entire programmes. But different house styles are evident even when all three were operating in full documentary mode. The commercially produced *This Week* and *World in Action*, tackling increasingly controversial topics, were more streetwise than their BBC counterpart. But *World in Action* specialised in narrated films, while *This Week* foregrounded presenter-journalists.

The Negro Next Door opens on a point-of-view shot (a full minute long!) taken from a car driving down a Leeds terraced street, under a soundtrack in which presenter Desmond Wilcox summarises the film's purpose. The sound says *current-affairs reportage*. The images say *documentary-film-making*. The combination announces the programme's dual status. Thereafter the film is structured by its interviews, punctuated by actuality shots and Wilcox's off-screen musings. Scenes are shot and shown chronologically. And dialectically: Wilcox (both heard and seen) interviews two white women about their black neighbour; then interviews the neighbour; then brings both parties together for an excruciating but instructive encounter. Finally, he speaks again to the white women, capturing their furious reactions to the filming of the previous scene. While race divides these women from their neighbour, class tensions clearly underlie the relationship between the film-makers and their subjects.

Using relatively mobile equipment that captures live sound, the film creatively treats actuality by intervening in it: techniques since refined (or corrupted: delete according to taste) by reality television. Here, the purpose is high-minded. The film explores prejudices much of its audience will have shared with the women, clearly in the 'I'm not racist but . . . ' category: not irredeemably malevolent but with some appalling attitudes. Among the ironies of their testimony is an admission by one that her Catholicism should probably entail her being more tolerant towards her black neighbours: her denomination and her Irish surname suggest she has roots in an earlier migrant group despised in its day. The film doesn't pick up on this, but it proves much of her resentment derives from misunderstandings both innocent and wilful. As one of Wilcox's interjections has it: 'There always *is* another side of the coin, isn't there?' His subject turns on him: 'Would you like to see your oldest daughter marry a coloured man?' She claims his facial expression proves he wouldn't. From the film alone, it's impossible to tell: his face is off screen at the time. It was brave to allow this accusation into the final edit.

The thrust is liberal but the treatment of race has dated. Wilcox originally wanted to end the film with a question to the viewer: 'Would you let *your* daughter marry a negro?' This exposes some of the programme-makers' assumptions about their documentary's audience. Might black people not also have been watching?

Prod Co: Rediffusion; **Dir**: Peter Robinson; **Prod**: Cyril Bennett; **Phot**: Ron Osborn.

Neil Kinnock
1987 – 10 mins
Hugh Hudson

This General Election broadcast is the party political film best remembered by UK voters, though rarely thought of as a documentary. It has a stronger case for being classified as such than many films celebrated as documentaries.

Then-fashionable cinema director Hugh Hudson was hired to make a film promoting the Labour Party to 1987's voters by focusing on its leader Neil Kinnock, a good if verbose Welsh orator harshly mocked by tabloids for lacking his opponent Margaret Thatcher's gravitas. The film sought to capitalise on his strengths, while neutralising criticism. Hudson brought feature-film production values (reminiscent of his similarly slick *Chariots of Fire* [1981]) to textbook documentary materials. These include interviews with Kinnock and political associates like James Callaghan and Denis Healey; faded stills of a youthful Kinnock and his family; and footage of major speeches. Last but not least, Hudson directed the iconic aerial footage of Neil and Glenys Kinnock walking hand-in-hand over sea cliffs.

These components are combined to build up a documentary portrait. Often they're juxtaposed to add force or meaning. This is classic documentary syntax: generating associations through considered use of image and sound. A straightforward example is the interpolation of shots of Kinnock, at his desk soberly going through papers, into an interview with Barbara Castle rebutting criticisms of his youth and inexperience. A more emotive instance occurs later, when Hudson cuts from one of Kinnock's best-known speeches, about his political values, to a series of family photographs framed along a wall. These are symbols of continuity, family strength and the distance the working class had come thanks to opportunities provided by moderate socialism. Kinnock was a transitional figure, exercising his rhetoric to apply beliefs rooted in post-war politics (here personified by Castle, Healey and Callaghan) to the Thatcher era in which they were being overturned. The film, too, has a transitional status within political communications history, combining faith in the public's receptiveness to an openly ideological pitch with polished projection of personal image. It was criticised then precisely for being too glossy, though it was initially popular enough to be selected for a repeat screening two weeks after its original broadcast (unusual: the normal convention was for different material to fill each of a party's several allocated television slots).

It's a good film in many respects. But as a doc-with-a-purpose *Neil Kinnock* can much more easily be judged than most other examples, and quickly found wanting. Labour lost the election. The Thatcherite revolution proceeded apace. Some claimed the film had not merely failed to avert but actually exacerbated this outcome. It was increasingly ridiculed as *Kinnock: The Movie*. This is perhaps due to its few but fatal artistic weaknesses. Hudson detracts from the power of a strong sequence, Kinnock's attack on the extremist Militant Tendency at Labour's 1985 conference, by introducing music. His intention is to underscore the drama of the moment. Instead he destroys it. And elsewhere, music adapted from Beethoven's *Ode to Joy* pushes the film over the edge, cheapening its sentiments, shifting attention from the message towards the film-making itself. This is bad documentary – and bad propaganda – technique.

Prod Co: John Gau Productions; **Spons**: Labour Party; **Dir**: Hugh Hudson.

New Year's Eve (*Police*)
1982 – 45 mins
Roger Graef, Charles Stewart

American-born Roger Graef is the UK's best-known exponent of Direct Cinema, a misnomer when applied to Britain where it's been confined to the small screen, popularly labelled 'fly-on-the-wall' film-making. Graef hasn't worked exclusively in this idiom. But he evolved a signature style based on its rigorous application in (series such as *Decision* [1976]) produced by his company Films of Record for the BBC and independent television. For these studies of the inner workings of institutions, the company integrated itself into its subjects' working environments, filming from unobtrusive physical positions, avoiding reconstruction, staging, commentary, interviews, even camera lighting. The films, austere but dependent on high shooting ratios, contained such eye-opening content that they achieved very respectable ratings as well as critical acclaim. This is certainly true of Graef's landmark BBC series *Police*. The rationale for the project was as follows:

> the Police probably get more airtime than any other section of society. But the picture presented is usually inaccurate – either too basic, too bland or too sensational. The time is ripe for a series which shows policemen as they really are.[44]

The Thames Valley Police Force was selected as the series' subject, for several reasons. It policed an area which was a UK microcosm (geographically and ethnically mixed), and easily accessible from London and Bristol. Above all, its Chief Constable was enthusiastic, following intensive courting by the producers: 'We are asking for . . . more access than any television team has yet won . . . we have made it clear that we do not expect access to be withdrawn when things go wrong.' The top brass were influenced by the success of *Sailor* (1976), a previous BBC series going behind the scenes of a disciplined organisation. Many later judged their openness naive, as the effect was ambivalent at best. The depiction of officers' insensitive handling of a rape victim in the episode *A Case of Rape* caused such controversy that national changes to police procedures followed.

However randomly 'observational' *Police*'s content, each episode was edited into recognisable documentary narrative shapes: the progress of one investigation; the work of a single department; the experience of an individual; the policing of an event; and, in the first episode, a passage of time, New Year's Eve. In swift succession, opening sequences show a station party contrasted with two drunk and disorderly incidents. There are moments of low-key drama and humour arising from events and characters, but mostly a sense of things simply unfolding. A main storyline does develop, however, centred on a raid on a house in which a man is supposedly loose with a gun. This turns out to be untrue, and the man an innocent, rather sweet character traumatised by what in retrospect was a police overreaction (though viewers are left free to draw their own conclusions). His solicitor later sought to prevent a repeat transmission on the grounds that its first screening had had negative effects on his client's life and mental health.

The aesthetics as well as the ethics of films like *New Year's Eve* are endlessly debatable. Proponents argue that they penetrate the reality of the institutions governing our lives more deeply than other versions of documentary. Detractors decry their faith in 'raw' material to interpret itself as naive, even duplicitous (exploiting that 'rawness' to disguise inevitable intrusions of subjectivity, particularly into editing). A more reasonable conclusion is that Direct Cinema is simply *a* style of documentary like any other, equally capable of being used effectively, ineptly, fairly and unfairly. In this case, millions found the style compelling. As to its fidelity to the 'reality' of the events of New Year's Eve 1981: from the film itself, it's impossible to say.

Prod Co: BBC Bristol; **Co-dir/Prod**: Roger Graef; **Co-dir/Phot**: Charles Stewart.

Night Mail
1936 – 24 mins
Harry Watt, Basil Wright

Readers seeking an historical account of *Night Mail* are directed towards
a comparatively mountainous literature, including a forthcoming 'BFI
Classic'. Suffice to say the following: it's jointly credited (for production
on some prints, direction on others) to Harry Watt and Basil Wright. Watt
represented one documentary tendency (human interest, bringing facts
to life); Wright personified another (the lyrical touch). The extent of their
individual contributions caused later dispute. But *Night Mail* is the
achievement of a unit, not auteurs. And the decisive contribution was
from two artists from outside cinema, far more prestigious (now, not
then) than Watt, Wright, any of them. *Night Mail* is two separate films in
one. Thanks to the final sequence, added late in production, in which
Auden's verse and Britten's music combine with admittedly splendid
images and editing, it lodged itself in the memory banks of a culture, of
many who've seen it, of many more who only *think* they've seen it.
A close viewing reveals the impressive economy with which the whole
film is put together. And the first twenty minutes of narrative and
explanation, sometimes boring, are essential to the meaning of the last
four. But it's those final minutes that make *Night Mail*, with *Drifters*, one
of only two 'compulsory' films on this or any other list of British
documentaries.

  If *Drifters* is British documentary's *Birth of A Nation* or *Potemkin*,
Night Mail is its *Stagecoach* (1939) or *Singin' in the Rain* (1952): instant
archetype, freshly minted. Like *Stagecoach*, it distils much of its genre's
recent history into something novel. Its framework is a journey, shot from
numerous angles. Its detailed content is numerous work processes both
explicated and enlivened. It includes some observational and a great deal
more reconstructed footage (the carriage scenes were shot in a studio).
Workers playing 'themselves' (or the 'types' to which they belong) bring
both authenticity and awkwardness. It has striking images and flat ones;

sound experiments that work, others that don't come off. And all its patterns are knitted into bigger ones. A nation is revealed communicating with itself in the midst of a humdrum daily life suddenly made complex, exciting. The cross-country trip lets the camera take in farmyard views and pithead glimpses. Auden bridges divisions: 'letters for the rich, letters for the poor'. Less often remarked upon are the connections made between England and Scotland. The subject is the

Full steam ahead: the *Night Mail*

London–Glasgow mail train. Pivotal to the narrative section is the changeover between English and Scottish staff at Crewe, and the vital switch, prose to poem, occurs as the train crosses the border. Some Scots prefer to deny it, but Britain and its Empire were Anglo-Scottish, not English, inventions. And the documentary movement was an Anglo-Scottish mix. Watt was from Edinburgh, Wright from London. *Night Mail*'s final sequence has two alternating movements. The famous, pressing couplets delivered by unit member Stuart Legg in BBC (GPO?) English are balanced by the gentler passages: 'all Scotland awaits . . . working Glasgow, well set Edinburgh, granite Aberdeen', read in the Scottish accent of John Grierson.

Prod Co: GPO Film Unit; **Prod**: Harry Watt, Basil Wright; **Prod**: John Grierson; **Asst Dir**: Pat Jackson.

Nightcleaners
1975 – 90 mins
Berwick Street Collective

> If we take it seriously, it could provide a basis for a new direction in
> British film-making.[45]

British film-making was conspicuously unaffected by *Nightcleaners*. But
the film *was* taken seriously: seriously enough to have provoked heated,
even violent reactions prompted, oddly, by its form more than its subject.

That subject was the campaign to unionise and to improve
conditions for London's female army of nightshift office-cleaners.
Actuality records of demonstrations were made. Sympathetic interviews
were filmed with the exploited workers – and subversively revealing ones
with their patronising bosses. Instructive comments from articulate
campaigners were recorded. The shooting schedule was unusually long,
allowing coverage of the campaign's progress over two years, attention
to individuals as well as the group and reference to the era's wider
upheavals. And much footage, unusual for the time, was taken of the
cleaners at work in ghostly office blocks, sometimes sharing their
thoughts with the crew as they dusted desks, vacuumed floors and
brushed toilet bowls. Still, the expected result was standard-issue agit-
prop, of the sort film collectives then specialised in (Marc Karlin and
Humphrey Trevelyan, two of the Berwick Street Collective, had previously
been involved in Cinema Action).

As the rushes were spliced, a different film emerged.

Events play out of sequence. Images shrink or slow down to the
point of abstraction. Clapperboards are left in takes – and retakes.
Scenes start in the middle of actions, end before their completion.
Sometimes the audio is removed, sometimes it's the pictures that are
missing – black leader is inserted at numerous points. Some of those
involved in the campaign (though not, reputedly, the nightcleaners

A grainy de-dramatised image from *Nightcleaners*

themselves) were perturbed. Had the political documentary, the one they'd signed up to, survived its unexpected collision with experimental cinema? By wilfully threatening its own coherence, was the film undermining its subject? Cultural commentators took up the debate. Supportive pieces, including a famous analysis in theoretical journal *Screen*, applauded *Nightcleaners*' challenges to viewers. Sceptical ones charged the film with pretentious obscurantism.

Since then, the film has been one of those more often culturally referenced than actually viewed. When it is viewed, the results are surprising. Perhaps later, mainstream breaches with classical narrative (think *Memento*) have made earlier, avant-garde ones less disturbing than they once were. In any case, *Nightcleaners* simply isn't, now, the forbiddingly difficult piece its reputation says it is (certainly less difficult than the unreadable *Screen* article). Its effect *is* initially disorienting, but viewers gradually attune to the rhythm, as if to real events reworked by a daydream playing in the overworked, under-slept brain of someone who has been up all night – murky, but with its own meticulous logic.

The function of these distortions is, in fact, a documentary one. Numerous individual editing decisions highlight facets of events which wouldn't otherwise reveal themselves: when the sound is sucked out of a conversation, we take a deeper look at the listener's eyes, telling a different story than the speaker's words. More generally, we start making connections a conventional edit wouldn't have allowed. Intangible – but real – processes lurking beneath visible ones become apparent: economic and political, cultural and psychological forces. But we're constantly aware that the material could be re-edited again, to different effect: every truth revealed is open to challenge.

Even viewers disagreeing with its politics may find this film compelling, because it never stops offering them unusual food for thought. In that sense, *Nightcleaners* is *more* accessible than less adventurous counterparts.

Prod Co: Berwick Street Collective.

O'Connell Bridge
1897 – 1 min

This film shot by a Frenchman in Dublin is scarcely less of a British documentary than anything else placed on celluloid in the nineteenth century. When a camera operator representing the Lumière brothers arrived in the British Isles in late 1897, he became the first of many foreigners to disembark with the aim of documenting them on film (witness Robert Flaherty, Jean-Luc Godard and hundreds of TV crews). And when, having filmed in London and Liverpool, he crossed the Irish Sea, he traversed no national boundaries. Dublin was the second city of Britain's Empire (so it was said – it was also said of at least three other British cities . . .). And at this formative time, with language no barrier to films without sound, their distribution was anyway an international business. The mixed programmes in which they were seen included films of multiple national origins and in several nascent genres. Of which, the actuality films of places across the globe are those for which a *documentary* function can most persuasively be argued. They brought the world before people who wouldn't otherwise ever travel long-distance. In this case, to the only bridge in Europe whose breadth equals its width.

Two decades later, dramatic events hastening Ireland's breakaway from the Union took place extremely close to O'Connell Bridge. But what we see is a peaceful, relatively prosperous British city. The film relies for movement on the people and transport busily moving before the motionless camera: the fulsomely dressed lady on the bicycle, the bowler-hatted man crossing the street, the horse-drawn coaches with their advertising hoardings. As such, this is a typical Victorian 'street scene' in form and in content. From such rudiments grew one kind of twentieth-century documentary, the documentary of place. The operative contrast is with travelling shots taken from *on board* transport, shots describing journeys rather than points of termination (on the same trip, the Lumières' camera recorded its departure from Dublin station).

Among twenty-*first*-century media it is CCTV and webcam footage that initially come to mind: like them, this film feels far more neutrally 'observational' than anything 'documentary' has to offer (at the time of writing there are at least two live webcams of O'Connell Bridge online, neither replicating the 1897 camera position). But look again. The film's extreme brevity entails the closed structure of a documentary more than the open-endedness of automated cameras' raw output, in turn ensuring our 'observation' is heavily mediated by the film-maker's decisions. Daniel O'Connell's imposing statue at right foreground, and at left background the Nelson pillar (a symbol of Britishness, later destroyed) make for an attractive composition. And from this perspective, we can take in buildings to our right, pedestrians passing us laterally and traffic moving towards and away from us. The merit of one street scene over another is almost always down to camera positioning enabling footage both visually pleasing and instructive of the place in which it's taken. This is also true of webcams. But like a documentary film-maker, and unlike a pointer of webcams, the Lumière operator also had to select his moment. Moreover, he intervened in it. A close viewing of the opening frames indicates that the nearby horse-drawn cart was placed there by him, and begins moving past us at his express instruction.

Prod Co: Lumière; **Phot** (probably): Alexandre Promio.

Out to Play
1936 – 10 mins
Harold Lowenstein

Out to Play, an obscure film by an obscure director, refuses any of the obvious categorisations of 1930s' documentary. Neither avant-garde nor political, nor made by the documentary movement, it is an entertainment short intended for cinema distribution but produced outside the studio system with evident creativity and an unusual style. Though a seamless mixing of the planned and the spontaneous is common in 1930s' documentary, their usual proportions are here reversed. The film catches children playing, fighting and dancing in a park and in the streets and is dedicated to the London children who unconsciously form its cast. Of course, this underplays the amount of direction that would have been necessary (one wonders in particular whether the close-up of a child crying was achieved by serendipity or intervention). The film does, though, anticipate by many years not only some better-known observational documentaries about children, but also several of the trappings of Free Cinema, minus its self-importance. Filmed entirely in unglamorous exteriors, it privileges the evocation of atmosphere over the taking of individually 'well-made' shots and is largely devoid of plot. It's all rather delightful (weird end-title, though), a bit too ramshackle but compensating with its *joie de vivre*.

The track includes tinkly music, children's laughter, ambient sound and the odd effect synchronised to the action. Its (female) voiceover is posh but gentle, unsentimental ('they invent their own games; they have little respect for their mothers, for coppers, even for crossing signs') and used only to introduce sequences, before the film submerges the viewer into the children's world. Adults occasionally appear, sometimes as victims of pranks supplying the few brief stretches of storyline, elsewhere evoking vanished backstreets of organ-grinders, street vendors and horse-drawn carts.

Little seems to be known about director Harold Lowenstein, though his brother-in-law Philip Leacock, employed on *Out to Play* as a teenaged assistant, was later a successful documentary and feature director. Lowenstein appears to have hovered on the edges of 1930s' cinema culture, and his filmography suggests an erratic directing career including brief later stints with the Realist Film Unit and British Transport Films, where he was remembered as a likeable aesthete.[46] Later he made several films dealing with clinical child psychology. Back in 1937 he had written:

Pavement life seen in *Out to Play*

A child psychologist told me, when I was preparing [*Out to Play*] that he always saw the director behind the child's acting. The director was trying to depict behaviour alien to the child's natural feelings. The healthy child has an endless curiosity, he wants to know all about the inside of the camera, and until he has found out (even at the expense of our valuable stock inside!) we cannot expect him to co-operate with us. That is the key to filming children. We must inspire them with confidence in us, and make them feel that we are all having a grand game, and that the way to be good at the game is to do certain things in front of the mysterious black box when it starts to whirr.[47]

Prod Co: Short Film Productions; **Dir**: Harold Lowenstein; **Phot**: Edwin Catford.

Portrait of a School
1957 – 24 mins
Vivian Milroy

Associated Redifussion Presents: Portrait of a School. Cut to a lively
exterior shot: young girls and boys, presumably children in the school's
playground. An archetypal documentary scene but strangely, on the next
cut, we seem to be in a different school, with older pupils, all boys. To
their left a man watches. Cut to close shot: still looking right, he turns to
face and address us. This is to be a portrait of a secondary modern
school, taking us behind the scenes for one day so we can better
understand the education Britain's children, 'your kids and mine', are
getting. This sounds rather Griersonian, implying a better-informed
populace will be better bound to its social institutions. But, as delivered
by a presenter suddenly present in the institution's midst, this
announcement has clearly moved beyond the ageing conventions of
large-screen documentary.

The unnamed presenter conducts several interviews: individual
interrogations of the headmaster and of a parent in her home; group
encounters with teachers and pupils. These are techniques
overwhelmingly associated with television. But frequently a teacher or a
pupil will himself introduce a scene, addressing the audience head-on.
Equally frequently, they act out scripted scenes, as in several meetings in
the headmaster's office, and a weird bit in which he chairs the school
parliament. Such reconstructed actuality – 'typicality', perhaps – was of
course widespread in past documentary. But here it might equally be a
legacy of the live acted 'documentaries' which seem to have been a
significant part of the BBC's early 1950s' output.

The decaying acetate negatives of *Portrait of a School* are physical
survivors of *commercial* television's early days (ITV began broadcasting in
1955) and the print made from them is an interesting document of those
days. It would be unwise to draw conclusions about 1950s' TV
documentary from the few easily viewable examples but this one

certainly offers intriguing pointers. Several modes alternate, frequently interacting within single scenes. Some became conventions, others disappeared from mainstream documentary. The mixture strikes us today as highly peculiar: as if the reporter were a documentary *deus ex machina*, arriving to prompt the school into Brechtian enactment of itself. The perfunctory style of the filming heightens the weirdness, but suggests that in 1957 it might not have been unusual.

All of this interacts with the social content. Secondary moderns were the schools where those who failed the '11-plus' exam were sent before comprehensive education was introduced. This one is unnamed but seems to be in London, possibly Wimbledon (check the noticeboards), with a lower-middle-class intake, and with greater focus on technical than academic education. The boys are equally gauche as interviewees and as actors. The headmaster is silver-tongued and suavely confident, the teachers a rum bunch: one would think twice before entrusting one's children to some of them. However, while the head and the dog-collared chairman of governors present a cautiously sunny view, several moany teachers offer grim comments on crumbling infrastructure, low salaries and enormous classes.

Executive producer Caryl Doncaster already had an estimable documentary track record, dating from a period working under Paul Rotha, no less, when he briefly ran the BBC's Documentary Department. She helmed several BBC drama-documentary series on social issues then became an early producer of *This Week*. *Portrait of a School* aside, director Vivian Milroy seems to have worked almost exclusively in drama and animation, before disappearing from recorded film and television history in around 1960.

Prod Co: Associated Rediffusion; **Dir**: Vivian Milroy; **Exec Prod**: Caryl Doncaster.

A Portrait of Ga
1952 – 4 mins
Margaret Tait

The films of Margaret Tait happily lack the cold, arbitrary pretensions of many experimental films. But her filmography illustrates well the typical conceptual relationships between the traditions of experimental (a.k.a. artists' a.k.a. avant-garde) film-making and of documentary. Some artists' films experiment within the framework of a fiction (as in Tait's *Blue Black Permanent* [1992]), some are abstract (Tait's *Calypso* [1950]). Others use photographic material from the real world, but principally as raw material for experimentation (*Colour Poems* [1974] mixes actuality footage and animation sequences).

It is when experimental films are not only of but *about* their subjects, that they clearly step into the documentary tradition, even if only at its margins. Most of Tait's films are in this category and many have recognisable documentary formats: representations of places, often in her native Orkney Islands, and of people. Though she rejected the documentary label, this was simply because her miniaturist portraiture techniques were so unconventional compared with most documentary production:

> The contradictory or paradoxical thing is that in a documentary the real things depicted are liable to lose their reality by being photographed and presented in that 'documentary' way, and there's no poetry in that. In poetry, something else happens. Presence, let's say, soul or spirit, an empathy with whatever it is that's dwelt upon, feeling for it – to the point of identification.[48]

Tait's intimacy with the subject of her early film *A Portrait of Ga*, her elderly Orcadian mother, is a given, but this isn't a mere home movie. Or rather it's not *just* a home movie, because it sets out to communicate its feelings to unrelated viewers miles and years away. Considering its graceful slowness, it's surprising, on a close viewing, just how many frequently unusual, indoor as well as outdoor, shots of the subject have been so carefully combined to build up its portrait. Simple lilting but sparingly used music, shots of water and of landscape and Tait's commentary, oblique and direct at the same time, are also parts of the picture. Tait's casual cut to a close-up of her mother as her commentary refers to her own children and to her mother's own mother, is (like her brief reference to the Orkneys' Viking heritage) typical of her unobtrusive creativity. These snatches of past and future sit inside a film mainly consisting of snatches of the everyday present: Ga slowly unwrapping a boiled sweet and placing it in her mouth, digging a flowerbed, dancing for the camera, looking at a book.

'My mother lives in the windy Orkney islands. It's certainly a wonderful place to be brought up in.' The film's final line is as deceptively simple as the film it ends. *A Portrait of Ga*, a true documentary even if an untypical one, looks at the familiar world in such as way as to glimpse, but never to pin down, the inner truth behind its appearance.

Prod Co: Ancona Films; **Dir/Phot**: Margaret Tait.

The Punk Rock Movie
1978 – 86 mins
Don Letts

The Punk Rock Movie was, in its own words, 'filmed entirely on location in Super 8mm', not by a professional observer or reporter of its events, but by a participant. In 1977, Don Letts was a young black DJ at the Roxy, a venue that became an HQ for British punk rock, then a burgeoning underground movement. He began filming the bands, on and off stage in available light, with a handheld camera containing sound-synchronised Super-8 stock (a not inconsiderable investment: such stock, unlike today's mini-DV tapes, didn't come cheap). After plenty of material had been shot and processed, it was assembled to feature length for cinema release in 1978, by which time punk had gone overground. Since then, punk has become virtually a heritage concept, an iconic foundation for much of today's popular culture. So the value of *The Punk Rock Movie* is that it's a record of punk not just from the inside, but in the present tense, as juvenile, basic, as alternately thrilling and wretched as its subject.

> Every generation needs its own soundtrack. In 1977 punk rock was it. It inspired some people to pick up guitars, I was inspired to pick up a movie camera.[49]

This is documentary film-making as stimulated by punk's DIY ethos, and infused with its aesthetic: as cheerfully contemptuous of good film-making, conventional or experimental, as punk was of bubblegum pop and progressive rock.

The film begins and ends with shaky, zoomy footage of the Sex Pistols performing 'God Save the Queen'. In between it shows performances by a host of bands including the Clash, the Slits, Subway Sect, X-Ray Spex, a pre-goth Siouxsie and the Banshees and a pre-'White Wedding' Billy Idol and Generation X. These are interspersed with footage of fans (including an excitable young Shane MacGowan in a union jack blazer), backstage conversations, street scenes, a police raid on a clothing store, tour bus hi-jinks. Letts himself is briefly seen (on the bus) and heard (in conversation with Siouxsie, and earlier with a policeman asking him to stop filming). Despite graphic scenes of drug-taking and self-mutilation, there's a sweetness about much of the film, reflecting the innocence in punk behind the exterior that Middle England found threatening: many scenes, of bands and fans larking about for the camera, are like moments from countless Super-8 family home movies. A few moments reflect the contact between punk and reggae, often attributed to Letts personally – he intends to develop this theme in a future 'director's cut' of the film.

Punk was musically limited, and the evidence is here for how mediocre – if not plain awful – many bands were (for every Clash there's an Eater . . .), but it vitally refreshed the popular music palette. *The Punk Rock Movie* is similarly a frighteningly narrow template for documentary film. But it presages the development of a 'punk' culture in its own medium, which wouldn't really flower until much cheaper technology came along.

Prod Co: Punk Rock Films, Notting Hill Studios; **Dir/Phot**: Don Letts; **Prod**: Peter Clifton.

A Queen Is Crowned
1953 – 80 mins
Castleton Knight

> J. Arthur Rank has the honour to present the Technicolor Film Record of
> the Coronation.

The film trade had marked earlier coronations: this time it had
competition. The BBC transmitted Queen Elizabeth II's coronation live to
millions, prompting a spurt in television sales. More saw it in others'
homes than in their own: the acclaimed broadcast supplied many with
their first memory of staring at a television set. Cinema couldn't compete
with the immediacy, but could supplement it with its own unique selling
points. Pathe's *Elizabeth Is Queen* and Rank's *A Queen Is Crowned* were
commemorative documentaries, fixing the ritual as colour spectacle. The

Pomp and ceremony: *A Queen Is Crowned*

British Film Academy gave them special certificates of merit as 'historical records of exceptional quality', the cinema community simultaneously tugging its forelock and patting its own back for enhancing an event celebrated as Britain's moment of reinvigoration.

The splendidly named Castleton Knight helmed Rank's version. This newsreel veteran was a specialist in documentary spectacles such as the official 1948 London Olympics film. He used expert cinematographers, and narration was written by respectably voguish playwright Christopher Fry and read by theatrical treasure Laurence Olivier. Of four reels, the middle two are devoted to the Westminster Abbey ceremony, filmed from a necessarily restricted range of angles serving the intention of presenting it as a sacred rite. The final reel records the parades (emphasising colonial allegiances, in evolution from Empire to Commonwealth). The first reel sets the others up with a sketch of Britain. Olivier reads Shakespeare's 'This England' passage. Scotland and Wales are included but much more briefly (an imbalance replicated in the ceremony itself, officiated by the Archbishop of Canterbury but with a token role for the Church of Scotland Moderator, cutting an odd figure in dark Presbyterian garb amid High Anglican finery). More interestingly, cities and industry are virtually excluded in favour of the postcard rural imagery preferred by cultural conservatives.

The Queen is a leading player among an ensemble cast of dignitaries. The star is the crown itself: physical artefact, national symbol. The film is often *excruciatingly* dull, but seen on a large screen, in the right mood, it's possible to give in, gradually mesmerised by the hushed pageantry. Afterwards, the colours linger in the mind, rich reds and purples. Fry's text is certainly deepest purple, Olivier's delivery alarmingly hammy. Fry's fashionability would soon retreat as Angry Young Men advanced. 'Method' would undermine Olivier's pre-eminence. Television would usurp cinema's documentary role. In due course, radically different documentary methods would be applied to the Queen in *Royal Family* (1969): further ahead, outside documentary, lay *Spitting Image* (1984–96) and Princess Diana's *Panorama* (1995) confessions (as this book went to press, a new BBC documentary, *A Year With the Queen*, became controversial because of misleading editing of a trailer – bringing debates about documentary's ethics and aesthetics to the front page). Britain's world status would continue to decline. The parades were literally rained on as if qualifying their own fleeting grandeur: Reel 4's cameramen struggle to maximise the colours against stubbornly dreary conditions.

Astonishingly, this was 1953's most successful film at the UK box office. A trade review recorded: 'With sedate dignity the opening show played to a packed house with standees in the rear, and a line outside it', adding that it 'immediately strikes one with the vast superiority of the motion picture screen to the television camera.'[50] Restored prints can recreate the sensual effect on 1953's viewers. Recreating the feelings invoked, for monarchy, for Britain and for cinema, is now impossible.

Prod Co: J. Arthur Rank Film Productions; **Prod**: Castleton Knight.

Returning the Serve (*Loyalists*)
1999 – 50 mins
Sam Collyns

In television's maturity, its documentary subgenres have intermingled as documentary cinema's had. *Returning the Serve*, second episode of the three-part *Loyalists*, typifies this by blending archive-based history, interview-driven testimony and presenter-led investigative journalism, a particular combination conceivable only when dealing with recent history: here, that of Ulster Loyalist paramilitarism. This episode covers the decade from the mid-1970s, one of failed political initiatives and horrific sectarian bloodletting.

Returning the Serve operates strictly within television conventions. Nonetheless, within that framework it's a documentary *film*, attentive to structure and impact in ways that become fully apparent on a second viewing. But the series' chronological, factual approach leaves the viewer to sense Loyalism's tragic Celtic paradoxes: prepared to bear arms against the state to demonstrate an equivocal 'loyalty'; committed to Britishness of a sort but hostile to the English; haunted by community memories of the Somme but willing to visit brutality upon its neighbours; resentful of Catholics' attempts to escape from downtrodden circumstances similar to those of working-class Protestants from whose ranks the UVF and UDA were exclusively drawn.

Three documentary strands each lend authority.

Presenter Peter Taylor's concerned but balanced professionalism contrasts with, say, John Berger's passionate partisanship, but references to his history of reporting from Northern Ireland add clout. He even enters the narrative, momentarily, via footage of a mid-1970s' encounter with Ian Paisley. Taylor typifies the journalist-as-documentarist tradition. He compiled and presented documentary reports for commercial television's *This Week* and *TV Eye* (1978–86), and the BBC's *Panorama*, *Brass Tacks* (1977–) and *Public Eye* (1966–), then fronted entire programmes on terrorism and Northern Ireland. *Loyalists* was the second series in a trilogy on the Troubles' major antagonists, with *Provos* (1997) and *Brits* (2000).

Extensive (and expensive) archive footage is another feature of authoritative history documentaries, BBC programmes, particularly, benefiting from access to past productions. Films spanning years tend to suggest their shifts by the period look of their footage: here, video's witness to 1985's Anglo-Irish Agreement protests feels much more contemporary than 16mm's to the 1974 Ulster Workers' Strike.

The testimony (securable on the strength of the journalism) is the most remarkable element. Interviews are with Unionist politicians (including Paisley), devastated acquaintances of Loyalists' victims and several formerly imprisoned Loyalist terrorists. Viewers were both impressed and disturbed by the candour of the latter, filmed quite close-up before austere black backgrounds.

They all accept personal responsibility, but have different reactions to it. Gusty Spence and David Ervine, who had become conciliatory politicians, are reflective (not apologetic). Others, like Jackie MacDonald and Gorman McMullan, are matter-of-fact or defiant. One, Billy Giles, is deeply remorseful and he literally haunts the film. Giles refers to having been pulled, from the moment he pulled the trigger on a Catholic victim, into a dark place from which he never returned. Five months before transmission, unable to live with his history, he hanged himself. The film opens with a clip from Giles's interview and ends with Taylor reading Giles's moving suicide note over a family photograph, then a shot of his grave.

Prod Co: BBC; **Dir/Prod**: Sam Collyns.

The Rival World
1955 – 26 mins
Bert Haanstra

The Shell Film Unit was 1930s' documentary's second most highly
regarded organisation. Initially the GPO Film Unit's private-sector
doppelgänger, it was much longer lived, operating under Ministry of
Information sponsorship during World War II then serving its parent
company, Shell Oil, for decades into the post-war age. Shell's films were
designed for a cumulative but subtle impact on the public. With direct
references to the company reduced to the minimum, they epitomise
public relations at its most enlightened – or insidious, depending on your
viewpoint. Certainly the unit made films on themes more elevated than
product promotion. Many popularise science; some deal with
technology's socially beneficial applications. After the war, there was an
increasing internationalism in production and in themes, reflecting the
sponsor's multinational character. These predilections are combined in
The Rival World. GPO graduate Stuart Legg produced it; he had become
the unit's leading light alongside another documentary movement
stalwart, Arthur Elton. But it was directed by Bert Haanstra, who soon
became one of the Netherlands' best-loved directors (he later disowned
this film). And it covers a societal, technological theme with particular
reference to the role of the United Nations.

Highly praised, it enjoyed a long life in Shell's non-theatrical library,
and an updated version was prepared in 1974. The time-lapse
cinematography is good and studio-shot wildlife close-ups eerily
effective. The straightforward, measured commentary adds statistics and
historical references to assiduously compiled sequences. Various
processes are shown in action. In short much of it typifies a conventional
documentary approach some were anxious to break away from (the Free
Cinema gang despised Shell). The subject is mankind's struggle against
insects bringing damage to health and crops. Although a worldwide
issue, a clearly British presence, reflecting the UK's colonial history, is

discernible in the film. And although a topical issue, the title suggests an almost metaphysical collision. What lifts *The Rival World* above mundane moments is the astonishing spectacle of wildlife film meeting social-problem documentary then literally turning into war movie.

> 'The battle moves from ground to air.'
> 'The orders are to attack.'
> 'We need faster communications, a better organisation, a bigger army.'
> 'It is Kill – or Be Killed.'

Other parts of the film match the bellicose commentary. The music, annoyingly tinkly in places, is elsewhere pugnacious. There are frequent shots of 'control rooms'. There is the obligatory reference to the 'good foreigners' with whom humans have come to terms: silkworms, bees and butterflies. And the film has its highlight battlescene, a disturbing spraying sequence in which thousands of locusts spatter against plane windows leaving messy pools of blood behind, ending in a close shot of grounded, twitching creatures and a wider shot of their mass graveyard.

Shell, now reviled by many as the archetypal corporate empire, here produced a film that is literally humanistic. *The Rival World* shows genuine concern for the welfare of people of all races across the globe, matched by disgust for those parts of the natural world that threaten it. It assumes an uncomplicated faith in technology to solve human problems by pursuing those threats to destruction.

Prod Co: Shell Film Unit; **Dir**: Bert Haanstra; **Prod**: Stuart Legg.

Royal Family
1969 – 90 mins
Richard Cawston

Buckingham Palace's solution to a plethora of filming requests received
in connection with the Prince of Wales's investiture was a
groundbreaking feature-length film made with its collaboration,
documenting the Royal Family's life and function. By joining the
institutions recognising the communicative value of documentary, the
aloof monarchy was consciously modernising itself. By 1968, ensuring
maximum reach for a documentary meant working with television rather
than with cinema producers (the film was, uniquely, co-produced by
public and commercial television). And it meant accepting current
documentary practices, including unrehearsed scenes recorded with

Cameras turned on the Windsor clan for *Royal Family*

lightweight cameras and microphones. The Royals had never previously allowed mikes near them.

The choice of Richard Cawston to helm the project was masterfully apt. Now little spoken of, Cawston should be massively important to documentary historians, having pioneered uniquely televisual documentary forms with excellent films like *On Call to a Nation* (1958) and *This Is the BBC* (1960). Later as head of BBC documentary production, he demanded civilised, 'objective' film-making. The Palace could rely on him to fashion an intelligent, contemporary film, tasteful and not remotely subversive. Writer Antony Jay said,

> we weren't making a public relations film about the Royal Family, but neither were we doing an analytical or critical study . . . it was not really possible to make critical remarks, particularly true after the immense help and extensive concessions and permissions given to the film team. No judgments could be made, either good or bad by the commentary; it was for the audience to make their own.[51]

From some perspectives, this merely begs the question. Tony Garnett observed: 'Richard Cawston . . . can publish a document saying "we must be impartial" and then he does a film which, as a republican, I claim is a public relations exercise for the Royal family.'[52]

It's certainly a superb primer for The Well-Made Documentary. When its title belatedly appears over bucolic footage of a contemplative Prince Charles, viewers are signalled that this is an absorbing *film*, not a diverting 'programme'. This material is revisited at the end, the circularity sealing the film's tone: unobtrusively artful. *Royal Family* has a classical structure, a year in the life of the Queen, shot largely in sequence though subtly manipulated in the cutting room. The framework allows considerable scene-by-scene variation. Spectacular ceremonies alternate with moments apparently caught by chance (though some were certainly semi-staged: the Queen's 'impromptu' visit to a Balmoral corner shop!). A busy summer of engagements is compressed into montage. Coverage of Royals on duty is presented alongside the hitherto less visible side of the coin, as in a family picnic scene. The climax, a lengthy elucidation of the sovereign's constitutional functions, is immediately followed by a family chat around the lunch table (very stiff, but perhaps not Cawston's fault: maybe the Windsors are really like that).

Interestingly, the unit used 35mm for exterior setpieces, 16mm for interior conversational scenes, expecting the 16mm to be blown up. It gradually became clear that the unprecedented intimate footage would be the unique selling point: the 35mm was reduced and the final assembly edited on 16mm. Cawston's involvement was conditional on independence from interference while shooting, but the Royals had final cut approval. They requested no changes. The controlled application of modern television methods to humanise the monarchy must have seemed benign: bringing it closer to its subjects. Royalist viewers will be predictably enchanted, republicans duly appalled. But the film's ultimate effect wasn't beneficial. It marked a changing relationship between monarchy and media, ultimately impossible for the monarchy to control.

Prod Co: BBC, Independent Television Authority; **Dir**: Richard Cawston.

The School
1978 – 18 mins

Liberation Films was a film collective at the pragmatic end of the activist spectrum, concerned more with community politics than class war or formal experimentation. It was also willing to take on commissioned work provided that this didn't conflict with its political values. *The School* is a nice, if modest, example of politically aware documentary informing another busily evolving genre. As a 'trigger' film it exemplifies a break from the prevailing didactic model for educational film-making. Not made for television, it was available for hire by schools from libraries, also including 16mm prints of previously broadcast schools programmes.

Trigger films presented viewers with an open-ended situation of some kind, almost always without commentary, never telling the viewer what conclusion to draw – at least not directly. The immediate purpose was not to instruct, but to trigger debate. It wasn't a new concept but it became widespread in the 1970s. Not all audiences were young: trigger films were used in workplaces, for instance. But they suited schools aiming to balance tuition with discussion, particularly in parts of the syllabus dealing with older pupils' personal development. This Health Education Council-sponsored film was one of a series on smoking. The collective produced other HEC series on sexually transmitted diseases and mental health. Rather than informing or moralising, they all raise questions.

The trigger film's most common mode (adopted by other films in this same series) was fiction. Short dramas showing conflict between characters with different viewpoints were found to be good triggers. But *The School* is an example of a trigger *documentary*, documenting discussions similar to those it was intended to stimulate. It consists of two conversations between mixed groups of teenagers, under the headings of 'Morning' and 'Afternoon'. They're divided by an 'ad break', in which they enact their own homemade anti-smoking public-information fillers: the sole break from an otherwise deliberately pedestrian realism. The discussions themselves are set up, but their content is unscripted: the pan-and-zoom vérité style indicates that participants were speaking freely (though careful viewing reveals several initially unnoticed edits). The microphone occasionally drops into the frame. Collective member Geoff Richman joins in the conversation several times. Mild swear words are used.

The first discussion covers school, careers, role models, advertising. Once smoking is brought up, differing views are shared and challenged. One teenager is not interested in smoking. Another smokes socially. Another has unsuccessfully tried to give up. And so on. Naturally, the HEC was more interested in discouraging smoking than promoting a truly take-it-or-leave-it attitude. So, like other trigger films, this one slightly loads its content while still allowing viewers to make up their own minds. But surveying teenagers' genuinely wide-ranging attitudes now seemed as cost-effective a way of tackling the issue as hectoring them.

Though not part of the film's purpose, it's interesting to observe the group dynamics, between the voluble and the more introverted teenagers. It would be equally interesting to be a fly on the wall of a 1978 classroom discussion 'triggered' by this film.

Prod Co: Liberation Films; **Spons**: Health Education Council.

Seven Up! (*World in Action*)
1964 – 45 mins
Paul Almond

The *Seven-Up* cycle, in which Michael Apted returns to a group of people every seven years, probing their changing fortunes and perceptions, has become a cherished franchise: one of the few documentary projects to have penetrated national imagination as deeply as popular fiction. This makes it difficult to view the very first film in its original 1964 context free of preconceptions created by its unintended sequels.

That context was weekly series *World in Action*. From its offices (as invigorating to work in as the GPO Film Unit's thirty years earlier) a passionate group of journalist-film-makers reinvented factual television, putting Manchester-based Granada at the forefront of 1960s' documentary culture. They took certain changes wrought on documentary by television further than they had yet gone: documentary as proactive investigation, even exposé. But they also returned to a notion of documentary as film-making capable of exciting citizens into engagement with social reality: the series intended 'to cater for those who want to know in an idiom which is incisive', reducing 'discussion to a minimum, substituting instruction delivered in a dramatic, even at times a thrilling, manner'.[53] It dispensed with presenters, returning to stentorian Voice of God, but not implying omniscient objectivity: it editorialised, provocatively.

This context is important to the original *Seven Up!*, billed as a *World in Action* special because it ran for fifty minutes with breaks rather than thirty. And because it was an ambitious state-of-the-nation statement (rather than a specific report like the following week's edition on pirate radio). It documented the lives of twenty seven-year-olds from 'startlingly different backgrounds': working-class Londoners, middle-class Liverpudlians, privately educated scions, a rural lad and orphanage boys. The idea of Britain as constituted of disparate microcosms had a documentary ancestry, brought up to date here by mobile observational footage contrasting classroom and playground milieus. Modern use is made of point-of-view shooting and live sound.

But where many earlier documentaries implied that microcosms could bind, the emphasis here is on social division. The film's thesis comes close to vulgar Marxism: British lives are determined early on by the social classes in which they begin. This is established partly by making

Children brought together by the makers of *Seven Up!*

shifts from one locale to another particularly pointed (cutting from noisy primary-school canteen to formal prep-school lunch), also by leading narration. But it depends more on two devices particular to contemporary television. One is extensive interviewing of thirteen of the children, about class, race, sex and aspiration (also pointedly cross-cut: a posh boy confidently outlines his Oxbridge future; cut to a mixed-race orphan who asks 'what does university mean?'). The other is a particularly televisual kind of 'set-up' scene, a catalytic intervention by the film-makers. At the beginning and end of the film, the children, who would otherwise never have met, are brought together, for a party, and visits to a zoo and an adventure playground.

Apted's later films (on this one, he was number two on the production to Paul Almond) became increasingly complex – as adult lives do, as did Britain's social structure. But the original film has its own compact charm and clout. Its somewhat (but not wholly) dated adult analysis, when combined with a glimpse into childhood's eternal mystery, yields a moving expression of an exciting moment in documentary.

Prod Co: Granada Television; **Prod**: Paul Almond; **Exec Prod**: Tim Hewat; **Researcher**: Michael Apted.

The Shadow of Progress
1970 – 27 mins
Derek Williams

A documentary subgenre temporarily thriving from the late 1960s in response to the first phase of popular concern about green issues consisted of environmentalist films paid for by major oil companies. This peculiar fact takes us to the conflicted heart of sponsored film-making. *The Shadow of Progress*, the best entry in this ecological cycle, was a late high point for the declining 'prestige' documentary, thus highlighting its complexities.

Where firms like Shell had in-house documentary units, others, like British Petroleum, outsourced film production to independent producers, often forging close relationships with particular units. BP worked regularly with Greenpark Productions, whose documentary work stretched from wartime Ministry of Information commissions to later films for public bodies like the COI and British Council as well as commercial concerns. With the involvement of the Film Producers Guild, *The Shadow of Progress* was commissioned as part of the International Year of the Environment, directed, like several of the BP-Greenpark productions, by Derek Williams. The distribution history of this first-rate but forgotten film demonstrates that at its late date sponsored documentaries could still reach substantial audiences through print distribution and even by crossing to the small screen:

> *The Shadow of Progress* has now been translated into twelve languages and has had the staggering total of nine hundred 16mm and eighty 35mm prints made. In the UK it was borrowed three thousand times in its first year and was shown on both BBC1 and BBC2 with an estimated television audience of 12.5 million.[54]

The issues documented by *The Shadow of Progress* now seem comparatively slight. Yet it has an oddly timeless impact paradoxically attributable to its compromised industrial origins. Its underlying argument about the relationship of humans to natural resources is necessarily so broad that it remains applicable to the global-warming era and, by being conveyed through deliberately cinematic documentary methods, it transcends ephemeral reportage. Carefully composed images unfold at a meditative, almost hypnotic pace to melancholy music, befitting their faintly surreal content: thronging city crowds, armies of cars, vast graveyards for dead vehicles and dead television sets, belching chimneys, and the natural elements set against such human destruction and detritus. Though the detailed message is carried by narration, it is economical but also elegiac. Barely noticeable, but crucial and revealing, is the absence of synchronised sound: despite visibly high production values, *The Shadow of Progress* was shot silent. In practical terms this ensured its soundtrack could easily be translated for its intended international market. In creative terms, when synch sound was now routine for television documentary and newsgathering, it marked the film as prose-poem rather than investigation, observation or report.

Unsurprisingly, then, it weakens its grip when venturing into analysis. Pollution having been presented as an enigmatic philosophical problem, the cures outlined (recycling, water-quality controls, improved oil-tanker design) are disappointingly mundane. By comparison with, say, *The Rival World*, the film takes an ambivalent view of science and industry (as its reference to pesticide resistance demonstrates), but it is complacent, especially of course when confronting the oil industry's environmental responsibilities. The film's defects, then, are as closely bound up with the issue of sponsorship as its merits. They undercut its message, today more urgent: 'It is time to clean up and pay for it, time to accept that the free ride is over.'

Prod Co: Greenpark Productions; **Spons**: British Petroleum; **Dir**: Derek Williams; **Prod**: Humphrey Swingler.

The Shadows in the Cave (*The Power of Nightmares*)
2004 – 60 mins
Adam Curtis

The title suggests dark atavism, and maybe Platonic allegory. That a
current-affairs programme should draw on myth and metaphor for its
title might seem oddly grandiose. But the Cannes Film Festival felt that
The Power of Nightmares, the three-hour BBC series concluded by this
film, explored such hefty themes so distinctively that it requested its
reversioning as a feature film. Its mode of presentation – recent history
conveyed by narration over archive film – makes the series a familiar type
of modern television documentary. But its handling of it marks it as a
sophisticated twenty-first-century return to cinematic predecessors.
A range of mutually critiquing voices and a disparate array of pre-existing
images are assembled together in dramatic form with an omniscient
journalistic voice to table a thesis. This approach is a feature of the work
of producer and narrator Adam Curtis (there is no credited 'director'),
who reportedly prefers to be described as a journalist than as a
documentarist. He might equally be termed an accomplished, even
dazzling rhetorician, ironically so given that *The Power of Nightmares*
seeks to *challenge* prevailing rhetoric in post-millennial international
politics. Its argument is that, with the collapse of post-war dreams,
politicians have been driven to project a new role for themselves: to
protect their publics from the chimera, the frightening but deceptive
nightmares, born of the symbiosis of US neo-conservatism and Islamic
extremism, each feeding off exaggerated fears of the other.

Given these dramatis personae, the first two episodes range mostly
across the US and the Middle East. But Britain is a significant presence in
the third film, *The Shadows in the Cave*, albeit a subsidiary one reflecting
its junior status in the War against Terror. The several 'British' sequences
typify the film's methods. In the first, occasioned by Britain's arrival in
Afghanistan, a brigadier's battle-hungry bragadaccio is undermined by

his later sheepish admission to an interviewer that no Al-Qaeda have been captured. A later section on Tony Blair, drawing on several different speeches, is a more complex deconstruction of motives. Other sequences are panoplies of fast-moving, sometimes incongruous images of Western, including British, life. They include a scene added for the repeat screening after the Law Lords had ruled that UK detention of suspects without trial was illegal. The film makes many uncompromising statements: for instance, that Al-Qaeda doesn't exist. But its inventive, frequently witty ways of playing with source material from news bulletins to *The Thief of Bagdad* keeps it light on its feet. Some viewers claimed it was peddling conspiracy theories. It's definitely manipulative (its makers would presumably argue that they are countering more prevalent, pernicious media manipulations).

Compilation films were once often described as having been fashioned from 'found footage'. Although this is literally true, the suggestion that material is somehow stumbled upon is misleading. The sourcing of archive material is complicated, and archive-based documentaries like *Shadows* are as crucially dependent on the skill of their footage researchers, as personal case-study documentaries are on people researchers. It's also very costly. It is difficult to imagine any UK broadcaster other than the BBC (with privileged access to its own archive and relatively large resources to put into accessing others') attempting as archive-rich a programme as this. The large number of rights interests in the film's visuals and accompanying music has restricted the subsequent commercial availability of *The Shadows in the Cave* and its fellow films.

Prod Co: BBC; **Prod/Sc**: Adam Curtis; **Phot/Asst Prod**: Lucy Kelsall.

Snow

1963 – 8 mins
Geoffrey Jones

Geoffrey Jones was an individualist who embraced industrial film-making as consistent with a personal style, one blending movement and sound into a joyous, rhythmic whole. Obvious comparisons are animators Len Lye and Norman McLaren, transposed to post-war live action.

Jones joined the Shell Film Unit under Sir Arthur Elton, via art studies and a period in advertising. On the strength of his Shell work, he attracted Edgar Anstey's attention but by this time had formed his own company. Hence, when Jones was commissioned in 1962 to make a film for British Transport Films on railway design, he was working not within the BTF unit but as an outside supplier: film units sometimes contracted with external producers on occasional projects, sometimes to the consternation of employees frustrated by the more specialised assignments going outside. Most viewers wouldn't have picked up on this distinction buried in the credits but would have grasped that this film was different. *Snow*'s title, flashing repeatedly on a screen abruptly switching between monochrome and colour, announces it as fresh.

Snow was a by-product of the design project for which Jones had been shooting research footage for four months. Luckily, the end of the financial year was looming and spare cash available. Anstey agreed to his proposal that another film be completed first, just in time for the footage to be shot prior to that winter's snow melting. The award-winning classic that emerged from the editing room compresses the railways' dedication to coping with blizzard conditions into an eight-minute montage cut to music. It's crisply invigorating enough to induce brief amnesia about British trains' notorious inability to cope with harsh weather conditions.

Shimmering camerawork catches the bright white of the snow against the dull of workers' jackets and the glistening sunshine. Gurning faces of men feverishly turning handles, drums beating as snow is kicked up by onrushing engines, wheels turning, electric guitars twanging as steam clouds billow, thrilling travelling shots of landscape pulling away from the viewer, a horse speeding across a field as the music speeds up . . .. As with older films trading in the visual commotion generated by the movement of trains, we wonder: how much is this documentary and how much an experiment in exciting the senses?

Certainly, the style could quickly become gimmicky and limiting. This running time feels about right. But the editing, interlocking events that took place separately if in close proximity, swiftly communicates the cause-and-effect chain linking the different physical processes depicted. Inherent in the concept approved by Anstey, crucial to the finished film, was the contrast, positively *driven* home by Jones's percussive editing, between comfortable well-served passengers and the tough work of the men struggling to keep the line clear. Other films articulate similar points, but the exciting imagery is effective in communicating them subliminally. The crescendo is built around increasingly insistent cuts between a

Steam, snow, machine and men in 1963's *Snow*

passenger eating in the buffet car and snow shovels furiously at work, a distant echo of the old dignity-of-labour theme wrapped up in a modern customer-facing public-relations package.

British Rail's snow-encrusted train insignia are briefly incorporated into the film's sequencing: subtle public-sector brand reinforcement. Many BTF productions adopt stately pacing in pursuit of timelessness, which has actually (if attractively) dated some of them. *Snow* achieves timelessness by feeling like 1963, the year to which Philip Larkin dated Britain's ambivalent emergence from heavy weather.

Prod Co: British Transport Films, Geoffrey Jones Films; **Spons**: British Rail; **Dir**: Geoffrey Jones; **Prod**: Edgar Anstey; **Phot**: Wolfgang Suschitzky.

The Song of Ceylon
1934 – 40 mins
Basil Wright

The Song of Ceylon was the outcome of a project that had
metamorphosed in several ways. Under sponsorship from the Ceylon Tea
Propaganda Bureau, it was initiated at the Empire Marketing Board.
Before its completion, the EMB's film group had mutated into the new
GPO Film Unit: Stephen Tallents had moved to the General Post Office,
taking Grierson and co. with him, initiating the documentary movement's
second phase. As for the Ceylon material, it was commissioned as a
series of short travelogues but spawned an ambitious forty-minute film
transforming travelogue (exotic animals, eye-catching scenery, quirky
foreign customs) into dreamlike tone poem. Achieving theatrical release,
it furthered the movement's burgeoning cultural credibility and quickly
came to epitomise 'poetic', 'impressionistic' documentary.

   As with many such films, 'poetry' was generated at two distinct
stages. Basil Wright and assistant John Taylor shot large quantities of
material, sometimes with sketchy, intuitive senses of its eventual use
(some of this was actuality footage, some staged: the memorable scene
of a man paying homage to a huge Buddha is filmed in numerous takes
from multiple angles). Only during editing did the film find its intricate
design, a documentary 'song' in four movements. Its effectiveness arose
partly from its technical limitations. The GPO staff, crucially including
Cavalcanti, devised a complex experimental soundtrack mixing effects
and voice to accompany the silent footage. This included extensive
quotation from a seventeenth-century sailor's account of Ceylon: Lionel
Wendt is credited for voicing 'Robert Knox in the year 1680'. The implied
present tense suggests time's barriers breaking down, as does the film's
non-linear progression. This tends to position Ceylon as an almost
ahistorical entity. An illustration of Wright's subjectivity and disinterest in
analysis is his awe for the iconography of Buddhism, overlooking the
presence of Ceylon's substantial Hindu, Muslim and Christian minorities.

The first section, 'The Buddha', is an impression of religious and cultural practices. The second, 'The Virgin Island', comes closest to the intended travelogues (contrary to what most books say, the four travelogues *were* in fact produced out of Wright's footage, though it's unclear how involved he was in their editing).[55] It's also, with fishing and agricultural scenes, the most factually informative, and, with imagery of children, the most empathetic. The next chapter, 'The Voice of Commerce', highlights the film's most controversial aspect, its ambivalence towards British imperialism. Its opening right-to-left pans, and backward travelling shots taken from a train, run counter to the leftward panning and forward tracking frequenting the rest of the film. The brisk Englishness of its collaged voices reading memos and market reports, and listing products and services further disrupts the earlier harmony. But the final section, pretentiously entitled 'The Apparel of a God', returns to ritualistic images of worship and dance, as if synthesising the verse and chorus of Ceylon's 'song'.

Academic critics have since argued every possible position on the film's portrayal of colonialism and its subjects (and its debatable propaganda benefits to its sponsor). Wright's vision is respectful and heartfelt, but partial. Years later, in comments written for Ceylonese film buffs, he observed:

> You now have your own film-makers. There is no longer any need to bring people like myself to make an outsider's view of your country like *Song of Ceylon*. I for one look forward to seeing more and more, and better and better films from a nation from which, nearly 30 years ago, I received such friendliness, hospitality and inspiration.[56]

Prod Co: GPO Film Unit; **Spons**: Ceylon Tea Propaganda Bureau; **Dir**: Basil Wright; **Asst Dir**: John Taylor.

Song of the People
1945 – 26 mins
Max Munden

A leftist take on national history mounted as a jaunty docu-musical, *Song of the People* is as bizarre as it sounds and a delightfully untypical piece of British cinema.

The Co-operative Wholesale Society, better known today for low-cost supermarkets than for its history as part of the Labour Movement, was one of that movement's few parts to give sustained attention to film-making. It had commissioned actualities in the Victorian era, and had its own film unit by the 1940s. *Song of the People*, though, was entrusted to an outside unit. Its end credits socialistically list numerous contributors, spurning standard pecking orders specifying individual roles. Several were significant industry names: for instance, Sydney Box, in a

Newly politicised, a throng of workers sings a *Song of the People*

production capacity, and Muir Mathieson, whose musical work graces countless features and documentaries (including five in this book).

A group of factory workers played by actors (look out for Bill Owen, of *Last of the Summer Wine* fame) begin singing a ditty referencing kings, queens and key dates. But a foreman confronts this 'Great Men' textbook history. 'Workers of Today, listen to the Voice of Yesterday. We are History, We are the Working Man. The great unwashed. *Ours* was the dirt of *their* profit.' He takes them through a series of historical tableaux enacted by non-professionals playing their own oppressed ancestors as if in a cinematic village pageant. Tyler's rebels, Diggers (proto-Cooperators), Luddites, Chartists: each generation leaves martyred ghosts and hard-won advances. Etchings and documents are also used, and the film switches to compilation form as the history lesson moves into the twentieth century. Skilled assemblage of footage conveys its struggles, culminating in a world war against Nazism.

All accompanied by song! The startling mix of perky populism and historical sweep distinguishes this film from standard po-faced, issue-based left-wing documentary. But its politics put it well to the left of anything that came out of the documentary movement, frequently persuaded into mingling past and present in service of Whiggish, even Tory history. *Song of the People* subverts, reclaims, such films' imagery: rural churchyards and swaying crops, industrial smoke and steam, children at play, flowing waters signifying time's passage. 'Made for the People, with the People, by some of the People, sponsored by the CWS in the year 1944 in the belief and faith that the people are the End and the Beginning', it shares with – *A Diary for Timothy* and *Land of Promise* hopes that a new social order can be forged in war's wake but is more radically grassroots than either. Its multiple voices and a radio broadcast 'calling all workers' could almost be direct references to Rotha and Jennings respectively.

The documentary movement's house journal gave a cautious review,[57] damning with faint praise but factually fair in its criticism of earthbound direction by journeyman documentarist Max Munden, fresh from several MOI productions at Verity Films. He shows some visual imagination (great use of superimpositions, and some terrific street scenes) but less panache than the imaginative concept deserves.

Politically, the *Song* hits certain disturbing notes, the most jarring its sunny regard for Stalin's Soviet Union, a dishonourable naivety too typical of its time. In this context, the foreman's role in the film is fascinatingly ambiguous: re-educating the workforce into egalitarian collectivism by standing apart from them, a messianic leader communing with the truth of their history on their behalf. On the other hand, few British films so courageously excoriate imperialism. Harrowing overseas footage accompanies urgings that British workers also fight for those 'oppressed in England's other name . . . tell it to the Indians . . . to the Irish, from New York to County Clare / And tell it with humility because before we didn't dare.'

Prod Co: Horizon Film Unit; **Spons**: Co-operative Wholesale Society; **Contributors included**: Max Munden, Ray Elton, Phil Cardew and his Band.

South – Sir Ernest Shackleton's Glorious Epic of the Antarctic
1919 – 80 mins

By joining heroic expeditions, cinematographers fashioned a reliably exalted variety of 1910s' and 1920s' documentary. Mixing narrative excitement, visual spectacle, patriotism and travelogue exotica, content was invariably determined by the unpredictable fates of the missions in which the film-makers' own were potentially entwined. Herbert Ponting's footage of Scott's Antarctic expedition established a model, not least by underwriting that expedition with its anticipated sales. Another famous project was Australian Frank Hurley's documentation of the 1914–16 Imperial Trans-Antarctic Expedition.

The Shackleton-led crossing of Antarctica failed, its ship trapped then later crushed by pack ice, but ensuing collective heroism ultimately resulted in the crew's safe return. Hurley captured many of these events, often imaginatively, sometimes bravely, on film and photographic stills edited with intertitles to create the classic documentary feature film starkly entitled *South*. It makes varied use of existing documentary techniques. For instance, expedition members are often 'introduced' while engaged in technical processes (an approach still adopted in films documenting team efforts) but *South* also takes the more commemorative approach. There is a 'group photo' scene actually mixing film and stills, and the film begins with studio portraiture of leading expedition members, filmed after their return (in military attire to defuse potential disapproval: the expedition having sailed, with full official backing, just as war broke out). Most impressive are the camera's varied viewpoints of the ship's journey. The film's late interruption by over fifteen minutes of Antarctic natural-history footage is exasperating, but most contemporary viewers hadn't seen penguins or sea lions in motion: these boring scenes were once enchanting. Crowd-pleasing anthropomorphism also explains *South*'s likeable lavishing of attention on the expedition's canine contingent (and its failure to comment on the dogs' puzzling non-appearance in later sequences: they had been shot and eaten).

The film was ambitiously reconstructed and restored in the 1990s, resulting in a widely available tinted-and-toned version recreating the original release's colours. This draws attention to the 'role that archives play in mediating our access to moving image heritage'.[58] The films in this book have *all* been archivally mediated but in varied, usually less spectacular, ways. The particular archival practice of *restoration*, when applied to documentaries, suggests a relationship between their aesthetics and their technical quality. Lesser versions preserve the 'actuality' better than its 'creative treatment'. Hurley's restored cinematography is sporadically stunning, as in the high-vantage shots of the ship cracking the ice ahead. *South*'s informative DVD commentary[59] points out that the mast's crucifix-like shadow adds a spiritual dimension to the composition: perhaps unconsciously, perhaps not. The commentary also implies that *South* was (when shot if not when edited) an overhang product of a civilisation presently destroying itself back in Europe. That civilisation's cultural artefacts are usually disconcertingly alien now. The cold, forbidding *South* is no exception. Yet later documentaries can be found echoing it. And British culture retains a peculiarly resilient fascination for its deepest theme: failure.

Prod Co: Imperial Trans-Antarctic Film Syndicate; **Phot**: Frank Hurley.

S.S. Skirmisher at Liverpool (Mitchell and Kenyon 235)

1901 – 2 mins

In 2005, Mitchell and Kenyon upgraded from academic footnote to household name. This turnaround illustrates how film history, popular and learned, is influenced by the survival, availability and certainly also the visual quality of materials. This rediscovered collection of 800 negatives of late Victorian and Edwardian films was systematically preserved then circulated to millions via a television series and other products.

Future histories may reach settled judgments on Mitchell and Kenyon as neither marginal nor central presences in their own industry. But they won't rob them of a place in the early twenty-first-century public's imagination. They owe this partly to the attention brought by the rediscovery of so much lost material, partly to the humour and humanity the films display. The collection's consisting almost entirely of 'actualities' was important. Among scholars, this bolstered a movement towards taking early non-fiction film as seriously as the development of fictional narrative. For general audiences, it offered captivating views of their great-grandparents' Britain. In this sense, the films are 'documentary' if employed as an adjective, furnishing fascinating photographic evidence. But few are 'documentaries', the noun applied to the films in this book: a valuable reminder that 'documentary' and 'non-fiction' are not interchangeable terms.

The unclear context of much early film-making renders the distinction especially hard to apply there, but less so in this case. The basis of most of Mitchell and Kenyon's activity is known to be commissioning by fairground operators. The normal brief was to film local scenes, crammed with local faces, for screening to local audiences. Clearly there is no documentary intent in this highly commercial enterprise, and little documentary effect for its audience. Take the firm's 'factory-gate' films: their viewers were already familiar with their workplace entrances, their streets, their families, neighbours and themselves. That was the point.

But the exceptions prove the rule, and *S.S. Skirmisher at Liverpool*[60] is an intriguing one. The opening scene is observational reportage. Passengers clamber aboard ship, women in hats or shawls (and a nun in a habit), men in bowlers or homburgs. The remainder of the film consists of shots of the army of staff manning the boat. To build up a composite portrait of the ship's employees, these are all staged (to varying extents). Men swabbing the deck, crew filing past, domestic staff primly posing, even the ship's cat held up for the camera! Filming planned with evident care compresses an entire staffing structure onto less than three minutes' worth of film stock.

Some of the imagery has a disquieting stillness, and a lineage in portrait photography traditions. But its artful deployment parallels the increasing sophistication of more purely cinematic conventions. Just as the travelling shots that initially constituted entire films – phantom rides – became incorporated into multi-shot narratives, these tentatively

Staff of the *S.S. Skirmisher at Liverpool*

animated portraits are combined with other material to build a structured documentary account. No mere hangover from older photographic practices, the composed 'cameo' portrait reappears, briefly, in many later documentaries.

Mitchell and Kenyon's film-making isn't usually stylistically refined. Crowds are martialled skilfully, camera placement often judged well. But their sophistication lies elsewhere, in the economic process by which they came to be commissioned, shot, processed and screened. Yet on this occasion the result is a relatively advanced proto-documentary. The great quality of most of the films is their vital yet fleeting spontaneity. Viewed alongside them, this more poised dispatch from the past is equally poignant.

Prod Co: Mitchell and Kenyon.

Sunday by the Sea
1953 – 14 mins
Anthony Simmons

A review praised *Sunday by the Sea* for injecting 'a welcome personal note into British "documentary"'. A trade write-up labelled it 'a diverting trifle for the masses'.[61] They were both right. Its freewheeling, personal style and semi-professional production conditions unassumingly pre-date Free Cinema. Yet it seemingly seeks more to entertain than to impress. In 1953 there was no obvious pigeonhole for it and apparently there still isn't.

Anthony Simmons's film is a leisurely yet intricate portrait of Londoners enjoying a day out at Southend-on-Sea, beneath a soundtrack medley of cockney music-hall songs. An East-End companion piece, *Bow Bells*, was made in 1954 by the same team using a similar musical-documentary approach. A revealing direct comparison between *Sunday* and Lindsay Anderson's *O Dreamland*, shot at Margate funfair later in 1953, is there for the taking. They both apply comparable mixes of observation and evocation to similar milieus, but *feel* entirely different: *Sunday* bittersweet and affectionate, *Dreamland* sour, even contemptuous. Would it be too crass to attribute this disparity to class? (Simmons's background was working-class London Jewish, Anderson's upper-middle-class Anglo–Scottish.) It certainly proves that sensibility is as crucial as subject to documentary's meaning. Equally revealing are the films' respective fates at the hands of critical history. *Sunday* won a Venice Grand Prix, received theatrical distribution, was enthusiastically reviewed by the likes of Dilys Powell, but has since been overlooked. *O Dreamland* was shelved for three years before Anderson resurrected it for the first Free Cinema programme, and has been in the canon ever since.

But *Sunday* is also echoed by John Taylor's much-loved 1957 *Holiday*, for British Transport Films, a paragon, presumably, of 'unFree' cinema (while Sunday's music-hall concept itself echoes John Krish's

Young and old enjoy *Sunday by the Sea*

earlier 1953 film *The Elephant Will Never Forget*). And while the involvement of Leon Clore and Walter Lassally reinforces the Free Cinema link, their genre-spanning careers expose British film's fuzzy boundaries. Clore produced numerous traditional sponsored documentaries (some directed by Simmons) before and after Free Cinema. Simmons's own later output has been eclectic, stretching from cult feature films to episodes of primetime TV series.

The songs, bound to Lassally's impressive camerawork by Lusia

Krakowska's adept editing, allow mood switches from rollicking to melancholy. But they're also, if you want to hear them that way, ancestral voices binding transient experiences (children's swinging and sliding, teenagers' courting, grown-ups' sunbathing, pensioners' impromptu knees-ups) to communal memory. The apparently improvised observation of spontaneous holiday-making superficially brings this film closer to what audiences today expect of 'documentary' than other 1953 films contrived in the wartime tradition. But Simmons had mapped out the film's overall shape to the songs' final order in advance of filming, and Lassally wrote of the shooting of both *Sunday* and *Bow Bells* that:

> the bulk of both films is made up of shots 'set up' for the camera. In some cases, of course, like the man asleep in the car in *Sunday by the Sea* shots were snatched without the subject's knowledge. But cameras make quite a racket . . . though it is sometimes possible to obtain effective shots of people truly engrossed in what they are doing, the action usually has to be more or less staged. We ask people to do for the camera something that they are accustomed to doing every day, or we get them to repeat an action they have just been doing, or occasionally we simply ask them not to look at the camera while they go on working or playing.[62]

However it was achieved, the result is beguiling.

Prod Co: Harlequin Productions; **Dir/Sc**: Anthony Simmons; **Prod**: Leon Clore; **Phot**: Walter Lassally.

Supersocieties (*Life in the Undergrowth*)
2005 – 50 mins
Stephen Dunleavy

For three decades, David Attenborough has been best known for fronting BBC nature programmes. On account of series like *Life in the Undergrowth*, he more than anyone personifies British documentary for the general public. This is apt because these programmes have not only been of consistently high quality (not to mention enormously popular at home and abroad); they also fuse the deeply rooted natural-history tradition in British documentary film with a significant television tradition that Attenborough helped develop long before becoming synonymous with wildlife subjects.

As Controller of BBC2 then director of BBC programming in the years 1965–72, Attenborough's commissioning decisions helped the 'prestige authored documentary' become a mainstay of British television. The prototype was the 1969 series *Civilisation*, in which art historian Sir Kenneth Clark presented an overview of Western history via narration and pieces to camera delivered in settings across the globe, interspersed with impressively filmed colour photography of artefacts and landscapes. This mix was taken up by presenters such as Jacob Bronowski and James Burke covering science subjects, and Robert Kee (or, recently, David Starkey and Simon Schama) presenting historical ones – and by hundreds of others.

Each episode of *Life in the Undergrowth* is billed as 'By David Attenborough': documentaries in this format highlight the authority of presenters over their subject matter. But they also implicitly emphasise the role of top-drawer film units, and lengthily expensive shooting schedules, in visually rendering it. This combination was ideally suited to natural history, as in Attenborough's cycle of series initiated by *Life on Earth* (1979).

Having previously focused on mammals and plants, in *Life in the Undergrowth* Attenborough turned his attention on invertebrates. Oliver

Attenborough and friend meet state-of-the-art cinematography in *Supersocieties*

Pike, a predecessor of today's nature film-makers once wrote that 'ants, and other small insects that move as rapidly as ants, are some of the most difficult things to photograph':[63] this 2005 series depended on recent advances in camera lenses to enable both a literal and a thematic deep focus on insects and spiders in their own habitats. Significantly, the series is a photographic crossbreed, having been shot on a mixture of film, high-definition video and even mini-DV for certain sequences (interestingly, extensive silent shooting is still common in nature films).

Such technology equips *Supersocieties*, the last episode in the six-part series, to make the point that insects are 'not the blindly mechanic robotic slaves we once thought' (and as many nature documentaries have portrayed them), are instead members of societies as complex in their way as ours. This thesis is advanced by textbook documentary means of a series of case studies: sand wasps, bees, wood ants, harvester ants, termites and matabele ants. After a climactic battle sequence in which the matabele ants launch a devastating attack on a termite colony in stunning close-up, the camera pulls back to the presenter. Prestige authored documentaries usually end with a concluding piece to camera: Attenborough points out that invertebrates are far more crucial to the ecosystem than mammals.

Prod Co: BBC; **Prod**: Stephen Dunleavy; **Series Prod**: Mike Salisbury.

The Sword of the Spirit
1942 – 15 mins
Henry Cass

The Sword of the Spirit was a religious movement founded early in
World War II, stressing the spiritual truths underlying the Allies' material
efforts. Though ecumenical, it was Catholic-led, Vatican-sanctioned and
headed by England's most senior Catholic, Cardinal Hinsley. Its story, the
patriotic contribution of British Roman Catholics to the wartime struggle
of their Protestant majority nation, had possible value to the
propagandist portrayal of that struggle, especially in largely Catholic
countries. Via the MOI, the Foreign Office sponsored a film at the
request of British diplomats in Latin America (hence the Spanish subtitles
on some prints). It was supplied by Sydney Box's company Verity Films
and helmed by a future feature-film director. (Verity was an example of a
commercial film unit largely outside the documentary movement;
incidentally, it continued making documentaries into the 1970s.) Graham
Greene, an admirer of British documentary, was approached to script but
wasn't available;[64] another RC convert, actor and writer, Robert
Speaight, was commissioned instead.

Though The Sword of the Spirit isn't a brilliant film, it nicely
exemplifies the many wartime documentaries intended solely for overseas
distribution – never to be screened in the UK. Its four distinct parts also
usefully isolate different wartime documentary tactics. The first
introduces Britain's Catholic community in newsreel style, compilation
footage with swift superimpositions and urgent narration. Catholicism's
troubled British history – reformation, recusancy, persecution, migration,
emancipation – is ignored, in favour of its present fortitude in the face of
enemy bombs. The next section is centred on Hinsley lecturing the viewer
about the Sword of the Spirit and the justice of the cause. The third part
personalises the first by employing acted reconstruction in both its
wartime guises. First, an actual past event is recreated before the
cameras, nuns rescuing sacraments from a burning chapel. Then,

everyday experience is evoked by the enactment of a typical, rather than specific, occurrence. During an air raid, a young priest provides comfort to sheltering parishioners and the last rites to one departing soul. The final sequence concludes the film with a factual survey of Catholic war contributions (decorated laymen; the RAF's Polish Squadron) and a mass held on a ship's deck, 'part of the freedom of the future for which Britain fights'. Britons of earlier centuries might have been surprised indeed to find themselves fighting for this particular freedom.

It's all well crafted but somehow, and interestingly, unconvincing. The imagery is in place: icons, rosary beads, the devout prayerful beneath imposing crucifixes. The visual motif, fire, is found in other Blitz films, but not with such theological overtones. But there's a slight, nagging diffidence about everything, as if Catholicism's passion were being refracted through a polite, faintly embarrassed Anglican sensibility.

Prod Co: Verity Films; **Spons**: Ministry of Information; **Dir**: Henry Cass; **Prod**: Sydney Box, James Carr.

Television Comes to London
1936 – 18 mins
Dallas Bower, Gerald Cock

Britain's first ever television documentary *Television Comes to London* was broadcast at 9.05pm on 2 November 1936, as part of BBC television's first day's output, then repeated several times over the next few days. With its light style, firm voiceover and dependence on dramatic music to maintain excitement it resembles contemporary newsreels. Like most newsreels, it is informative in content but is designed principally to divert and entertain. However, it does so by classic documentary means: going behind the scenes to see a product being made.

The film begins by showing how Alexandra Palace had to be reconstructed as television's first base, then focuses on the technology enabling transmission from there. As the film explains, the BBC initially made use of both the main competing television systems, those of John Logie Baird and of Marconi-EMI. Baird is seen personally, while his rivals receive slightly more extensive technical coverage. The viewer is left to guess at the delicate politics behind the arrangement, necessitating the balanced treatment. After some fine exterior shots (distant silhouetted figures working atop transmitters) the film reaches its dramatic highlight. Mechanics and make-up equally in place, the switches are thrown, the generators turned, and television goes on air. These actions were, of course, filmed several days before the great event, though some of the film was unstaged (its most spontaneous human moment is supplied by a staff member acting as guinea pig for an earlier camera test). Barring a final passage showing off the BBC orchestra at work, the rest of the film consists of music-hall star Adele Dixon's rendition of the specially written song, 'Television', itself a repeat having been part of a variety programme screened six hours earlier: 'A mighty maze of mystic magic rays . . . The busy world before you is unfurled, its sounds, its tears and laughter . . ..'

A cutaway purports to show two delighted viewers watching at home. In fact, no more than about 300 well-off early adopters in range of the transmitter could have watched this first broadcast.

Of the two men credited for 'production', Gerald Cock was the corporation's first Director of Television: as such, he briefly appears in the film. The other, Dallas Bower, had come from the cinema industry. The year before Bower had written a book, *Plan for Cinema*, envisaging a future in which cinema would become a yet more spectacular medium, precisely because television would take over many of its functions of informing and entertaining the masses. *Television Comes to London* begins to do exactly that. It's much less ambitious and creative than the previous year's GPO release *BBC: The Voice of Britain* (about the radio service), but much more prescient. The BBC's contribution to British documentary has since dwarfed that of any other organisation.

Prod Co: BBC; **Prod**: Gerald Cock, Dallas Bower.

Time Is
1964 – 29 mins
Don Levy

Time is: a feature of the universe? A property of subjective perception? Or an illusory, even dangerous human construct? Few films tackle headier themes than this, the most splendidly offbeat documentary discussed herein. Yet it was less aimed at late nights in smoky art-house cinemas, than at rainy classroom afternoons, flickering onto roll-up screens while clattering its way through teachers' 16mm projectors.

The books and films published under the heading *The Ancestry of Science* – what would now be termed a multimedia project – were the brainchild of Stephen Toulmin and June Goodfield, noted names in their fields (Toulmin is an eminent philosopher in the analytic tradition; Goodfield became a prolific writer on technology's implications). Seeking collaborators, they approached the Slade School of Art, in close proximity to their London offices, where Thorold Dickinson had established a pioneering film programme. A young Australian named Don Levy had been one of his first students. Levy too would become a significant though mysterious figure in *his* world: the very different one of experimental cinema. He is credited with directing, photographing and editing *Time Is*.

This unusual collaboration was an apt metaphor for one of the project's aims, to bridge the chasm dividing Humanities and Sciences: the 'two cultures' famously diagnosed by C. P. Snow. It also explains the film's distinctive character – as if the Gaumont–British Instructional team had come under the temporary influence of hallucinogens. The strange bedfellows of sensible educational documentary and eccentric experimental film-making are brought together, and both surprisingly enhanced. The education becomes more arresting and the experimentation more accessible. Many viewers leave the film unaware of its pedagogic function.

In classic classroom style, *Time Is* has lucid narration, clearly delivered in a middle-class (female) voice, though one free of plumminess and prone to deadpan wit. It is intended more to spark interest than to inculcate information. Where it conveys facts these are imaginatively illustrated: electrons, positrons and gamma ray photons by a man, a woman and a speeding car; matter and anti-matter by positive and negative film of the same image. But it dwells as often in metaphysics as in physics, pondering simultaneity and change, cause and effect, and Ancient Greek paradoxes. These themes cue a dazzling array of experiments with form: slow trancelike sequences and furiously edited ones; reversed, repeated and out-of-focus shots; actions sped up, slowed down or freeze-framed; double exposures, clear frames, black frames, discordant sounds and total silence. Yet every device has a clear documentary purpose.

Moreover, the images have figurative, not abstract content – all are taken from the perceptible world of bullfights and bottle factories, rugby matches and mushroom clouds. Some were shot for the film, others 'found' (this film is also in part a compilation film). The effect is to encourage viewers to reconsider the mystery of the familiar and enjoy its absurdity (prompting the film's occasional droll social commentary, as in a witty visual satire on former prime minister Harold Macmillan).

It's easy to guess at *Time Is*'s stimulating effect on intellectually curious sixth-formers and first-year undergraduates, because it remains exciting viewing. The only slightly dated touch is the music by Ravi Shankar and a host of other Indian musicians, probably intended, ironically, to transport audiences from their immediate cultural surroundings. The film-makers couldn't have guessed that the sitar was about to be temporarily popularised, creating in the West a perennial association between Indian string music and 1960s' counterculture.

But then time, as it passes, always brings surprises.

Prod Co: Nuffield Foundation Unit for the History of Ideas; **Dir/Phot/Sc/Ed**: Don Levy; **Prod**: June Goodfield, Stephen Toulmin.

Today We Live: A Film of Life in Britain
1937 – 23 mins
Ruby Grierson, Ralph Bond

One of the few Depression-era British films *about* the Depression, *Today We Live* is a fascinating compendium of documentary's pre-war styles and themes. Part sermon, part compilation film, part re-enactment, it integrates Ruby Grierson's warmth, Ralph Bond's left-wing commitment, producer Paul Rotha's visual rhetoric, and the social concern of all three. This absorbing film was released into cinemas as well as non-theatrically (in a different version entitled *Today and Tomorrow*). Strand, the production company, made particular efforts to get its documentaries theatrically released. This interesting organisation was, together with the Realist Film Unit, the leading pre-war independent documentary unit. This meant that they were not based within a particular state or commercial organisation, and could work for various funders,

Coal-gathering: a desolate shot from *Today We Live*

occasionally undertaking non-sponsored projects. Such independent units would proliferate after the war.

The preface is very Rotha, at first a miniaturised remake of *The Face of Britain*, compressed, visually, into a swift array of images representing Britain's mixed legacy, bucolic and industrial. But communicated verbally through insistent analytical commentary (written by Stuart Legg) echoing, as much of late 1930s' documentary did, the influential, unusually sober newsreel *The March of Time*. This influence persists into the introduction's second movement, an historical compilation. The Great War is pinpointed as 'the climax and close of a long era in English social life'; the Depression encapsulated in images of inequality (flat caps versus top hats). So we arrive in the present, still with desolate, boarded streets, idle pits and desperate people. A young Donald Alexander, later official film-maker for the nationalised coal industry, took the startling, oft borrowed shots of men gathering coal atop windswept slagheaps.

The film switches to narrative mode. Hereafter, human beings filmed by Bond and Grierson embody the two Britains thus far abstractly established, in what are effectively two parallel films. These are factually based and 'played by the villagers of South Ceney, Glos.' and 'the unemployed men of Penrith, Rhondda', the former directed by Grierson, the latter by Bond (and Alexander). Both narratives focus on an individual, a Mrs Harrison and a John Adlam respectively, but as a way into what are community portraits. The narratives match quite closely. From a radio announcement heard in both places, both sets of villagers hear about the national voluntary organisation that commissioned the film. Both have meetings to discuss grant applications. Both set to work building community centres, which are finally seen in use. The social differences are marked. The Welshmen discuss their grant over beer and sandwiches, the shire-dwellers in a village hall meeting laden with hatted ladies, polite applause and the obligatory vicar. A football match is contrasted with a church-hall social. Once the buildings are up, they are used in one case for male crafts like shoe-making, in the other for PT (a vaguely surreal scene), amateur dramatics and country dancing. Both films almost have different genders: women virtually absent from Bond's, while dominating Grierson's. Both also have contrasting, surprisingly complementary styles. The Rhonnda film is more impassioned and more visually impressive, with its frequent, impactful camera movements past the men's expressive faces. The Gloucestershire one has tenderness and humour. The differences are encapsulated by Bond's heroic low-angle shot of three men against the sky, and Grierson's affectionate, amused glance at two ladies delightedly watching the dancing.

The use of synchronised sound on location was very advanced. Both directors complement actuality shooting with scenes both scripted and improvised to enable two communities to document themselves for a higher purpose. Legg's concluding phrases state that the voluntary work celebrated by the film can merely ameliorate 'fundamental problems that lie at the very root of our existence'. 'Only by working together can we hope to solve them': these words are as far as the film can go, verbally, in advocating socialism. But the final tracking shot over which they are read – a group of impoverished men crouched against a wall, one with a baby in his arms – strikes a resonant note of compassionate protest.

Prod Co: Strand Film Company; **Spons**: National Council of Social Service; **Dir**: Ralph Bond, Ruby Grierson; **Prod**: Paul Rotha; **Sc**: Stuart Legg.

Touching the Void
2003 – 106 mins
Kevin Macdonald

Joe Simpson's 1998 book *Touching the Void* describes his and Simon
Yates's 1985 ascent of an Andes mountain, the disasters of their
descent, culminating in Yates cutting a rope connecting him to Simpson,
and Simpson's miraculous escape from a deep crevasse (Yates having
concluded he must have died there).

In 2003 a documentary adaptation was released into cinemas,
holding its own against other features, winning the best British film
BAFTA. Some cinema documentaries had appeared in preceding years,
including the same director's Oscar-winning *One Day in September*
(1999), and few more have followed, certainly none as successful. But
Touching the Void resuscitated the idea of a British non-fiction cinema,
becoming a reference point in all discussions of documentary's future:
the doc that had 'crossed over'. This was noteworthy precisely because
of Britain's strength in documentary television, a cinema analogue
seeming conceptually superfluous. *Touching the Void* poses intriguing
questions. What is specifically cinematic about it: subject, style or mere
contingencies of production and distribution?

As to the latter, the credited organisations straddle cinema and
television industries: Pathe, distributor; the Film Council, public funder
(it inherited the BFI's funding responsibilities in 2000); FilmFour (Channel
4's feature-film arm), commercial funder. Each is duly represented on the
executive producer list. But actual production was by experienced factual
television company Darlow Smithson. The producer was its CEO John
Smithson, with journalist and project initiator Sue Summers. They initially
assumed this was a broadcast project, albeit prestigious, but quickly
concluded it had cinema potential and began developing a feature,
pitching it to funders with the advantage of rights to a best-selling book
on their hands. They hired Kevin Macdonald, a director with unusual
awareness of documentary's cinematic past. Their subject resonated with

that history. Two other films in this book are heroic expedition stories released as cinema features. Unlike them, *Touching the Void* recounts the mission only in retrospect, with no actuality record available – and uses that mission as a Documentary MacGuffin for the human story flowing from its disastrous curtailment.

But the film's fulfilment of its big-screen potential is principally down to stylistic choices rendering it 'cinematic' in paradoxical ways. Structurally, it's absurdly simple, reduced to two staple television elements: interviews with Simpson, Yates and base-camp companion Richard Hawking; and dramatic reconstruction with actors showing the events described. The interviewees, driving the narrative, were shot before black screens, close up, facing the camera: a TV device distilled to essentials. But the film's makers blew another factual television ploy up

Reconstruction in *Touching the Void*

to cinematic proportions. Preconceptions of reconstructions as filler to replace unavailable footage are here dispelled: they're filmed both with fidelity and at blockbuster quality for visceral and emotional impact.

A third strand, the subjects revisiting Siula Grande (necessary in any case to advise the reconstructions) was abandoned as narratively overcomplicated. It saw light of day as a DVD extra. Simpson experienced post-traumatic stress there, but was happy to endorse the film. Yates wasn't. He curtailed involvement following the trip, perhaps fearing the film showed him in a bad light, though it makes it clear that at the crucial moment he had little choice other than to cut the rope. For many viewers he's the more likeable man: when Hawking admits his preference for him over the driven Simpson, he acts as audience surrogate.

If this were primarily a climbing film it wouldn't have had such success. It's essentially character study. By avoiding comment, symbolism and lyricism, whenever its interviewees make a profound statement it's exactly that: as when lapsed Catholic Simpson comments that close to death he felt no compunction to turn to God.

Though slightly overpraised, *Touching the Void* deserved its success. Still, its peculiarly 'tele-cinematic' style doesn't leave much more of a primer to wannabe crossovers than to trust their story and find a style that suits it.

Prod Co: Darlow Smithson; **Dir**: Kevin Macdonald.

Tracking down Maggie
1994 – 83 mins
Nick Broomfield

It is slightly unfair to represent Nick Broomfield, an undeniably important director, by one of his weaker films. But *Tracking down Maggie* well illustrates the strengths and weaknesses of Broomfield's mature style, as emerging in his films of the time.

> I always wondered who the real Maggie Thatcher was . . . how little I really knew about the woman who has dominated our lives for the last fifteen years.

These snatches from Broomfield's garrulous narration for *Tracking down Maggie* encapsulate the reasons why it is, fascinatingly, a flawed film. They imply enquiry into Thatcher's political legacy and a concealed inner life, but make the enquirer, not the enquiry, the subject of the thoughts. Broomfield famously structures documentaries around his own making of them: turning investigative documentary processes into visible stylistic tropes, turning him into the recognisable 'star' of his films. This style has won him unusual success, in cinema as well as television, and has valuably expanded the documentary audience. But it has also attracted accusations of egotism which the director rejects:

> There's no other way of telling the story when you are confronted with somebody who absolutely refuses to be interviewed and who refuses to talk about these issues. The only way to do it is to use yourself as this character who is investigating Margaret Thatcher.[65]

Broomfield adopts a quintessentially English (and bourgeois) persona: affable, self-deprecating, perhaps disguising a manipulative side. *Tracking down Maggie* is seemingly patterned on Broomfield's 1991 *The Leader, His Driver and the Driver's Wife* in which, to hilarious and telling effect, he sought to interview South African supremacist Eugene Terreblanche, eventually successfully. In the case of Margaret Thatcher, whose book-signing tour Broomfield pursues across London and then the US, it becomes obvious early on that he won't secure an interview. Partly to mitigate this, he pursues parallel avenues of investigation. Some are quirkily humorous, as in a visit to Thatcher's home town in Lincolnshire, where he encounters a lady in possession of her former loo. With more serious intent, but without the rigorous underpinnings of investigative journalism, the film follows accusations of immoral arms-trading against Thatcher's son Mark. The director also supplies interpretive comment over library footage and stills of Thatcher in her youth and in her prime.

The film otherwise depends on the drama, humour and insights generated by its main predicament. Various supporting characters among Thatcher's entourage fill the vacuum left by the film's uncooperative lead. After a decade in which restricted access and control over information has become the norm for celebrities as well as politicians, Broomfield's offence at this now seems naive. Thus, certain pivotal moments work against the film rather than in its favour. Broomfield's car is driving by Thatcher's: he calls out at her, taps the window, and Thatcher neither responds nor acknowledges him. But, in the same circumstances, would anyone?

The film communicates its view of Thatcher as arrogant, humourless and narrow-minded, with some unattractive people around her. And it has some strong moments, including the breathtaking mendacity of her press aide when confronted by Broomfield (whom he has spent the film avoiding) in the final shot. This ends on a pan across to Broomfield, with his trademark headphones and boom shrugging at the camera.

Tracking down Maggie was televised in Channel 4's prestige doc-slot *True Stories*, as was *The Leader* and the earlier *Driving Me Crazy*). The next day, even *The Guardian*'s reviewer professed a modicum of sympathy for Thatcher *vis-à-vis* Broomfield: a sign of the film's faults, but also that, four years after her prime ministerial resignation, Mrs T.'s divisive shadow was fading.

Prod Co: Lafayette Films; **Dir**: Nick Broomfield; **Prod**: Nick Broomfield, Rita Oord.

Two Victorian Girls (Yesterday's Witness)
1970 – 30 mins
Stephen Peet

In 1968, Stephen Peet persuaded his BBC superiors Richard Cawston and David Attenborough to commission six films under the title *Yesterday's Witness*, arguing that they would make interesting but inexpensive television, filmed in black-and-white by tiny crews in just one or two interior settings. Their 1969 transmission was so successful that Peet ended up producing some eighty episodes over the next dozen years, directing many himself, such as *Two Victorian Girls*, among the second batch of films produced under the series umbrella.

Television producers had been using synch interviews to place personal recollection of historical events on film for several years. *Yesterday's Witness* was the first project in which reminiscence itself was the theme, and on-screen statements the core component around which entire films were structured, establishing the 'oral history documentary' as a viable form in its own right. These films proved eye-opening for younger viewers, coming at a time when many survivors of late nineteenth- and early twentieth-century events still walked the earth. Now they're long since gone, this is even truer.

As the strand became familiar, viewers increasingly wrote in suggesting suitable interviewees. Still early in the programme's run, *Two Victorian Girls* originated from the producers' advertised search for survivors of the pioneering female typing pools of the late Victorian era. It is based around interviews with two of them, Frances 'Effie' Jones, 94, and Berta Ruck, 91, intercut with period photographs, including stills of the young Jones and Ruck (later, incidentally, a prolific author of romantic novels). The series' makers successfully resisted any temptations to patronise or editorialise, and aimed at sympathetic curiosity rather than nostalgia. The two women tell their stories fluently, humorously, intelligently – offering considered retrospective comment on their generation's assumptions, neither simply accepting nor rejecting them.

Viewers warmed to Jones, Ruck and other episodes' 'witnesses', finding it 'refreshing that no "professional" was present to put words into their mouth'.[66] This is actually a paradoxical tribute to selflessly skilled film-making that worked hard to become imperceptible, introducing creative treatment not just at the editing but also the shooting stage. The director-interviewer perched himself uncomfortably under the lens so that interviewees faced it (and the audience) directly, rather than 'over-the-shoulder' as had become the norm. Transcripts of rushes show the key passage of *Two Victorian Girls*, Ruck's comments on unquestioned ('of course') assumptions of the Victorian era, was, in its final form, coaxed from her by her sympathetic director, though based on her spontaneous observations. Oral history as a branch of documentary film-making is a different animal than oral history as a branch of historical research.

Initially screened as a general-interest late-night BBC2 programme, repeats were handled by BBC Schools. Unlike textbooks, and unlike other types of documentary, films like *Two Victorian Girls* gave the youth access to the modern past as privately experienced.

Prod Co: BBC; **Dir/Prod**: Stephen Peet.

UCS I
1971 – 22 mins

The youth radicalism of 1968 interacted with 16mm's increasing affordability, portability and live-sound capability to produce a new generation of oppositional documentarists. Numerous 'collectives' sprang up, making leftist films outside the mainstream industry throughout the 1970s: Newsreel Collective, Women's Film Group, Sheffield Film Co-Op, Amber, Four Corners . . . each differently positioned on the political and stylistic continuum. The most broadly representative and best known is Cinema Action, formed by Gustav 'Schlacke' Lamche and Ann Geddes in 1968 and joined by many collaborators in the following years. Most members (not all) had middle-class origins but a genuine commitment to working-class protest, their early output principally consisting of films supporting specific industrial actions. Editorial control was often shared with, even ceded to the campaigns for which the films were made. At a stretch, these films could therefore be argued to constitute a form of 'sponsored' documentary mutated outside the cosy post-war consensus, now beginning to break down.

In this context, *UCS I* is significant, documenting and supporting an iconic 1970s' industrial action. Shipbuilding in decline, Edward Heath's Conservative government refused a £6 million loan to bankrupted Upper Clyde Shipbuilders. Led by Jimmy Reid and Jimmy Airlie, the workforce staged not a strike but a 'work-in', proving the yards could stay functioning with union stewards in charge. The only cameras allowed inside were Cinema Action's. The footage of meetings is fascinating, but the action's leaders would only approve an edit from which material recording internal disagreement was excluded. *UCS I*, energetic and energising, combines on-the-spot synch-sound reportage with effective thematic cutaways. Reid's fiery oratory opposing 'the Scotland of the lairds and the lackeys', in the name of 'the real Scotland, the Scotland of the working people' is a recurring element. Workers' comments are recorded, often suggesting a masochistic ambivalence about shipbuilding: wanting to keep the yards open to avoid unemployment, but characterising the work as unforgivingly tough. The film ends with Airlie's sober but trenchant comments, followed by a postal address (handwritten) to which donations could be sent. Some 1930s' films ended similarly (see, for instance, Donald Alexander's more moderate mining film *Eastern Valley* [1937]).

The most calculated moment is the politically pivotal one: silence descends, screen fades to black, then we see a locked gate, the yards now under union control. Uninformed modern viewers will probably assume, wrongly, that the action was doomed. Historians are divided about its ultimate legacy but it was initially successful to the extent that two of three yards remained open. Documentaries from past eras can often feel more like science fiction than contemporaneous feature films, and this is as true of the militant *UCS I* as of, say, *A Queen Is Crowned*. Post-Thatcherite viewers will be astonished by its forceful display of union power and collective action. Such industrial politics had just a decade left to run.

Cinema Action later took the subject (and some of the footage) in different documentary directions. *Class Struggle: Film from the Clyde* (1977) was a reflective narrative account of the entire dispute. *Rocking the Boat*, further from the events (made for Channel 4 in 1983) was a politicised contribution to oral history documentary. Of its earlier films, one collective member said: 'you needed to be there on the spot. It wasn't a documentary you were trying to make. You weren't trying to record history. You were trying to make history.'[67] *UCS I* is indeed a campaign tool, but a documentary nonetheless.

Prod Co: Cinema Action.

The Vanishing Street
1962 – 20 mins
Robert Vas

Hessel Street, Whitechapel, London E1 is now an unremarkable inner-city side street, commercial at one end (a café, small businesses, Halal butchers), residential at the other (concrete blocks, housing a mainly Bengali-descended population). Its descendants dispersed to the suburbs, there is no discernible trace of the area's predominantly Jewish population of fifty and a hundred years ago. The street's ghosts might dimly recognise the commercial buildings but not the 1960s' blocks that replaced rows of close chimneyed terraces in the joint name of slum clearance and post-war reconstruction.

Documentary-makers have often been motivated to record things about to disappear. In 1962, financing from the *Jewish Chronicle* and from the BFI Experimental Film Fund enabled the vanishing of the old Hessel Street to be recorded on 16mm film by Robert Vas, a Hungarian refugee who had grown up in a Jewish ghetto. Near the beginning of his film we see officials surveying the area. At its end we see architects' models, the first blocks dwarfing the small street, and the bulldozers making space for others. But Vas's film is neither angry nor really remorseful: its main purpose is to commemorate and celebrate the community and its heritage, using an almost wordless mixture of long, medium and close shots of people and activities, and evocative family photos from the more distant past.

Although the film appears slackly structured, it's actually divided into five loose sections. The soundtrack for the first and third, recorded on audiotape, alternates and mixes atmospheric street sounds, snatches of conversation and Yiddish songs. The images are shots of the street, of its kosher butchers and fishmongers, and sights that caught Vas's attention but are edited into the film as if knitted into a tapestry, part of the whole though briefly standing out: a gramophone player, feet tramping the street, an old woman pulling a box, dolls at a thrift shop, pots and pans. Above all: faces, in lively conversation or in solitary thought.

After both sections come quieter ones. The film's brief second section shows local workplaces: a barber's shop, a sewing-machine plant, and – not for the squeamish – a kosher slaughterhouse (dead birds reappear on the vanishing street's markets). The fourth section is filmed inside a synagogue: great shots of young boys and girls, expectant, bored or nervous.

Then the final section, about the street's imminent disappearance: Vas frames the street as filtered through the council official's viewfinder. This doesn't distance us from the vivid scenes we've seen, but makes us feel their transient tininess. A montage of carefully composed shots of local scenes precedes the final demolition.

Vas's previous film *Refuge England* (1959) was part of the final Free Cinema programme. By 1962, Free Cinema's leading lights had largely abandoned non-fiction and were embarking on feature-film careers. Vas (and Michael Grigsby, also represented in the final programme) remained true to documentary, thus inevitably advancing their careers mainly through television. Grigsby was already at Granada; Vas, after a period at the National Coal Board, joined the BBC, remaining there until his premature death. But their two independent, BFI-funded shorts (Grigbsy's *Tomorrow's Saturday* [1962] and Vas's *The Vanishing Street*) remain two of their best films.

Spons: BFI Experimental Film Fund, Jewish Chronicle; **Dir/Phot/Ed**: Robert Vas.

View from an Engine Front – Ilfracombe
1898 – 4 mins

A record of a genuine trip through the Devon countryside into Ilfracombe, which would have been identical if no camera had been present: documentary or not? A clutch of *View from an Engine Front* films was made in 1898 by the dynamic Warwick Trading Company led by Charles Urban: many, like this one, photographed by then employee Cecil Hepworth. They belonged to the newly imported 'phantom-ride' format, films in which the cameras were attached to the front of trains, enabling viewers to experience their movement vicariously. Similar films came to be shot from the tops of trams. Given their popularity, they are of obvious importance to scholarly study of early film history, but also interesting, in hindsight, in relation to later documentary. In the first place, emphasising kinetic *journey* rather than the more static sense of *place* in equally popular views of British street scenes and panoramas of exotic foreign locations, they crudely prefigure a significant strand of factually based film-making. Second, considered as a group, these films provide another test case for early actuality films' inconsistently 'documentary' relationship to the reality on which they rely.

Viewing them as part of mixed programmes of short films of several types, audiences presumably recognised their greater factual basis. But the 'reality' of some of the phantom rides is essentially a convenience, their sole purpose being to recreate from this source material the sensation of movement. The Ilfracombe ride, with its exciting, wildly winding railtrack, and the bright vista that emerges from out of a tunnel, certainly shares that sensationalism, but boasts other virtues derived mostly from its interesting location. The film feels like it is continuous but was filmed on two rolls of celluloid. The first covers hilly country, the second continues the journey into town, terminating at the station. The documentation of the ruggedly attractive scenery, of the track's unusual, increasingly steep incline and of the processes involved in signalling trains and bringing them to a stop, add both picturesque and, yes, documentary qualities to the phantom ride's more basic pleasures.

Before long, the phantom ride would disappear into other films, fiction and non-fiction, where it can still be found today. The travelling point-of-view shot is often included in documentaries in which a journey is undertaken, to aid viewer empathy or to add visual variety. When not attached to particular characters or events, it often serves to introduce the audience to a locale or to create the impression of travelling from immediate surroundings into a film's interior world. Employed well, it can still have a powerful effect.

Prod Co: Warwick Trading Company.

Vox Nova Scientiae
1936 – 13 mins

Gaumont–British Instructional was established in 1933, a smallish outpost of the production, exhibition and distribution empire Gaumont-Pictures Corporation. With the involvement of Bruce Woolfe and several of his past directors, GBI pursued a similar educational mission to British Instructional Films, but with greater efforts to get films into actual classrooms. Participation by educationalists and by the British Film Institute added gravitas and public service, a little at odds with Gaumont's commercialism. GBI's business setting may ultimately have stymied its saturation of the unprofitable schools market, which didn't have enough projectors to go round.

But it kept itself busy. In 1936 alone, some ninety-five films were released. One, *Vox Nova Scientiae*, was a promotional documentary for GBI and GB Equipments, which supplied the projectors. Its seven film extracts (introduced by a narrator) handily encapsulate the output of the decade's leading purveyor of educational film, showing how it was marketed to teachers.

The films' reliability is established by listing expert consultants, Julian Huxley the best known today. As for the extracts, slices of antique pedagogery are easy to chortle at: clipped accents; clipped techniques; clipped worldviews. A reviewer approvingly described these films as 'deliberately made elementary' to 'keep the minds of the audience clear and simplify the argument'.[68] Yet even mere lectures permit subtle variation and creativity. Think back to your own teachers, good and bad, and it's obvious. No lecture gets its points across just by being lucid – tone of voice is crucial.

Varied visuals are deployed, some tried and tested (via time-lapse, a thistle grows in seconds), others feeling more contemporary (an over-cranked camera slows down footage of swimmers in a PE film). *Circulation* is introduced as an 'object lesson in the use of the diagram'. But it's the voiceovers that principally differentiate the approaches. *The Plover*, for infants, mixes facts with gentle anthropomorphic humour.

Cathode Ray Oscillation, for adolescents, features 'perfectly timed commentary which merely directs the attention'. A female narrator adds a warmer feel to *Circulation*. *Analysis of Exercise* is more imaginative: two voices, male and female, working with the images' rhythm.

These are fascinating examples of their type. But only one of the seven extracts has an inherent significance. *Coal* (also released theatrically, as *The Mine*) was a process documentary promoted for inclusion in geography lessons, and the first film shot underground in a working British mine. It was shot silent (decades later, the NCB's cameramen were *still* shooting silent). Nonetheless, silence broken only by voiceover lends the other films a static, airless quality – dispatches from a disconcertingly tidy universe unique to their genre. *Coal* does rely on authoritative factual commentary, but blends this with effects, ambient sound and authentic-sounding dialogue between Midland-accented miners. The technical imagery is pulled direct from the adult world, its meaning completed only by the close-ups of miners' faces supplying the human dimension.

Director J. B. Holmes (also behind *Cathode Ray Oscillation*) was an adept film-maker whose career straddled sectors. After making many of these commercially produced classroom films, he went on to adult documentaries at the GPO, Strand Crown and British Transport units. Here he combines a realism eschewed by other extracts with a straightforwardness absent from more artistically self-congratulatory films. This suggests relatively progressive educationalism, bringing into schools a glimpse of a milieu beyond the upper-middle-class drawing room, part of Britain's social as well as physical geography.

Prod Co: Gaumont–British Instructional Films.

A Wedding on Saturday
1964 – 40 mins
Norman Swallow

How strongly does the technology involved in making documentaries
affect their meanings? Films made with new tools often make interesting
test cases: *A Wedding on Saturday*, shot largely on videotape, is one. The
few shots on film emphasise the dissimilar, grainless texture of the rest.
When classic film techniques are replicated on this new medium, the
impact is slightly different: cutaways, like *Wedding*'s repeated cuts to a
fruit machine, seem less pointed, more conversational. Video recording
also affects tempo. The necessity of constantly emptying and replacing
the magazine could be avoided, leaving events and conversations
uninterrupted for potentially longer periods. This gives *A Wedding on
Saturday* a fluidity it wouldn't have had as a film production (to
complicate things, the entire film was subsequently transferred to
16mm).

   More important is whether the video camera transforms the material
it is documenting: a particularly interesting question when the subject
has a history of having been documented on film. The eponymous
wedding is merely the pretext for this film. Its subject is the close-knit
community in which the wedding takes place, the Yorkshire mining
village of South Elmhirst. A history of ennobling documentary is
suggested by the archive film footage of miners underground. So when
we see miners emerging from their pit, showering, eating and chatting in
the canteen, it's as if they're emerging from subterranean myth into
daylight (the daylight in which their industry would, a few years later, be
engulfed by bitterness and harsh economic realities). This matches the
underlying theme: the long-term changes in working-class expectations
and aspirations. The film-makers aim to show that sweeping
generalisations can't be made. Many conversations in the film register
differing opinions, and the film is structured to suggest a three-
dimensional view of the community it portrays: the wedding crosscut

throughout with numerous other scenes. These valuably portray the relatively un-'swinging sixties' that most Britons inhabited. There are regular cuts to a man laughing uproariously. When finally shown in context, it transpires he is laughing at his own racist joke.

This was one of a handful of 1964 Granada documentaries made on two-inch video, an experiment helmed by Norman Swallow and Denis Mitchell. Some sources list Mitchell as director of *A Wedding on Saturday*, but (as with many 1960s' programmes) no one is credited with direction. In this case Swallow as producer was creatively in charge. As a pathbreaking maker of BBC current affairs television in the 1950s, then a resourceful, articulate Granada film-maker, he probably had a deeper effect on factual television than the more strikingly individualistic Mitchell did. But they shared several tendencies – some became standard television practice, some didn't. These imclude immersion in their subject, often necessitating a lengthy research before any cameras could roll: Swallow spent several weeks getting to know the people of the area and them used to his presence. When the cameras do roll, they show an interplay between careful planning and spontaneous happening: Swallow selected the setpieces in advance but had no script or firm expectations. And, back at base, the film-makers had licence to edit creatively:

> Conversations were broken up, so that Mr. X, who in reality had spoken to Mr. Y, was shown as though he were speaking to Mr. Z . . . ideas which had been raised quite independently were placed side by side, either because they illuminated the same theme or because together they made an effective counterpoint. There were, of course, scores of ways in which that same material might have been edited . . . the way I finally chose was a reflection of what I thought about those Yorkshire miners and their families, and was in this sense as much my own view of life as theirs.[69]

Prod Co: Granada Television; **Prod**: Norman Swallow.

Western Approaches
1944 – 82 mins
Pat Jackson

Western Approaches' roaring waves may recall *Drifters*. But the lifeboat adrift beneath suggests *In Which We Serve* (1942).

> So the two pre-war worlds of feature and documentary have, during the war, made contact. *Western Approaches* is perhaps the perfect example. Is it feature? Is it documentary? Or is it some new fusion of both schools?[70]

Self-described documentaries that were also entirely acted fiction films pre-dated war's outbreak. Noted examples were late-period GPO films like Harry Watt's *North Sea* (1938). War intensified the need to document and concurrently to dramatise the many detailed facets of collective effort. Having its participants act out realistic stories set in their own professional locales seemed an effective device, hence the plethora of 'story documentaries' from the Crown Film Unit, like Watt's *Target for Tonight* (1941).

The Western Approaches command was an important Royal Navy division, responsible for protecting merchant shipping against the Germans' attempted blockade. Jealously admiring *Target for Tonight* (RAF-themed), its commander-in-chief requested a similar treatment of its own Atlantic activities. The film that eventually surfaced, under GPO alumnus Pat Jackson's direction, surpassed its inspiration, proving the apotheosis of Crown's narrative phase. It is of feature length, outstandingly photographed in Technicolor by Jack Cardiff (who came with the colour system), with a haunting score, and pushing documentary so close to fiction that it goes over the edge. It was also so expensive and time-consuming to produce (two years in the making) that it brought the wartime story-documentary cycle to its end.

Western Approaches brandishes documentary credentials in its opening declaration: 'the players are not professional actors but serving officers and men of Allied Navies and Merchant Fleets'. These men enact a story with five settings: a lifeboatful of torpedoed merchant sailors, the ship rescuing them, its convoy and command centre, and the German U-boat seeking to sink it. Each strand is intercut, indicating that they are happening simultaneously, though they were filmed as separate parts of the schedule. On the other hand they were filmed with a documentary fidelity to real processes and lived experiences. The lifeboat scenes at the film's heart were shot, dangerously and exhaustingly (and, amazingly, with synchronous sound) in a real lifeboat. Virtually everyone but Jackson was beset by seasickness. The 'players' bring trustworthiness to the story, without the awkwardness that makes many of the story documentaries embarrassing today. And the tone is kept sober, heroism associated with pragmatism: 'things are not too good. They could be a darn sight worse.' Such 'documentary' sobriety had seeped into conventional feature films. Meanwhile, *Western Approaches* crosses onto fiction's territory: in a climactic death scene, and in the U-boat sequences, acted in German, accompanied by dramatically sinister scoring, and increasingly urgently crosscut with those in the more naturalistic settings.

These touches (which don't entirely come off) were the director's doing, and he was well aware of their significance:

> I realised that I would be betraying the sacred tenets of 'documentary' as currently accepted. I never had any qualms about it. The camera, if it is to capture its maximum capacity to convey the most compelling illusion of reality, must be free to see what the dramatist wants it to see. To truncate its power by restricting it to illustrate a commentary is 'creative interpretation of reality' in a straitjacket. There is no message unless it makes the heart beat faster and brings laughter or a tear to the eye.[71]

Prod Co: Crown Film Unit; **Spon**: Ministry of Information; **Dir/Sc**: Pat Jackson; **Prod**: Ian Dalrymple; **Phot**: Jack Cardiff.

Westward Ho!
1940 – 8 mins
Thorold Dickinson

The years 1939 to 1945: Britain's divisions were bridged by its collective war effort – if superficially, temporarily, sometimes chaotically. The same could be said of the war contributions of various sectors of Britain's film industry, all of them sanctioned, many directly sponsored, by the state. Initially disordered government policy and arrangements for film propaganda crystallised into shape over the course of 1940. While many films were for overseas distribution, medium-length domestic ones aimed at general morale-raising formed the backbone of non-theatrical programming, while a continuous cycle of shorter films communicating specific urgent information was distributed free to cinemas. Produced under the aegis of the Ministry of Information, some were supplied by film units rooted in the documentary movement, others from within the commercial industry. *Westward Ho!*, the very first of these 'five-minuters', was made by the company running Denham and Pinewood Studios. Feature film-maker Thorold Dickinson directed using technicians from recent studio projects. Shooting began the day after his melodrama *Gaslight* (1940) was released. Astonishingly, prints began screening two weeks later.

'Controlled Evacuation, planned and executed in good time, is right.' The closing title spells out the message, exemplifies its clear but nuanced delivery. Dickinson was inspired by a newspaper letter from a mother objecting to the evacuation of city children to rural areas. He seeks first to reassure urban parents that procedures are being efficiently, humanely implemented, then to underline the policy's bitter necessity. The first objective is achieved via a documentary account of one infant group's evacuation from London to Devon, expertly telescoped into a short running time. The final two minutes engage with the second task. Female continental refugees, superimposed on a map of Europe, emotively beseech the British audience to learn from the tragic

consequences of delayed evacuation in their own countries. A staunch
Scottish soldier's grim determination concludes the film.

The softer first section, like many wartime documentaries dealing
with subjects of family interest, uses a female narrator, the sterner
conclusion a male one. Dickinson's credit for 'reporting' rather than
directing seems appropriate for a film as reminiscent of newsreel's brand
of realism as of contemporary documentary's. But it would be hard to
make clear distinctions between this and films by documentary
specialists. The multi-voice soundtrack (short passages of first-person
narration by children) echoes their documentary experiments.

The music (derived from 1936 sci-fi classic *Things to Come*) is too
unyielding, almost competing with the words. Otherwise, this is
tremendously effective, economical documentary-making for a time of
crisis. The camerawork is stylish without being florid – fluid coverage of
the station crowds; well-handled travelling shots from the train window.
His very purpose being to neutralise heartfelt fears, Dickinson neither
dares nor need stress the situation's poignancy. Despite – because? – of
its outward stoicism, this is a touching film. Parents, in particular, may be
choked up by scenes of their 1940 counterparts waving off the
evacuation trains, and by later shots of plucky, even cheeky, young faces.

Prod Co: D&P Studios; **Reported by**: Thorold Dickinson; **Phot**: Desmond Dickinson.

When the Dog Bites
1988 – 50 mins
Penny Woolcock

The week of its broadcast, the listings page suggested with somehow apt bemusement that viewers were in for an offbeat documentary:

> A fresh look at Consett, the former steel town, in which an escapologist does his tricks, a drag act sings *There'll Always Be an England* and local people talk about their experiences. Plus drama sequences in which Bill tells Rose that making a fortune is easy.[72]

If the film sounded intriguing, its first shot was amazing. From a godly vantage point above the town centre the Steadicam swoops . . . follows a woman crossing the road in a fancy-dress leopardskin, catches up with the raucous throng swarming the opposite pavement . . . ground-level now, close up and almost among them it follows their massed, purposeful stride down the street . . . trails them into a pub and finally circulates excitedly among the revellers inside. One continuous shot, like a Mitchell and Kenyon community street scene remade by Orson Welles! The referencing of *Touch of Evil* (1958) is intentional, and locals' numbers had swelled even above normal Saturday-night levels, as word of the filming had spread.

   The 1980s brought many documentaries about Northern industrial decline. Solemn stridency was expected of them, playful bravura wasn't. There's nothing as jaw-dropping in the rest of the film, but it stays surprising by mixing modes and moods like the manic-depressive place it depicts: ghost-town-meets-party-town, a defunct steelworks where its soul used to be. Snatches of staged symbolism sporadically disrupt the film. Threaded through it is the fictional relationship of Rose and the self-deluding Bill (a stock British tragic-comic character: think Harold Steptoe). As well as appearing in discrete scripted and acted scenes, they occasionally pop up in the settings for the film's observational and interview sequences. Many interviews are oddly filmed: in black and white or in unusual settings like a swimming pool. The two dozen interviewees, none named, range from bored teenagers and middle-aged unemployed to spokespersons for the emerging post-industrial, non-unionised Consett. Their non-local accents stand out. So does the Standard English of director Penny Woolcock's offscreen questions (a touch of the Molly Dineens).

Woolcock occasionally annoys when being different for the sake of it, but then she wasn't aiming for the ascetic rigour of a *Nightcleaners*. However she faced comparable controversy when the film was screened in town (Trade Films, funded under the 1980s' Workshops Agreement, distributed its work locally as well as providing some of it to Channel 4 for national broadcast):

> a councillor sprang to her feet, absolutely apoplectic with rage, and shouted: 'Why don't you just go back to the gutter where you belong?' and people cheered. But when it came out on television the response was very different in that we got tons of mail, a lot of it from people in the South who said what a kind film it was and how it made you really like the people in it, whereas on the whole people in the North were offended on behalf of Consett.[73]

Woolcock admits that it was a learning experience but has continued to specialise in unconventional studies of marginalised communities, from drama-inflected documentaries (*Shakespeare on the Estate* [1994] is especially recommended) to docu-styled fictions.

Prod Co: Trade Films; **Dir**: Penny Woolcock; **Prod**: Belinda Williams, Ingrid Sinclair.

Winter (Secrets of Nature)
1923 – 12 mins

H. Bruce Woolfe, British Instructional Films' (BIF) presiding spirit, followed a cinematic path combining commercial imperatives with edifying aims. BIF's productions were descended from earlier film-making that could be described as 'broadly educational'. Charles Urban's declared allegiance to 'the more permanent uses of the Kinematograph, namely its application to purposes of instruction, and the widening of general knowledge'[74] could easily have served, later, as BIF's mission statement. One Woolfe collaborator was Percy Smith, responsible for 1910's pioneering *Birth of a Flower* under Urban. Another was Oliver Pike, who had been shooting birds (cinematographically speaking) since 1907.

Given such roots, BIF's productions look antique, but feel oddly more modern than many later *Zeitgeist*-courting documentaries, especially to factual television addicts who will catch their distant echoes. One strand of BIF's output dealt with recent human history: World War I films blending actuality footage and reconstructions. Another dealt with natural history. *Secrets of Nature*, a series started in 1923, had several contributors (usually uncredited) specialising in different aspects of filming the natural world on location and in laboratories. Individual issues are therefore surprisingly diverse. *Winter* illustrates this by combining several elements in a single piece, from mammal and insect close-ups to time-lapse micro-cinematography – Smith's specialism. Technical standards are high. But there is more than this: an opening stylised shot of a leaf falling before the camera, dramatic compositions of barren trees against winter fields, luminous footage of a glistening spider's web, a superbly photographed sequence of a farmer and horse ploughing a field. OK, this isn't Dovzhenko, exactly . . . but by linking and rhyming the lives of human, animal and plant, above ground and below, *Winter* takes on a modestly pantheistic quality. And its compound portrait of a rural winter crams a lot into a short space without seeming rushed.

Documentary of the 1930s would have its own pastoral side, but often juxtaposed with industrial or urban Britain in the name of broader social engagement. We might expect that next generation of hungry film-makers to have instinctively disliked their more staid predecessors. In fact some seem to have had considerable if grudging respect for the achievements of Woolfe and his colleagues. A great historian of British cinema later stated that 'the excellence and popular success of the *Secrets of Nature* films was one of the few bright features of the British film industry during the twenties'.[75] Given that she was referring to a series of one-reel films screened near the bottom of most cinema bills, this is damning comment on a decade of national cinema, and remarkable tribute to a series of ingenious factual films punching well above their weight.

Prod Co: British Instructional Films.

Wisdom of the Wild
1940 – 10 mins
Mary Field

Gaumont–British Instructional's bread and butter was its long-running *Secrets of Life* series, effectively continuing British Instructional Films' *Secrets of Nature*. *Wisdom of the Wild*, mixing concise zoological explanation, ingenious cinematography and jolly anthropomorphism, was made to its pattern. But, unlike that series, it was sponsored, by the British Electrical Development Association. Passing references to electricity might suggest a shaping of the series' conventions to serve promotional ends, but the purpose turns out to be far more serious.

'The squirrel in the tree, the fox below, the birds, insects: all know that a time of plenty will not last forever.' The film proceeds to celebrate the astuteness of rural creatures via multiple case studies: the wise snail, the economical caterpillar. Rabbits don't waste food. Cattle methodically consume their week's rations. The leafcutter bee plans the feeding of her growing grubs. Honey-bees store their food over winter. A sparrowhawk family carefully shares out its babies' food. 'Badgers, like most Britons, are meat-eaters but when this one is convinced that there are no more rabbits about he trots away to the woods and makes a vegetarian meal off the bark of a tree.'

By now every 1940 viewer has clocked The Message. There can be few clearer demonstrations of the extent to which documentary was co-opted to Britain's war effort than the finessing of even nature films to its ends. Finally the film turns to the human world, simultaneously switching style. 'Like the bees, the Ministry of Food is collecting food.' The remaining scenes are mostly staged ones in which the narrator banters with actors playing typical members of the public ('Madam you haven't got half the sense of a leafcutter bee!'). These techniques are also found in wartime work by more self-consciously advanced film-makers.

For documentary historians, a valuable aspect of this minor film is its crowded credits list. Listed collaborators include Percy Smith, Oliver Pike and J. V. Durden (biochemist and maker of noted science films including the pro-eugenics *Heredity in Man* [1937]). Narrator E. V. H. Emmett voiced countless GBI fil.ms, the parent company's newsreel Gaumont–British News, many documentaries and some feature films. His is *the* quintessential, much parodied newsreel voice.

Director and educationalist Mary Field spent years with BIF and GBI and was later a leading light in Rank's Children's Entertainment Division and the Children's Film Foundation. She was one of Britain's most successful female film-makers though hardly a feminist role model: note *Wisdom of the Wild*'s bouts of jovial sexism. Though this film is for grown-ups, Field's commitment to engaging juvenile audiences, combined with her films' undertones of domesticated English conservatism suggest a cinematic Enid Blyton, but with documentary rather than fantasy as her default setting.

Prod Co: Gaumont–British Instructional; **Spon**: BEDA; **Dir**: Mary Field.

Yarmouth Fishing Boats Leaving Harbour
1896 – 1 min

By alphabetical coincidence, the last film in this book is the earliest. Victorian actualities had no on-screen titles: *Yarmouth Fishing Boats Leaving Harbour* is so called because of how it's referred to in contemporary sources, and because it contains shots of boats taken from the harbour at Great Yarmouth. It was among the crop of British films made in 1896 for projection to audiences. The year before, all films were still being shown only in kinetoscopes (peepshows). *Yarmouth Fishing Boats* was one of several early films serendipitously rediscovered just in time for the UK's cinema centenary, severely deteriorated prints urgently copied to more stable stock.

Britain's film industry emerged from the complicated series of comings and goings, team-ups and break-ups, of a small number of

Briefly glimpsed, *Yarmouth Fishing Boats Leaving Harbour*

people carrying a small number of cameras. The relationship of R. W. Paul and Birt Acres is a case in point. Jointly responsible for several key inventions and innovations in 1895, they had fallen out and were operating independently by the time Acres hand-cranked these three shots. Acres's career was the shorter and less influential, but he was Britain's first cinematographer and of interest to this book because he seems to have been drawn to the capacity of 'animated photographs' to document.

Putting early films into categories invented later is a questionable practice. Yet documentary roots can be found growing in this film, a point best made by comparing it with two 1895 films by the Paul–Acres partnership. *Rough Sea at Dover* (and the many succeeding films 'documenting' breaking waves) was 'actual' in subject but 'sensational' in purpose, whereas Acres here reproduces movement as a function of subject, one with some documentary interest for audiences, including the Royal Family to whom Acres screened this with twenty other films in July 1896. By contrast, Paul–Acres's *The Derby* (probably the oldest surviving British film) chronicles a newsworthy event, suggesting the future newsreel reportage film rather than the general-interest documentary sketchily rehearsed here.

A pioneering historian of our pioneering film-makers was frank about their productions' limitations: 'their merit relied almost entirely on choice of subject-matter, not on treatment. The more interesting the subject, the more successful the film. There was no creative process involved, except that some films were photographed better than others.'[76]

Maybe: it depends how 'creativity' is defined. Here, the film-maker *has* applied a basic measure of interpretation to his subject by his camera positioning and by his decision to take *these* three shots, of two different vessels at different distances from his vantage point.

Before long, admittedly, such films would seem prehistoric and fragmentary. This one's subject would, by another coincidence, prove popular for future documentary, would even one day furnish the certified masterpiece marking documentary's official coming of age (though, incidentally, 'drifters' were turn-of-the-century replacements of this film's trawler 'smacks'). But Acres's fishing boats are remote, shorn of context and deceptively unpeopled. The presence of more than one shot is the result not of subsequent cutting but of stopping and starting the camera. Nor does this prefiguration of editing-in-the-camera imply a film-maker constructing a narrative, merely one getting the most out of the short piece of stock in his camera. Depending on the speed at which it's projected, *Yarmouth Fishing Boats Leaving Harbour* runs about twenty seconds, coincidentally a typical length for very early webfilms.

Phot: Birt Acres.

Appendix

Several film-makers represented in this volume, spanning at least three generations, were asked for their opinion of Grierson's definition – creative treatment of actuality – and whether it applied to their films in the book. Their responses (in some cases edited for space reasons) make fascinating reading.

Wolf Suschitzky

(Cinematographer, many editions of *Mining Review* including two stories in *4th Year No. 12*; and *Snow*; also, one of the cameramen on *March to Aldermaston*. His grandson Adam was director of photography on *Lockerbie – A Night Remembered*)

Art usually came in the cutting room, in the editing. I tried to put on the screen what the director wanted. Some of them knew how they are going to cut the material and instructed me accordingly. My contribution was perhaps in the choice of lenses and in lighting. I was attracted to documentary because they stated that they wanted to make films which were useful to society, which did not exclude entertainment. I think it is true to say that we were amateurs in making films. We had to learn by making them. Grierson surrounded himself with university graduates. They read their Eisenstein and Pudovkin and looked at as many films as they could, to analyse them. The only one who had worked in a studio was Cavalcanti. He taught some of our directors a lot. As far as *Mining Review* goes – we certainly tried to make them look interesting. I don't think we wanted to make works of art.

Snow was different. I had worked with Geoffrey Jones before, and I had a good idea of the kind of film he wanted to make. He was an artist of sorts, always cut the films to music. *Snow* was perhaps the best film he ever made.

Walter Lassally

(Cinematographer, *Sunday by the Sea* and *Every Day Except Christmas*)
I would certainly agree with John Grierson's definition and add one of my own: 'Art is real life with the boring bits cut out.'

Anthony Simmons

(Director, *Sunday by the Sea*)
Directors are storytellers even if their material is simply happening in front of them. They choose the material they shoot, they put it together in the way they want the world to see it. Sometimes there's storytelling as well as documentary images (*Listen to Britain*), imagination as well as well-researched material, fiction as well as truth. I was mindful of this when I came to shoot my first 35mm film. I decided to fill the screen with faces of people I knew, people I'd grown up with

having a day out away from the grime – helped by Betty Lawrence with, or should I say guided by, a soundtrack of Victorian music-hall songs.

We could afford two weekends and a Bank Holiday. We had no long lenses, no hidden cameras. Mostly everything was handheld, Walter had just about time to focus and set the stop. Luckily we also had an editor, Lusia Krakovska, ready to spend hours adjusting every edit to the music-track: I'm amazed every time I see it.

We earned enough to reinvest the cash in our next film, *Bow Bells*, with a broader canvas and longer schedule. We couldn't find a song to close, so Betty and I made one up and shot the sequence with my wife and baby son, the only bit which wasn't as we found it – my first step into fiction. Heartfelt, just the same, and the creative treatment of reality, fact or fiction, has always remained the object of the game.

John Legard

(Editor, *Any Man's Kingdom*)
I worked with John Grierson when

he was executive producer at Crown Film Unit. We made a film about the West Indies called *Caribbean* (1951). He encouraged us in the editing to avoid the didactic where possible and be more impressionist – to catch the flavour of the islands (a touch of 'creative treatment of reality'?). It certainly worked and I was grateful for his wisdom and encouragement. He would probably have enjoyed *Any Man's Kingdom*. Visually it is a fairly conventional travel film. What makes it atmospheric and evocative is the soundtrack. The narration contains oblique historical references and provocative thinking and avoids stating what the audience can see for themselves (there were many lengthy humdrum travelogues in the cinema at that time). The music by Elisabeth Lutyens also adds texture, together with sequences using Northumbrian pipes and local dancing. In my experience Grierson, when able to concentrate on individual films, fully earned the 'Father of Documentary' soubriquet, and I like to think that this film would

perhaps have been given his 'thumbs up'. He may indeed have seen it. He came one day at Anstey's invitation to see a batch of the output and he did say 'Edgar has gone over the hills and far away' which *could* perhaps have been taken as a compliment.

Derrick Knight

(Secretary, the Committee responsible for *March to Aldermaston*, and one of its directors; director, *Education for the Future*)

We all agreed that we were making a film of record, partly motivated by the knowledge that the mass media might ridicule or ignore the marchers. I don't believe that anyone gave a toss about what their documentary forebears might have done, but they were good technicians and knew a thing or two about imagery and character. So what about the shadow of Dr John Grierson? I have said that it was a record but the means by which it was made must have pleased him. He must have approved the attempt at launching such a film into an international mass-media orbit. That's what he had been doing for thirty years. He must have been pleased that we were able to grasp the power of film to move and educate a wide public and he would certainly have been pleased with the *hommages* to his style throughout the film. Yet he was never a member of our group and as far as I know has left no commentary on the film.

In 1967 the Labour Party found itself in the unusual situation of having three spots booked in consecutive weeks and no firm idea of how to use them. I was in the party's media advisory group and was challenged to come up with ideas and warned that there was a minuscule budget . . . two films were made and a studio discussion spread the messages. Result? Good community education, films made out of the lives of ordinary people and putting them on a million or so TV screens. I believe that Dr John enjoyed this modest tribute.

John Krish

(Director, *I Think They Call Him John*; also uncredited assistant editor, *Listen to Britain*)

Grierson's definition seems clever, until you examine it, then it crumbles in your hand. He and his disciples believed they were the only ones making real films because they were using real people. So early on, in this wonderful, treacherous, creative, destructive, exhilarating film world he created the film snob. But real people don't necessarily make documentaries more real. In the wartime Crown classics, dialogue scenes between brave airmen, seamen or firemen often seemed stilted. That taught me the essential lesson – never extend non-actors beyond their limits.

In *I Think They Call Him John*, I recreated the Sunday of a real old man, taking three days to shoot it. John Ronson was a gallant old soldier and for his first shot had to walk into his sitting room. He marched in, as if on parade. I showed him how old people dragged their feet and he smiled, admitting that's how he was when there wasn't a film unit in his home. I directed his every move and used the camera as I always do: stay invisible, give people the illusion that what they're seeing is real.

I define documentaries as films that reveal so that those who see them say, 'I never thought of it like that . . . '. I don't care if it fits Grierson's definition. As a writer/director I had one aim, to reach the audience, and I used every means: real people, actors, sets, even fantasy.

Grierson dismissed *The Elephant Will Never Forget* as a glorified newsreel. I first saw *Drifters* at Hampstead's Everyman and missed the opening minutes but the usherette reassured me saying, 'Don't worry, luv, it's only an old film about 'errings.'

Joyce Robertson

(Co-film-maker, *John, Aged Seventeen Months*)
This film is an edited chronological record of what happened to 'John' – what we chose to include and what to omit has an impact on the final film. When editing, there is always a creative element, in that the editing is done to enhance the story that is being told, to help the viewer to concentrate and to understand more easily. My voiceover does not merely state that 'John' was crying . . . or 'John'

did not eat. It is a summary account based on our understanding of the child's experience and behaviour. The voiceover supplements and explains the story that unfolds in the film record. With editing and the informative voiceover, there is no doubt that Grierson would not have regarded the film as a 'mere record'. However, does this then mean that the actuality has had 'creative treatment'? If that means rearranging the record to suit the storyteller . . . then this film is NOT a documentary in Grierson's terms. It is a chronological record of actuality carefully edited to tell a poignant story.

Derek Williams

(Director, *The Shadow of Progress*)
Regarding Grierson's definition: while generally agreeing with it, I have little to add to that simplistic label. On the subject of documentary theory my generation was more preoccupied with *practical* problems. Because even documentaries cost money, the adjective 'sponsored' became almost inseparable from the noun 'documentary'. Its writers and

directors therefore faced the often insoluble task of reconciling industry's demands with sincerity of product and personal integrity. *Shadow of Progress* exemplifies such dilemmas. It divides into two parts: problems and palliatives. However, the remedies featured were piecemeal and failed to penetrate root causes. For this reason the film weakens during its second half. The other problem, again affecting all our movement, was poverty of outlet. Cinema distributors saw non-fiction as padding. Television fought shy of sponsored work. The sole outlets remaining were what was known in the business as 'non-theatrical'. Journalists, concentrating either on cinematic events or primetime TV, henceforward ignored documentary. It was this falling between all stools which led to the demise of the significant or influential documentary. In my view, nevertheless, our type and style of product had some validity in that it differed from its television equivalent in certain important respects: all, I think, deriving from the fact that its practitioners' motives were more aesthetic than journalistic. I do not regard *Shadow* as my best film, though the most successful, but I was able to be true to a basic tenet of documentarians, i.e., that one must show what one is talking about. This has long been abandoned by TV, with its diet of talking heads as a substitute for shot material. Another item on our forbidden list was wall-to-wall commentary. Our best writing was terse. True to our inherited tradition, the visual was always the senior element and the best visuals were those that could speak for themselves.

Eric Marquis

(Writer and producer, *Guinness for You*)
I have little memory of it. However, glancing at the list of awards which I called my 'bullsheet', I note that *Guinness* is somewhat derisively described, by me, as 'advertising' which tells us a little of what I thought of it at the time: twenty minutes or so of clever-dicky images, like an extended commercial, satisfying to the client since their product was on screen the whole time and for many clients that was nirvana! I wouldn't mention

Guinness for You in the same breath as either documentary or John Grierson – but you've obviously seen the film and may have your reasons for picking it up for consideration. If you asked me (which you haven't, but might!) I'd nominate my 1975 film *Seven Green Bottles* as an attempt at the 'creative treatment of actuality' shot.

[On re-viewing *Guinness for You*:] My first reaction has been reinforced (and multiplied). If you do not wish this disc returned, I will cheerfully burn it and wish that all other copies extant could also be destroyed! This seems a dreadfully ungracious response to your well-meant enquiry, but at least it's honest and I can only say that I am deeply ashamed of having had anything to do with the making of it. And you can quote me if you like.

Patrick Keiller

(Director, *London*)
Both *London* and *Robinson in Space* (1996) were conscious attempts to apply ideas and techniques from Surrealism, Situationism and their precursors to the predicament of the UK in the early 1990s, in the hope of changing this in some way, however slightly. As a goal, this was rather more specific than Grierson's formulation, though you could certainly see it in similar terms.

Andrew Kötting

(Director, *Gallivant*)
Reality as a poetic reinvention
Reality as assimilation collation and regurgitation
Reality as a means of implied truth
Reality as confabulation
Reality as Odyssey
Reality as 'landscape' processed by 'inscape'
Reality as hoodwink and communal conspiracy
Reality as look-at-me.

Brian Hill

(Director, *Drinking for England*; also executive producer, *24 Hours*)
Drinking for England could have been made to fit Grierson's definition of documentary. In the film we took real interviews from real people and literally gave them a creative treatment by turning those words into verse. The important thing about Grierson's

definition is that reality is treated in a creative way while still retaining the essential reality. This was done in *Drinking for England*. Too many documentaries ditch the reality in favour of what they imagine is creativity.

Michael Grigsby

(Director, *Lockerbie – A Night Remembered*)

The process began at the start of our long research period. On my first morning I stood outside our rented cottage, closed my eyes and listened to the gentle sounds of dawn Lockerbie – cattle, sheep, tractors. This soundscape of rural rhythms became the foundation from which we created the film.

First I tried to create the space to *feel* this small safe town in order to understand the longlasting effects of the sudden violence unleashed on the community. Then I created the space for people to express themselves in their own way, at their own pace. We did this through measured editing with the juxtaposition of evocative images and a strong soundtrack. Hopefully this treatment – creative

treatment – captures the essence of a small Scottish town coming to terms with its recent past.

Kevin Macdonald

(Director, *Touching the Void*)

I still think that Grierson's definition – broad as it is – holds up pretty well after almost eighty years. Although *Touching the Void* contains sections with actors I still see it as a documentary and think it falls within the bounds of Grierson's intentions. Without getting too historical, one can look at many of the early documentaries – produced by Grierson – and see that they are scripted and employ 'actors' – whether professional or not – but they also give priority to a sense of authenticity and contain moments of genuine spontaneity.

TtV was always conceived as a documentary. The 'reconstruction' using actors was only necessary because there was no other way to illustrate the story and to bring home to the audience the predicament the two climbers were in – to build on the interviews not to supplant them. Generally I hate dramatisation in documentaries, because it can never measure up to the 'real' elements – it feels 'cheesy' and lightweight. So before using it in the film I thought hard about how we might get over this hurdle – and the answer I came up with was simply to film the drama elements in as documentary a way a possible, i.e., to film them in the real places wherever possible and to put the actors through what Joe and Simon themselves had gone through in terms of wind, snow and difficulty of climbing. As much as possible I tried to 'observe' rather than self-consciously 'make a film'.

Eva Weber

(Director, *The Intimacy of Strangers*)
The Intimacy of Strangers is a modern-day love story, entirely constructed out of real, overheard mobile phone conversations. Urban living brings us into ever closer contact with strangers; and as the title suggests, this film explores the conflict between the private and the public, between being intimate yet removed, inherent in our use of mobile phones. While filming, we had no control over who we might be able to film on each day, what they might talk about and who they were talking to. We literally went to a location, and waited until we spotted somebody talking on their phone. As such, the film was entirely down to chance; yet, in the editing, we were able to weave these unmediated and random snippets of actuality into a narrative that reflects on the way we communicate and relate to each other today. Thus, I feel that Grierson's famous definition of a documentary film is very much relevant to this film, although I am not sure whether the film would fulfil some of his other criteria of what a documentary should do.

Notes

1. Brian Winston is notable among those who have challenged documentary; Stella Bruzzi among those who have provided rejoinder.

2. This influential phrase was coined by Tom Gunning and can be found in many of his writings and those of other scholars of early film-making.

3. Bill Nichols, *Introduction to Documentary* (Bloomington: Indiana University Press, 2001) and elsewhere.

4. Brian Winston, *Claiming the Real: Documentary Film Revisited* (London: BFI, 1995), p. 42.

5. Edgar Anstey, *The British Film Institute presents a series of programmes on: the documentary film in Great Britain* (pamphlet: London: BFI, 1951).

6. Paul Rotha and Richard Griffith, *The Film Till Now*, 4th edn (London: Vision Press, 1963), p. 736.

7. Simon Brown, email to author, 2006.

8. Ken Gay, letter to author, 2006.

9. Bectu History Project Interview, 1990.

10. Ron Craigen, Bectu History Project Interview, 1988.

11. Barbara Freese, *Coal: A Human History* (London: Heinemann, 2005), p. 245.

12. Julian Petley, 'Doing without the Broadcast Media', anthologised in Margaret Dickinson, *Rogue Reels* (London: BFI, 1999), p. 189.

13. Roger Manvell, *Film* (London: Penguin, 1944), p. 101. Manvell's championing of *Coal Face* was significant in establishing its subsequent reputation.

14. Monbiot: <www.monbiot.com/archives/2001/05/01/violence-is-our-enemy>; 'stylistic hard hitting films'.

15. VHS packaging.

16. Anstey, Ibid.

17. Newspaper quotes, in Lothar Prox (ed.), *Drifters* (Lindlar: Siebel Druck, 1986), p. 41.

18. John Grierson, 'Drifters', reprinted in Ian Aitken, *The Documentary Film Movement: An Anthology* (Edinburgh: Edinburgh University Press, 1998), p. 79.

19. Quoted in Prox, *Drifters*, p. 13.

20. Paul Rotha, *Documentary Diary* (London: Secker and Warburg, 1973), p. 103.

21. Sydney Box, *Film Publicity: A Handbook on the Production and Distribution of Propaganda Films* (London: Lovat Dickson, 1937), pp. 42–4.

22. Memo, 'Guinness for You', in Guinness Storeroom Archives.

23. Publicity handout: leaflet in BFI Special Collections.

24. Medical officer: Dr Connan quoted in Elizabeth Lebas, 'When Every Street Became a Cinema', *History Workshop Journal* vol. 39 (1995), p. 51.

25. Synopsis in *Radio Times* 23 November 1989, p. 69.

26. Stella Bruzzi, *New Documentary: A Critical Introduction* (London: Routledge, 2000), pp. 166–7.

27. BFI Special Collections, Paul Rotha collection 5/103 souvenir programme.

28. Bectu History Project Interview, 1988.

29. Interview in Eva Orbanz, *Journey to a Legend and Back* (Berlin: Volker Spiess, 1977), p. 41.

30. Introduction to National Film Theatre screening, April 2003.

31. Interview on *Thinking outside the Box* (CD-Rom produced by Documentary Film-makers Group, 2005).

32. Philip Donnellan, 'Memories of the Future', *Sight and Sound* vol. 2 no. 4, August 1992.

33. All quotes in Donnellan's unpublished memoir (consulted copy unpaginated).

34. James and Joyce Robertson, *Separation and the Very Young* (London: Free Association Books, 1989), pp. 89–91.

35. John Willis, 'Johnny Goes Home', *TV Times* 17 July 1975, p. 9. Next quote is from same source.

36. Bond, quoted in Bert Hogenkamp, *Deadly Parallels* (London: Lawrence and Wishart, 1986), p. 147.

37. Ibid,. passim.

38. Bob Neaverson, *The Beatles Movies* (London: Cassell, 1997), p. 110.

39. Keiller and Griffiths quotes in BFI Special Collections *London* correspondence files.

40. Preproduction report: production file for M.R. 4/12, held by BFI.

41. Mandy Rose, 'Through the eyes of the Video Nation', in Richard Kilborn and John Isod, *From Grierson to the Docusoap: Breaking the Boundaries* (Luton: University of Luton Press, 2000), p. 177.

42. Denis Mitchell, 'Through the Hours of the Morning', *Radio Times* 25 March 1959, p. 9.

43. Derrick Knight and Vincent Porter, *A Long Look at Short Films* (London: Pergamon Press, 1967). Incidentally, the same Derrick Knight whose film work is represented in this book

44. BFI Special Collections Roger Graef collection, feasibility study for controller. The next quote is from the same source.

45. Claire Johnston, Paul Willemen 'Brecht in Britain: The Independent Political Film', *Screen* vol. 16 no. 4, Winter 1975/76, p. 112.

46. The BTF memories are from a telephone conversation between John Legard and the author, 2006.

47. Harold Lowenstein, 'Can Children Act?', *Sight and Sound* vol. 6 no. 21, Spring 1937, p. 17.

48. Tait, quoted in Peter Todd and Ben Cook, *Subjects and Sequences: A Margaret Tait Reader* (London: Lux, 2004), p. 132.

49. Letts, frequently quoted as at <en.wikipedia.org/wiki/The_Punk_Rock_Movie>.

50. *Motion Picture Herald* vol. 1919 no. 11.13, 3 June 1953, p. 43.

51. Jay, interviewed in Alan Rosenthal, *The New Documentary in Action* (Berkeley: University of California Press, 1971), p. 211.

52. Garnett, interviewed in Orbanz, *Journey to a Legend and Back*, p. 66.

53. Duncan Crow, *World in Action '63* (London: World Distributors, 1963), p. 10.

54. Ken Gay, *Films and Filming* vol. 17 no. 10, July 1971, p. 84.

55. The four released travelogues were *Negombo Coast*, *Dance of the Harvest*, *Monsoon Island* and *Villages of Lanka*. Thanks to Jon Hoare for supplying this information.

56. BFI Special Collections, Wright Collection Box 6: Ceylon folder.

57. *Documentary News Letter* vol. 6. no. 51, 1946, p. 8.

58. Leo Enticknap, 'South', in Ian Aitken (ed.), *Encyclopedia of the Documentary Film* (London: Routledge, 2005), p. 1245

59. The DVD commentary is supplied by silent film expert Luke McKernan.

60. The film is also catalogued as *Cunard Vessel at Liverpool* (and released on DVD under this title); alternate titles are the result of the research carried out on the collection by the University of Sheffield in association with the BFI.

61. *Monthly Film Bulletin* vol. 20 no. 235, August 1953, p. 127; *Today's Cinema* vol. 81 no. 6803, 20 June 1953, p. 12.

62. Walter Lassally, 'Making *Bow Bells*', *Films and Filming* vol. 12 (1954), p. 6.

63. Oliver Pike, *Nature and Camera* (London: Focal Press), p. 209.

64. Source for Greene's abortive involvement: production file at the National Archives: INF 6/462.

65. Interview in Jason Wood, *Nick Broomfield: Documenting Icons* (London: Faber & Faber, 2005), p. 146.

66. Audience research document contained in *Two Victorian Girls* files at BBC Written Archives; these files also contain transcripts indicating the extent to which Peet 'coaxed' the interviewees.

67. Dave Douglass, interviewed in Dickinson, *Rogue Reels*, p. 274.

68. *Monthly Film Bulletin* vol. 3. no. 27, March 1936.

69. Norman Swallow, *Factual Television* (London: Focal Press, 1966), p. 186.

70. *Documentary News Letter* review, quoted in James Chapman, *The British at War* (London: I. B. Taurus, 2000), p. 137.

71. Pat Jackson, *A Retake Please!* (Liverpool: Liverpool University Press, 1999), p. 117.

72. *TV Times* 19 September 1988, p. 61.

73. Woolcock, interviewed in John Corner, *The Art of Record* (Manchester: Manchester University Press, 1996), pp. 153–4.

74. Kineto Catalogue, January 1912.

75. Rachael Low, *The History of the British Film 1918–1929* (London: Allen & Unwin, 1971), p. 130.

76. John Barnes, *The Beginnings of the Cinema in England* (Newton Abbot: David and Charles, 1976), p. 196.

Further Reading

Listed below is a selection of easily available books covering reasonably wide territory (inevitably excluding classic works no longer in print, and books and articles relevant only to individual films included in this Screen Guide).

Reference

Ian Aitken (ed.), *Encyclopedia of the Documentary Film* (London: Routledge, 2005).

Robert Murphy (ed.), *Directors in British and Irish Cinema: A Reference Companion* (London: BFI, 2006).

Theory

Bill Nichols, *Introduction to Documentary* (Bloomington: Indiana University Press, 2001).

Critical Commentary

Stella Bruzzi, *New Documentary: A Critical Introduction* (London: Routledge, 2000).

Michael Chanan, *The Politics of Documentary* (London: BFI, 2007).

John Corner, *The Art of Record: A Critical Introduction to Documentary* (Manchester: Manchester University Press, 1996).

Paul Ward, *Documentary: The Margins of Reality* (London: Wallflower, 2005).

Brian Winston, *Claiming the Real: Documentary Film Revisited* (London: BFI, 1995).

History

Ian Aitken (ed.), *The Documentary Film Movement: An Anthology* (Edinburgh: Edinburgh University Press, 1998).

Richard M. Barsam, *Non Fiction Film: A Critical History* (Bloomington: Indiana University Press, 1992).

Timothy Boon, *Films of Fact: A History of Science in Documentary Films and Television* (London: Wallflower, 2007).

James Chapman, *The British at War: Cinema, State and Propaganda, 1939–1945* (London: I. B. Taurus, 2000).

David Curtis, *A History of Artists' Film and Video in Britain* (London: BFI, 2006).

Margaret Dickinson, *Rogue Reels: Oppositional Film in Britain, 1945–90* (London: BFI, 1999).

Bert Hogenkamp, *Deadly Parallels: Film and the Left in Britain, 1929–39* (London: Lawrence and Wishart, 1986).

Web Resources

<www.screenonline.org.uk>
BFI's online guide to British film and television history, with growing coverage of non-fiction; text and images available to all web-users, moving image clips available in UK schools, universities and public libraries.

<www.bfi.org.uk/mediatheque>
Guide to material available at BFI's free onsite viewing facilities containing curated programmes of archive material: includes a programme based on the 100 films included in this book.

<www.movinghistory.ac.uk>
Overview of the collections of UK public film archives, in which factual film-making is strongly represented, with links to their individual websites.

<www.wildfilmhistory.org>
Online history of British natural history film-making.

<www.bufvc.ac.uk/newsreels>
Useful for exploring the interconnections of newsreels and cinemagazines with documentary.

<www.channel4.com/fourdocs>
Documentary interest site whose features include a few streamed classic documentaries as well as self-made docs uploaded by users.

<www.dfgdocs.com>
Resource guide aimed at current documentary-makers but also of wider interest; includes a directory of documentary films strongest on recent material.

<https://sheffdocfest.com>
<www.oxdox.com>
The leading UK documentary film festivals.

<www.dochouse.org>
Voluntary organisation supporting and promoting documentary in the UK; runs popular screenings of international and British works.

Index

Page numbers in **bold** denote the principal entry for a selected film; those in *italic* denote illustrations; *n* = endnote

24 Hours (2000) **9–10**, 248
1930s, documentary movement 4–5, 69, 104–5, 236
    criticisms 90, 245
    fusion of styles 209–11
    influence on later approaches 134–5
1950s, trends in documentary 159–60
1960s, mood/culture 109–11, 126–7, 186, 228

'access' documentary 134
Acres, Birt 239–40, 241
activist cinema 80, 130–1
    role in activist process 131
    see also politically committed film; protest
actors, use of 50, 106–7, 190

'actuality' 2–3, 223–4
Addinsell, Richard 54
Adlam, John 210
advertising 78–9
Airlie, Jimmy 219–20
Akomfrah, John 80
Al-Qaeda 182–3
alcohol
    consumption 58–60
    production/promotion 78–9
Aldermaston 124–5, 128
Alexander, Donald 24–5, 72, 210, 220
Alexandra Palace 205–6
Alice in Wonderland (1903) 17
Almond, Paul 177, 179
'amateur' film-making 134–6
Amber 219
The American Family (1973) 70
Analysis of Exercise (1936) 226
The Ancestry of Science 207

Anderson, Lindsay 64–5, 90, 124, 126, 197
Anglo-Irish Agreement (1985) 169
Anne, Princess *172*
Anstey, Edgar 11–12, 88, 90, 91, 120, 184, 185, 244
Antarctica 192–3
Any Man's Kingdom (1956) **11–12**, 243–4
Apted, Michael 177, 179
Arabic, films in 140–1
archives, role in preservation of documentaries 7, 193
Armitage, Simon 58
Armstrong, Franny 130–1
Artists Must Live (1953) **13–14**
Arts Council 14
Associated Rediffusion 142, 159

*At Work in Manchester
    and Milan
    (Neighbours) (1974)*
    15–16
Atkins, Humphrey 40
Attenborough, David
    200–2, *201,* 217
Attlee, Clement 106
Auden, W. H. 35, 148–9
audience, assumptions
    regarding 143
awards/nominations 31,
    182, 197, 212

babyhood 17–18, 52–4
Baby's Toilet (1905)
    17–18
BAFTA awards 212
Baird, John Logie 205
Balfour, Lady 132–3
Barry Langford (1963)
    127
The Battle of the Somme
    (1916) *19,* **19–21,**
    47, 49, 50
The Battleship Potemkin
    (1926) 56, 148
BBC: The Voice of Britain
    (1935) 206
BBC (British Broadcasting
    Corporation) 96–7,
    131
Broadcast Archives 7
    Community
        Programmes Unit
        134
    documentary style
        13–14, 142
    start of television
        operation 205–6
BBC Orchestra 13

The Beatles 109–11, *110*
*Beauty, Bonny, Daisy,
    Violet, Grace and
    Geoffrey Morton
    (1974)* **22–3**
Beckham, David 120
Beethoven, Ludwig van
    145
Benn, Tony 31
Berger, John 168
Bermondsey Borough
    Council 82–3
Berwick Street Collective
    151
BFI (British Film Institute)
    25–6, 74, 80, 116,
    212
    Experimental Film Fund
        221
BIF (British Instructional
    Films) 235, 238
Big Brother (2000–) 9
The Big Meeting (1963)
    24–6, *25*
Birth of a Flower (1910)
    235
Birth of a Nation (1916)
    148
Blag, Flaco 42
Blair, Tony 183
*Blue Black Permanent
    (1992)* 161
Boer War 20
Bogarde, Dirk 118
Bogside Community
    Association 134
Bond, Ralph 32, 104,
    209, 210–11
Boorman, John 126–7
Boulting, John 47
Boulting, Roy 47

Bow Bells (1954) 197,
    199, 243
Bower, Dallas 205, 206
Bowlby, John 98
Box, Sydney 78,
    189–90, 203
Box-office successes 167
Brass Tacks (1977–) 168
Britain
    character/identity,
        depictions of 39,
        55–6, 68–9, 76–7,
        85, 112–13,
        119–21
    foreigners' views of
        154
    see also British
        documentary;
        colonialism; social
        issues
Britain at Bay (1940)
    27–8
Britain on Guard (1940)
    see Britain at Bay
*Britain Under National
    Government (1934)*
    76–7
British Campaign to Stop
    Immigration 134
British Council 62, 180
British documentary,
    traditions/style 4–7
    (alleged) decline 5–6,
        30
    development(s) 4–5,
        151–2, 159
    female directors 30
    see also 1930s
British Electrical
    Development
    Association 237

British Industrial and Scientific Films Association 120
British Petroleum 180–1
Brits (2000) 168–9
Britten, Benjamin 35, 148–9
Bronowski, Jacob 200
Broomfield, Nick 94, 215–16
BTF (British Transport Films) 11–12, 24, 90, 91, 157, 184, 186, 197, 226
Buddhism 187–8
Burke, James 200
Burton, Richard 124
Bush, H. W. *82*

Callaghan, James 40, 144
Calypso (1950) 161
Cannes Film Festival 182
Cardiff, Jack 229
Caribbean (1951) 244
Carthy, Martin 75
Cary, Tristram 79
A Case of Rape (*Police*) (1982) 147
Cash, Johnny 100–1
Castle, Barbara 144
Cathode Ray Oscillation (1936) 226
Catholicism 203–4
Cathy Come Home (1975) 102
Cavalcanti, Alberto 33, 35, 187, 242
Cawston, Richard 97, 172, 173–4, 217

Central Electricity Board 68
Ceylon (Sri Lanka) 187–8
Channel 4 9–10, 80, 114, 212, 220, 234
Chariots of Fire (1981) 144
Charles, Prince *172*, 173
children 29–30, 156–8, *157*, 177–9, *198*
care of 72–3, 98–9, 246
see also babyhood; education; schools programmes
Children Growing Up with Other People (1947) 29
Children Learning By Experience (1947) **29–30**
Children's Film Foundation 238
Churchill, Winston 28, 48, 106
Cinema Action 31, 80, 151, 219–20
'cinema of attractions' 2–3
cinéma vérité 4
style, compared with British examples 92–3, 99
cinemagazine series 128–9
Circulation (1936) 225–6
Citizen 63 (1963) 126–7
Civilisation (1969) 13, 200
Clark, Kenneth 13, 112, 200

The Clash 163, 164
class 73, 124–5, 178–9, 210
disparity between subjects and presenter/audience 7, 44–5, 88–9, 122–3
Class Struggle: Film from the Clyde (1977) 220
Clore, Leon 38, 197–8
CND (Campaign for Nuclear Disarmament) 124–5
Co-operative Wholesale Society 189–91
Coal (1936) 226
The Coal Board's Butchery (*The Miners' Campaign Video Tapes*) (1984) **31–2**
Coal Face (1935) **33–5**, *34*, 84, 251*n13*
Cock, Gerald 205, 206
COI (Central Office of Information) 29–30, 140–1, 180
Collyns, Sam 168
colonialism, history/ attitudes 170–1, 187–8
criticisms of 191
Colour Poems (1974) 161
commercial television, documentary styles 142, 159
compilation films 7
The Complainers (1997) **36–7**

The Conquest of Everest
(1953) **38–9**
Conscious Cinema 42
Conservative party
criticisms 117–18
films made by/for
40–1, 76–7
(protests against)
policies 31–2,
219–20
see also National
Government;
Thatcher, Margaret
*Conservative Party
Election Broadcast
23/4/79* **40–1**, *41*
Consett (Yorks) 233–4
Contemporary Films 124
Conway, Mrs 15–16
Conway, Ted 15–16
Cooper, Budge 30
Countryman Films 38
Covent Garden market
64–5
Craigie, Jill 13, 30
Craignish Trust 92
Crowd Bites Wolf (2000)
42–3
Crown Film Unit 5, 29,
54, 91, 229, 244
Cummings, A. J. 69
*Cunard Vessel at
Liverpool see S.S.
Skirmisher at
Liverpool*
current affairs
programming 142
Curtis, Adam 8, 182
Cutting Edge (1990–) 37
Cutts, Graham 122
Cvitanovich, Frank 22–3

Dance of the Harvest
(1934) 253*n*55
Darlow, Michael 100
Darlow Smithson 212
DATA (Documentary and
Technicians
Alliance) 132
A Day in the Hayfields
(1904) 17–18
*A Day in the Life of a
Coal Miner* (1910)
44–6, *45*
The Death of Yugoslavia
(1995) 1
Decision (1976) 146
Deliverance (1972) 126
Depression (1930s) 76,
209–11
The Derby (1895) 240
Desert Victory (1943)
47–9, *48*
*The Devil Is Coming (The
Great War)* (1964)
50–1
Diana, Princess of Wales
166
A Diary for Timothy
(1946) **52–4**, *53*,
190
Dickinson, Thorold 207,
231–2
*Digging Deep see Mining
Review 4th Year
No. 12*
digital video 134–6
and political activism
42
Dineen, Molly 84–5, 94,
234
'Direct Cinema' 4, 29,
84, 99, 146–7

directors
crossover between
genres 126, 198
female 30
role of 215, 228, 243,
245–6
Dixon, Adele 205
documentary/ies
debatable classifications
78–9, 119–20,
144–5
definition(s) 2, 242–50
function 2–3
generic hybridity 3–4
long-running strands
142
see also British
documentary
'docusoap' 36–7, 70–1
Doncaster, Caryl 160
Donnellan, Philip 96–7
Dovzhenko, Alexander
235
D&P Studios 231
Drifters (1929) *55*,
55–7, 86–7, 148,
240–1, 246
Drinking for England
(1998) **58–60**, *59*,
248–9
Driving Me Crazy (1988)
215–16
Dublin 154–5
Durden, J. V. 237–8
Durham 24–6, *25*

Eastern Valley (1937)
220
Edinburgh, Duke of *172*
education 61–3, 82–3,
159–60, 175–6

see also schools programmes

Education for the Future (1967) **61–3**, 244

Edward VII 56

Eisenstein, Sergei 242

The Elephant Will Never Forget (1953) 197, 246

The Eleventh Hour (1980s) 80

Elizabeth II 112, *172, 173*

coronation 14, 38, *165*, 165–7

Elizabeth Is Queen (1953) 165

Elton, Arthur 79, 88, 90, 170, 184

Emmett, E. V. H. 238

Emmott, Basil 56

Empire Marketing Board 55–6, 187

Empo 35

The End of the Line see Johnny Go Home

environmental issues 170–1, 180–1

Erulkar, Sarah 30

Ervine, David 169

Essex, Tony 50, 51

evacuation 231–2

Every Day Except Christmas (*Look at Britain*) (1957) **64–5**, *66–7*, 243

Excalibur (1981) 126

exotic locations 38–9, 192–3

experimental cinema 2–3, 161–2, 207–8

exploration 38–9, 192–3

The Face of Britain (1935) **68–9**, 210

The Family (1974) **70–1**

farming 22–3, 235

Fasoli, Domenico 15–16

Fasoli, Signora 15–16

Feltham Sings (2002) 58

Festival of Britain (1951) 133

Field, Mary 15, 237, 238

Fiennes, Ralph 120

Film Producers Guild 180

FilmFour 212

Films of Fact Ltd 106

Films of Record 146

fishing industry *55*, 55–7, 86–7, 239–41

Five and Under (2002) **72–3**

Flaherty, Robert 154

Flanagan and Allen 112

'fly-on-the-wall' approach *see* Direct Cinema; docusoap

Foot, Michael 125

Ford, John 64

Ford Motors 64

Forty Minutes (1981–94) 84

Four Corners 219

Foxhunt see Mining Review 4th Year No. 12

France, documentary traditions/style 4, 62

Free Cinema 5, 26, 64–5, 92–3, 114, 124, 170, 197–8, 222

Freud, Anna 98

Fry, Christopher 166

Gaitskell, Hugh 24

Gala Day (1963) 25–6

Gallivant (1996) **74–5**, 248

Garnett, Tony 173

Gaslight (1940) 231

Gaumont–British Instructional 68, 225, 237–8

Geddes, Ann 219

General Strike (1926) 32

Generation X 163

George V, Silver Jubilee 104–5

Germany

co-productions with 15–16

war dead 20, 47–8, 51

Gervais, Ricky 37

Giles, Billy 169

Gilroy, John 79

Glazer, Jonathan 79

Godard, Jean-Luc 154

Goodfield, June 207

Goretta, Claude 64

GPO Film Unit 5, 27, 35, 170, 187, 206, 226

Graef, Roger 134, 146–7

Graham-Wilcox Productions 122

Grainger, Frank 87

Granada Television 114, 142, 177, 228

The Great Recovery (Britain Under National Government) (1934) **76–7**

The Great War (1964) 50–1, 92

Green, Herbert A. 104, 105

Green, R. 104, 105

Greene, Graham 203

Greengrass, Paul 126

Greenpark Productions 180–1

Grierson, John 4–5, 35, 38, 55–7, 68, 86–7, 96, 120, 150, 159
criticisms 245–6
definition of documentary 2, 242–50

Grierson, Ruby 88, 209, 210–11

Grierson Award 31

Griffiths, Keith 116

Grigsby, Michael 114–15, 134, 222, 249

Groser, John, Father 107

Group 3 38

Guerillavision 42–3

Guinea, Richard 15

Guinness, Arthur 79

Guinness for You (1971) **78–9**, 247–8

Gunning, Tom 251n2

Haanstra, Bert 170

Haig, Douglas, Field-Marshal 50

Hall, Stuart 81

Handsworth Songs (1986) **80–1**

Harris, Roy 137, 138

Harrison, George *110, 111*

Harrison, Mrs 210

Hawking, Richard 213–14

Healey, Denis 144

Health and Clothing (1928) **82–3**

Health Education Council 175–6

The Heart of the Angel (1989) **84–5**

Heath, Edward 219

Heathfield, Peter 31

Heaven 17 32

Henscher, Gordon 134–6

Hepworth, Cecil 17–18, 223

Hepworth, Elizabeth 17–18

Heredity in Man (1937) 238

Heroes of the North Sea (1925) **86–7**

Heron, Patrick 13

Hill, Brian 9, 58, 248–9

Hillary, Edmund 39

Hinsley, Arthur, Cardinal 203

Hoare, Jon 253n55

Holiday (1957) 197

Holmes, J. B. 11, 226

Holmes, Kelly 120

homelessness 102–3

housing conditions/policy 88–90, 106–8

Housing Problems (1935) **88–90**, *89*, 134

Howells, Kim 31

Hudson, Hugh 144–5

Hunt, John 39

Hurley, Frank 192, 193

Huxley, Julian 225

Hyks, Veronica 130–1

I Protest (1960) 128

I Think They Call Him John (1964) *91*, **91–3**, 245

Idol, Billy 163

Ilfracombe 223–4

IMF (International Monetary Fund) 42

Imperial War Museum 7, 50

industrial action 219–20

industry *see* fishing; mining; shipbuilding; steel

'interest' films 122–3

International Visual Communications Association 120

International Year of the Environment 180

The Intimacy of Strangers (2005) **94–5**, 250

The Irishmen: An Impression of Exile (1965) **96–7**

Isaacs, Jeremy 22

Isotype 106–7

Italian culture, compared with British 15–16

ITV *see* commercial television; *names of individual stations*

Jackson, Pat 126, 229–30
James, Sid 128–9
Jarrow March (1926) 125
Jay, Antony 173
Jenkins, Timothy 52–4, *53*
Jennings, Humphrey 5, 35, 52, 54, 64, 112–13, 138
Jewish Chronicle 221
Jewish communities/ identity 221–2
John, Aged Seventeen Months, for Nine Days in a Residential Nursery (1969) **98–9**, 246
Johnny Cash in San Quentin (1969) **100–1**
Johnny Go Home (1975) **102–3**
Jones, A. E. 8, 86, 87
Jones, Frances 'Effie' 217–18
Jones, Geoffrey 8, 184–6, 243
Jubilee (1935) 80, **104–5**, 134

Karlin, Marc 151
Kee, Robert 200
Keiller, Patrick 116–17, 248
Khan, Amir 120
Kineto 44
Kinnock, Gladys 144
Kinnock, Neil 144–5
Kino 105

Knight, Castleton 165, 166
Knight, Derrick (and Partners) 61–2, 244–5, 253*n43*
Knight, Marion 126–7
Knox, Robert 187
Kötting, Andrew 74–5, 248
Kötting, Eden 74–5
Krakowska, Lusia 198–9, 243
Krish, John 91–3, 126, 197, 245–6

Labour party/movement 24, 26, 28, 125, 132, 211, 245
criticisms 40–1
films made by/in support of 61–3, 82–3, 144–5, 189–91
internal differences 145
Lamche, Gustav 'Schlacke' 219
Land of Promise (1946) **106–8**, *107*, 190
Larkin, Philip 186
Lassally, Walter 197–9, 243
The Last Laugh (1924) 87
Last of the Summer Wine (1973–) 190
Lawrence, Betty 243
Leacock, Philip 156–7
The Leader, His Driver and the Driver's Wife (1994) 215–16

Legard, John 243–4
Legg, Stuart 150, 170, 210, 211
Lehmann, Beatrice 72
leisure activities 197–9
Lennon, John *110*, 111
Let It Be (1970) **109–11**, *110*
Letts, Don 163–4
Levy, Don 207
Liberation Films 175
Lindsay-Hogg, Michael 109
Listen to Britain (1942) **112–13**, 243
Livingstone, Ken 120
Loach, Ken 102, 130
Lockerbie – A Night Remembered (1998) **114–15**, *115*, 242, 249
Logue, Christopher 124
London 82–3, 94–5, 116–23, *117*, 128–9
class contrasts 122–3
Jewish community 221–2
social conditions 88–90, 102–3
London (1994) 74, **116–18**, *117*, 248
London 2012: Make Britain Proud (2004) *119*, **119–21**
London International Film School 94
London's Contrasts (Wonderful London) (1924) **122–3**
Longinotto, Kim 94

Look at Britain (1957)
    64
Look At Life (1959–69)
    128–9
Lowe, George 38
Lowenstein, Harold
    156–8
Loyalists (1999) 168–9
Lumière Company
    154–5
Lutyens, Elizabeth 11
Lye, Len 184

MacColl, Ewan 96
MacDonald, Jackie 169
Macdonald, Kevin
    212–13, 249–50
MacGowan, Shane 164
Macmillan, Harold 208
Malins, Geoffrey 19
Malleson, Miles 107, *107*
Mander, Kay 30
Manvell, Roger *251n13*
The March of Time
    (1964) 210
March to Aldermaston
    (1958) **124–5**, 242,
    244
Marconi, Guglielmo 205
Marion Knight (1963)
    126–7
Market Place (1959) 1,
    128–9
Marquis, Eric 79, 247–8
masculinity, treatments
    of 36–7, 59–60
Mass Observation
    movement 134–5
Mathieson, Muir 190
McAllister, Stewart 112,
    113

'McAlpine's Fusilliers'
    96–7
McCartney, Paul *110,*
    111
McDowell, J. B. 19
McKernan, Luke *254n59*
McLaren, Norman 184
McLibel (1998/2005)
    130–1
McMullan, Gorman 169
McPhee, William 'Billy
    Two-Tone' 102–3
Memento (2000) 153
Militant Tendency 145
Miller, Frank 122
Mills, John *107,* 107–8
Milroy, Vivian 159, 160
*The Miners' Campaign
    Video Tapes* (1984)
    31
*Miners' Festival see
    Mining Review 4th
    Year No. 12*
mining industry/
    communities 24–5,
    25, 33–5, *34,*
    44–6, *45,* 52,
    132–3, 220, 226
  leisure time 227–8
  protests against
    government policy
    31–2
  varying documentary
    approaches 25–6
*Mining Review 4th Year
    No. 12* (1951)
    132–3, 242
Ministry of Information
    29, 170, 180, 203,
    231
Mirren, Helen 120

Mirror (1994) **134–6**
Mitchell, Denis 22, 96,
    137–9, 228
Mitchell and Kenyon
    films 194–6, 233
Modern Times
    (1995–2001) 58
Monbiot, George 42
Monsoon Island (1934)
    253n55
Montagu, Ivor 32, 104
Montgomery, Bernard,
    Field-Marshal 47–8
Moore, Roger 120
morality, (debate on) role
    of TV in 70
Morning in the Streets
    (1959) 22, *137,*
    137–9
Morris, David 130–1
Morris, Gladys 74–5
Morton, Geoffrey 22–3
*Moslems in Britain –
    Cardiff* (1961)
    140–1
mountaineering 38–9,
    212–14
Mozart, Wolfgang
    Amadeus 112
Munden, Max 190–1
*The Murder of Billy Two-
    Tone see Johnny Go
    Home*
Murnau, F. W. 87
music, as documentary
    subject
  popular 100–1,
    109–11, 163–4
  wartime 112–13
music, use of 11, 32,
    33, 35, 39, 54, 65,

75, 95, 96, 114–15,
190–1, 197, 198–9,
205, 208, 232
failure of intended aim
145
Muslim life/society 140–1

National Coal Board 24,
132–3, 226
national cultures,
comparison of
15–16
National Film and
Television School
94
National Government
76–7, 104–5
natural history 192,
200–2, 237–8
Negombo Coast (1934)
253n55
The Negro Next Door
(*This Week*) (1965)
142–3
*Neighbours: Four
Families in Europe*
(1974) 15
Neil Kinnock (1987)
144–5
Neurath, Otto 106
New Year's Eve (*Police*)
(1982) **146–7**
Newsreel Collective 219
Nice Time (1957) 64
Night Mail (1936) 35,
114, **148–50**, *149*
night shift workers 84,
151–3
Nightcleaners (1975)
151–3, *152*, 234
Noel, J. B. 38

North Sea (1938) 229
Northern Ireland 168–9
Northumberland 11–12
nuclear power 125

O Dreamland (1953) 64,
197
observation,
documentary
approach based on
4, 29–30, 84–5,
155
O'Connell Bridge (1897)
154–5
The Office (2001–3) 37
old age 91–3, 134–6,
217–18, 245
Olivier, Laurence 166
One Day in September
(1999) 212
one-minute films
154–5, 239–41
compilation 9–10
Ono, Yoko *110*
Open Door (1973–83)
134
Open Space (1985–94)
134
'oral history
documentary' 217,
220
Orkney Islands 161–2
Out of Chaos (1944) 13
Out to Play (1936)
156–8, *157*
Owen, Alun 65
Owen, Bill 190

Paisley, Ian 168, 169
Panorama (1953–) 142,
166, 168

Parker, Charles 96
Parkinson, Harry B.
122
party political broadcasts
40–1, 61–3, 144–5
Pathe Pictorial (1919–69)
128
Paul, R. W. 239–40
Paul Rotha Productions
73
Peacock, Richard 97
Peet, Stephen 217,
254n66
*Personal Call see Mining
Review 4th Year
No. 12*
Pike, Oliver 200–1, 235,
237–8
Piper, John 13
place, documentary of
154–5
Platform Films 31
Platter, Enrico 15
The Plover (1936) 225
Police (1982) 146–7
police force 146–7
politically committed film
31–2, 40–1, 42–3,
68, 96–7, 104–5,
124–5, 151–3,
219–20
role of digital video in
42
see also party political
broadcasts;
propaganda
politics, international
182–3
Ponting, Herbert 192
Portrait of a School
(1957) **159–60**

A Portrait of Ga (1952)
161–2
Powell, Dilys 197
*The Power of
Nightmares* (2004)
182
Prague 42–3
presenter, foregrounding
of 200
'prestige documentary'
27, 180
'authored' 200–2
Priestley, J. B. 27–8
An English Journey
27
prison life 100–1
Promio, Alexandre 155
'promotional
documentaries'
78–9, 170–1
propaganda
anti-governmental
31–2
national 55–7
party political 40–1,
61–3, 76–7, 144–5
social 73
wartime 27–8, 47,
112–13, 203–4
protest activity
documentaries as
expression of
31–2, 42–3, 124–5
documentary coverage
80–1, 124–5, 128
Provos (1997) 168–9
Public Eye (1966–75)
168
Pudovkin, Vsevolod 242
The Punk Rock Movie
(1978) **163–4**

A Queen Is Crowned
(1953) **165–7**, 220

race 39, 80–1, 128,
140–1, 142–3
Radio Ballads 96
railways 11–12, 84–5,
148–50, 184–6,
223–4
Rain In My Heart (2006)
70
Rank Organisation 128,
165–6, 238
Read, John 13
Realist Film Unit 29,
157, 209
reconstructions
213–14
Redgrave, Michael 50,
52–3
Refuge England (1959)
222
Reid, Jimmy 219
Reisz, Karel 64, 126
Rescued by Rover (1905)
17
restoration 193
*Returning the Serve
(Loyalists)* (1999)
168–9
reviews 81, 167, 190–1,
197
Richardson, Ralph 50
Richman, Geoff 176
The Rival World (1955)
170–1, 181
R&J Films 86
Robertson, James 98–9
Robertson, Joyce 98–9,
246
Robinson, Peter 142

Robinson in Space (1996)
74, 117, 248
Rocking the Boat (1983)
220
Roddam, Franc 70
Rogue Males (1998) 37
Rommel, Erwin, Field-
Marshal 47–8
Ronson, John 91, 92–3,
245
Rotha, Paul 12, 68, 73,
106–7, 126, 132,
160, 209, 210
Rough Sea at Dover
(1895) 240
Royal Family (1969) 166,
172, **172–4**
Royal Navy 229
Ruck, Berta 217–18
Rushdie, Salman 81
Russell, Ken 126
Russian cinema,
influence on British
documentary 68
see also Soviet Union

Saatchi and Saatchi
40–1
Sailor (1976) 146
Savage, Dominic 36, 37,
94
Savile, Jimmy 71
Scargill, Arthur 31–2
Schama, Simon 200
Schlesinger, John 126
The School (1978)
175–6
schools programmes
15–16, 218
science 207–8, 225–6,
238

Scofield, Paul 118
seaside scenes/activities
        197–9, 223–4
Secrets of Nature
        (1923–33) 83,
        235–6
Seeger, Peggy 96
Seven Green Bottles
        (1971) 248
*Seven Up! (World in
        Action)* (1964)
        177–9, *178*
The Sex Pistols 163
Shackleton, Ernest
        192–3
The Shadow of Progress
        (1970) **180–1**,
        246–7
*The Shadows in the Cave
        (The Power of
        Nightmares)* (2004)
        8, **182–3**
*Shakespeare on the
        Estate* (1994) 234
Shankar, Ravi 208
Sheffield Film Co-Op
        219
Shell Film Unit 90, 170,
        180, 184
shipbuilding industry
        219–20
Short, Anthony 78
shorts 119–21, 128,
        134–6
    see also one-minute
        films
Simmons, Anthony 197,
        199, 243
Simon, Sir Ernest 107
Simpson, Joe 212–14,
        250

Singin' in the Rain (1952)
        148
Siouxsie and the
        Banshees 163–4
Slater, John 133
The Slits 163
slum conditions 88–90
Small, Heather 120
Smith, Percy 235,
        237–8
Smithson, John 212
smoking 175–6
Snow, C. P. 207
Snow (1963) 8, **184–6**,
        185, 242
social issues, treatment
        of 72–3, 88–90,
        91–3, 98–9,
        102–3, 151–3
The Song of Ceylon
        (1934) 81, **187–8**
Song of the People
        (1945) *189,*
        189–91
*South – Sir Ernest
        Shackleton's
        Glorious Epic of the
        Antarctic* (1919)
        192–3
Southend-on-Sea 197–9
Soviet Union 191
    see also Russian cinema
Spanner Films 131
Speaight, Robert 203
Spence, Gusty 169
Spice, Evelyn 30
Spinetti, Victor 92
Spitting Image
        (1984–96) 166
sponsorship 5, 79, 82,
        91, 92, 180

Sri Lanka *see* Ceylon
*S.S. Skirmisher at
        Liverpool (Mitchell
        and Kenyon 235)*
        (1901) **194–6**, *195,*
        254n60
Stagecoach (1939) 148
staged material, use of
        37, 44, 138, 159,
        173, 199, 211
    in war films 20, 49,
        229–30
Stalin, Joseph 191
Starkey, David 200
Starr, Ringo *110,* 111
Steel, Helen 130–1
steel industry 233–4
Stepney, housing
        conditions 88–90,
        89
Stewart, Charles 146
Stobart, Thomas 38
Storyville (2003–7) 131
Strand Film Company
        209–10, 226
structure (of
        documentary films)
        20, 29, 84, 106–7,
        109–11, 148,
        187–8, 203–4,
        210–11, 213–14,
        221–2
Subway Sect 163
Summers, Sue 212
Sunday by the Sea
        (1953) **197–9**, *198,*
        243
*Supersocieties (Life in the
        Undergrowth)*
        (2005) **200–2**, *201*
Suschitzky, Adam 242

Suschitzky, Wolf 242
Swallow, Norman 227, 228
The Sword of the Spirit (1942) **203–4**

Tait, Margaret 161–2
Tallents, Sir Stephen 55, 187
Tanner, Alain 64
Target for Tonight (1941) 229
Taylor, Basil 13–14
Taylor, John 11, 38, 88, 187, 197
Taylor, Peter 168, 169
technology, relationship with meaning 227
telephone conversations, overheard 94–5
Television Comes to London (1936) **205–6**
Temple, Julien 126
Tensing Norgay, Sherpa 39
Terraine, John 51
Terreblanche, Eugene 215–16
terrorism 114–15, 182–3
Thames Television 142
Thames Valley Police 146–7
Tharp, Graham 38
Thatcher, Margaret 31–2, 40–1, 144–5, 215–16
Thatcher, Mark 216
The Thief of Bagdad (1940) 183

Things to Come (1936) 232
This Week (1956–1992) 142, 168
Thompson, Tony 11–12
Thomson, Margaret 29–30
Time Is (1964) **207–8**
Today We Live: A Film of Life in Britain (1937) 209, **209–11**
Tomorrow's Saturday (1962) 222
Touch of Evil (1958) 233
Touching the Void (2003) **212–14**, 213, 249–50
Toulmin, Stephen 207
Tracking Down Maggie (1994) **215–16**
Trade Films 31, 234
trades unions 31–2, 219–20
  calls for formation 151–3
Transexual Liberation Group 134
transport 11–12, 84–5, 148–50, 194–6
Transport Commission 11, 12
travel films 74–5, 122–3, 187–8, 195–6, 223–4, 253n55
Trevelyan, Humphrey 151
A Trip to the White Sea Fisheries (1909) 86
True Stories (1990–2002) 216

Trueman, Brian 16
TV Eye (1978–86) 168
Two Victorian Girls (*Yesterday's Witness*) (1970) **217–18**, 254n66

UCS 1 **219–20**
Undercurrents 42
United States
  documentary traditions/style 4, 62
  penal system 100–1
  popular culture 100–1
Upper Clyde Shipbuilders 219–20
Urban, Charles 19, 44, 223, 235

The Vanishing Street (1962) **221–2**
Vas, Robert 221–2
Venice Grand Prix 197
venues, 'non-theatrical' 6, 92, 97, 105
Verity Films 203
Vertigo (1958) 85
Victoria, Queen 65
'video activism' 42
Video Diaries (1991–2) 134
Video Nation (1994) 134–6
video tape, introduction/ development of 227
  see also digital video
View from an Engine Front – Ilfracombe (1898) **223–4**
Villages of Lanka (1934) 253n55

A Visit to Peek Frean & Co's Biscuit Works (1910) 44
visual arts 13–14
Voss, Manfred 15
Vox Nova Scientiae (1936) **225–6**

war, treatments of 19–21, 50–1
  enduring images 20
  'faked' material 20
  impact on old soldiers 92
  limitations of documentary treatment 20–1
  see also names of specific conflicts; World War I; World War II
Warwick Trading Company 223
Watson, Paul 70–1
Watt, Harry 27, 114, 148, 150, 229
We Are the Lambeth Boys (1957) 64
weather conditions 184–6
webcam 155, 241
Weber, Eva 94–5, 250
A Wedding on Saturday (1964) **227–8**
Welles, Orson 233
Wendt, Lionel 187
Western Approaches (1944) **229–30**
Westward Ho! (1940) **231–2**
When the Dog Bites (1988) **233–4**

Wigan Coal and Iron Company 44
Wilcox, Desmond 142–3
Wilcox, Herbert 122
Wilkins family 70–1
Williams, Derek 180, 246–7
Willis, John 102–3
Wilson, Harold 61
Winter (Secrets of Nature) (1923) **235–6**
Winterbottom, Michael 126
Wisdom of the Wild (1940) **237–8**
Wolfensohn, James 42
women
  documentaries directed by 30
  employment/social role 72–3, 151–3
Women's Film Group 219
Wonderful Britain (1924) 122
Wonderful London (1924) 122
Woolcock, Penny 126, 233, 234
Woolfe, H. Bruce 225, 235, 236
working classes, (patronising) treatments of 73, 122–3
The World at War (1974) 50
World Bank 42
World in Action (1963–99) 142, 177
World of Plenty (1943) 106

World War I 193
  aftermath 210
  contemporary treatments 19–21, 47, 49
  retrospectives 50–1
  veterans 50–1, 92, 105
World War II 203–4
  aftermath 106
  domestic lives/ conditions 27–8, 52–4, 72–3, 106–8, 112–13, 231–2
  impact on documentary making 5, 38, 237
  military/naval operations 47–9, 229–30
Wright, Basil 35, 54, 148, 150, 187–8

X-Ray Spex 163

Yarmouth Fishing Boats Leaving Harbour (1896) *239,* **239–41**
Yates, Simon 212–14, 250
Yesterday's Witness (1969–81) 217
Young Children in Brief Sparation (1969) 98
youtube.com 135–6

List of Illustrations

While considerable effort has been made to correctly identify the copyright holders, this has not been possible in all cases. We apologise for any apparent negligence and any omissions or corrections brought to our attention will be remedied in future editions.

The Battle of the Somme, British Topical Committee for War Films; *The Big Meeting*, National Coal Board Film Unit; *Coal Face*, GPO Film Unit; *Conservative Party Election Broadcast 23/4/79*, Conservative Party; *A Day in the Life of a Coal Miner*, Kineto; *Desert Victory*, Army Film Unit/Royal Air Force Film Production Unit; *A Diary for Timothy*, Crown Film Unit; *Drifters*, New Era Films/Empire Marketing Board Film Unit; *Drinking for England*, Century Films; *Every Day Except Christmas*, Graphic Films; *Housing Problems*, British Commercial Gas Association; *I Think They Call Him John*, Samaritan Films; *Land of Promise*, Paul Rotha Productions/Films of Fact; *Let It Be*, Apple Films; *Lockerbie – A Night Remembered*, Castle Haven Digital; *London*, British Film Institute/Koninck/Channel Four; *London 2012: Make Britain Proud*, London 2012 Campaign; *Morning in the Streets*, BBC; *Night Mail*, GPO Film Unit; *Nightcleaners*, Berwick Street Film Collective; *Out to Play*, Short Film Productions; *A Queen Is Crowned*, © General Film Distributors; *Royal Family*, BBC/Independent Television Authority; *Seven Up!*, Granada Television; *Snow*, British Transport Films/Geoffrey Jones Films; *Song of the People*, Horizon Film Unit; *Sunday by the Sea*, Harlequin Productions; *Supersocieties*, BBC TV/Animal Planet; *Today We Live: A Film of Life in Britain*, Strand Film Company; *Touching the Void*, © FilmFour/ © Film Council.